Crime and Thriller Writing: A Writers' & Artists' Companion

Endorsements

With its stress on a writer's obligations to language and to humanity, as well as the necessary craft and graft, this guide to planning, writing and finally selling crime fiction hits just about every button square on. Michelle and Laurie are not only accomplished writers, but helpful and persuasive teachers, leading you from the perfect first sentence to the perils of plotting (Orderly or Organic anyone?) and beyond. Peppered with advice and inspiration from 20 or so established masters and mistresses of the genre, this is close to the perfect primer for any aspiring writer with echoes of murder and mystery in their bones. **John Harvey**

The good thing about the *Crime and Thriller Writing: A Writers' & Artists' Companion* is that, unlike many How To guides, it is not prescriptive. The authors, Michelle Spring and Laurie R. King, don't say there is a right and a wrong way of writing a crime novel. They accept that there are many equally valid approaches to the task, but then with practical advice and well-chosen exercises demonstrate how any writer can make their book better. There is also input from a distinguished list of Guest Contributors, whose short essays provide a wider perspective on the business. The *Crime and Thriller Writing: A Writers' & Artists' Companion* is full of invaluable, extremely sensible advice for every aspiring crime writer and I, as an experienced practitioner in the genre, also picked up some very useful tips. **Simon Brett**

Novels by Michelle Spring

Every Breath You Take (Simon and Schuster, New York; Orion, London, 1994)

Running for Shelter (Simon and Schuster, New York; Orion, London; Ballantine, New York and Toronto, 1997)

Standing in the Shadows (Ballantine, New York and Toronto; Orion, London, 1998)

Nights in White Satin (Ballantine, New York and Toronto; Orion, London, 1999; Ostara Publishers, 2010)

In the Midnight Hour (Ballantine, New York and Toronto; Orion, London, 2001)

The Night Lawyer (Ballantine, New York and Toronto, 2007)

Novels by Laurie R. King

The Kate Martinelli novels

A Grave Talent (1993)

To Play the Fool (1995)

With Child (1996)

Night Work (2000)

The Art of Detection (2006)

The Mary Russell novels

The Beekeeper's Apprentice (1994)

A Monstrous Regiment of Women (1995)

A Letter of Mary (1997)

The Moor (1998)

O Jerusalem (1999)

Justice Hall (2002)

The Game (2004)

Locked Rooms (2005)

The Language of Bees (2009)

The God of the Hive (2010)

Beekeeping for Beginners (an e-novella, 2011)

Pirate King (2011)

Garment of Shadows (2012)

Standalone novels

A Darker Place (1999)

Folly (2001)

Keeping Watch (2003)

Califia's Daughters (2004)

Touchstone (2008)

Books from 1993 to 1998 were first published by St Martin's Press, New York; books from 1999 to present by Bantam Books, New York. UK editions and other publications are listed on the website.

Crime and Thriller Writing: A Writers' & Artists' Companion

Michelle Spring and Laurie R. King

Carole Angier and Sally Cline, Series Editors

BLOOMSBURY
LONDON • NEW DELHI • NEW YORK • SYDNEY

BLOOMSBURY PUBLISHING PLC

50 Bedford Square
London
WC1B 3DP
UK

1385 Broadway
New York
NY 10018
USA

www.bloomsbury.com

First published in 2012 as The Arvon Book of Crime and Thriller Writing

This edition published 2013 by Bloomsbury

British Library Cataloguing-in-Publication Data
A catalogue record for this book is available from the British Library.

ISBN: PB: 978-1-4725-2393-8

Library of Congress Cataloging-in-Publication Data
A catalog record for this title is available from the Library of Congress.

Printed and bound in Great Britain

Contents

Preface to series

Who has not dreamed of writing a crime novel? Crime stories offer a classic structure – mystery, quest – and a solid base in research. We all read them and love them; and if we dream of writing at all, we think, *Maybe I could do this.* The message of this book is: with devotion and practice, we can.

This is the second in a new series of books on writing. Like the others, it is written by two distinguished writers in the field: in this case, one American and one British. In Part One they tell with riveting honesty why and how they themselves write about crime. In Part Two their twenty-six invited guests – all top practitioners, some British, some North American (and one Icelandic!) – add generous, lively and fascinating reflections on their trade. And in Part Three the two co-authors return, to offer a detailed practical guide to writing every kind of crime story, from classic whodunits to fast-paced thrillers.

We mustn't give the authors' secrets away, especially in a book about mystery.

But here are just some of their reasons to write about crime: for catharsis, and the thrill of research; to explore social questions without having to give answers, and to combine entertainment with the deepest exploration of the human soul. If these sound like reasons to do any kind of writing, that is because they are. This is not a book about crime writing, the authors say, it is a book about writing, crime.

All writers, not only crime writers, will enjoy it.

Carole Angier and Sally Cline, series editors

Introduction

by Michelle Spring and Laurie R. King

We are writers, and the books we write are crime novels. This delightful situation is one that neither of us expected. Neither of us came from a literary background. One of us was sidling towards middle age, the other only a few years younger, before we turned our hands to fiction. Michelle, for one, grew up in a time and place where reading was considered an eccentric pastime, and writing as a career was never considered at all.

Times have changed, and in this respect, for the better. As a population, we are now more educated and, in spite of competition from computer games and television, many of us have a hunger for reading. A staggering range of fiction is easily available from bookshops, supermarkets, online sellers, and (where they've escaped the cuts) libraries. Thanks to the spread of reading groups – virtual and real-life – the pleasure found in novels is once again a shared activity.

The idea of writing fiction is also less exotic than it used to be, and somewhat less the prerogative of the privileged. Writers seldom find their footsteps dogged by the paparazzi, but the names of authors such as Lee Child or Tess Gerritsen are widely recognised. Literary festivals, book events, blogs and interviews have made the route to writerdom more public than in the past.

Is it surprising, then, that more and more people aspire to write? Men and women fresh out of university commit to writing as a career. Mothers with young children try to shoehorn writing into their busy lives. People approaching retirement look to writing for fresh challenge and a supplement to the pension. The proliferation of courses in creative writing (and of books such as this one) is both a response to the demand from budding writers, and an invitation to people to regard writing as something they might try for themselves.

But though there is great enthusiasm for the novel, many people puzzle over making the leap from 'wanting to write' to actually doing it. Many are bursting with ideas and ambition, but unsure how actually to produce a work of fiction that is worthy of being read.

One aim of *Crime and Thriller Writing: A Writers' & Artists' Companion* is to help such people move from intention to result. This book says: You want to write? To write a crime novel or a thriller? Here's how to go about it.

By the way: unlike some guides, we don't suggest that writing is easy. Far from it. Writing takes imagination and commitment and mountains of hard work. But we do show how to lay the foundations, so that – if you put in the effort – you'll be able to direct it in a way that will produce the best novel possible.

The second, and perhaps the more important, aim of this book is to explore the nature of crime writing today. What exactly is this genre that occupies such a large portion of the shelves in any bookshop and many of the top spots in best-seller lists? What are the boundaries of the genre, and the subgroups within it? What are its roots in literary tradition, and where is it going today? Why is crime fiction so appealing to readers, and what propels some writers to devote their working lives to it?

In pursuit of our aims, we've enlisted the help of over two dozen of the best thriller writers and crime novelists working today. They give their highly diverse takes on crime and thriller writing, and provide the kind of insights that emerge only from experience. Their passion for story-telling and for the genre is illuminating and inspiring.

Having a substantial range of guest authors is one way of signalling an idea we regard as primary: there is no one way to write a crime novel. No single approach or 'formula' is right for everyone. People bring to writing their individual talents and convictions, and shape what they do accordingly. We hope that the arguments and examples and exercises in this book will nudge readers into cultivating their own views of what crime writing is and how it can be done.

The emphasis on diversity of approach extends to the two co-authors, as well. We have a great many shared views about crime fiction – what it is, and how it should develop – but we are by no means carbon copies of each other. In our 'Reflections', in Part One of this book, we lay bare our lives as crime writers, and our individual views on what we believe to be important and challenging about the genre. We describe our markedly different work habits. One of us begins a book with a carefully constructed outline; the other plunges in and leaves the specifics to the rewrite. The crucial thing is that both approaches do the business: both can produce great novels. By revealing alternative ways of getting the book you want to write on to paper, we hope to extend your range of options as a writer until you identify the approach that works, absolutely, for you.

This guide to crime writing is, in short, just that: a guide, not a recipe. There are two main authors and twenty-six guests in order to give a faint indication of the breadth of the genre and its writers. We all have to invent our own wheel in this business. What is comfortable for one writer causes another to look on in horror. One writer sits down to the keyboard only when mortgage payments threaten to overcome bank balance, while another clocks in at the same time every day – literally, with a time card. None (that we know of) follows the system of Kent Haruf, who composes on a manual typewriter with his knitted cap pulled over his eyes, but if you find that appealing, by all means try it, and do let us know how it works for you.

Crime and Thriller Writing: A Writers' & Artists' Companion might be considered a collection of Things We Wish We'd Known When We Started. Neither the co-authors nor their twenty-six crime-writing guests are keen to reveal the wrong turns taken and the hours wasted before each of us discovered our own right way to write. The goal of the present volume is to bring together some of the things we learned, to free your creative mind to soar while your feet are grounded on solid technique.

Find your way, experiment with differences, see what works for you. Have fun while you're doing it, because joy reveals itself in your work.

But above all – keep writing!

Notes on format and terminology

As well as serving as an up-to-date guide to the craft of crime writing, this book is designed for readers, whether writers or not, who are fascinated by crime fiction and are keen to get the inside story. The format of the book reflects this dual aim.

In Part One, Michelle and Laurie explore the experiences and skills that go to make up a successful crime writer, and reflect on what the genre is and where it's going. Don't expect to find a bland consensus here, as differences of approach – in plotting, for example – are fully aired. (Bullet points and unsigned portions of the book are joint ventures, but where sections of the book are written by one or other of the authors, her name will appear.) Our aim is to shed light upon the range of crime and thriller writing, not to insist on a one-size-fits-all formula.

In Part Two of the book, the breadth and variety of approaches to crime and thriller writing is underscored as twenty-six guest contributors, all established professionals, reveal key aspects of their craft, from passionate discussions of the purpose of writing, to techniques for creating suspense.

Laurie and Michelle take the reins again in Part Three, with detailed advice about the craft of crime writing, from the mechanics of plotting to the means of promoting a book. When we talk about publication, we mean the traditional publishing industry. Writers happy to upload their book online may be less constrained by some of the industry's requirements.

Fiction that includes country house detection and graphic serial killer novels makes for a broad church. Our guest authors represent every position on the crime spectrum and are content to be included in a book devoted to 'Crime and Thriller Writing'. But constant repetition is cumbersome, so we use 'crime writing' to mean all degrees within the spectrum, but 'thrillers' or 'detective stories' when we are looking at a particular type. (The 'spectrum of crime' is analysed below.) Similarly, because of the mix of nationalities, we chose to stick to British spelling, and trust the American eye will not stumble over 'plough' and 'colour'.

In North America, the umbrella term for 'crime writing' is often 'mystery'. In this book, the term 'mystery' will usually be reserved for the specific type of crime novel known also as 'traditional detective stories' or 'whodunits'.

Part 1:
On a life of crime

Reflections I

by Michelle Spring: Thoughts about crime

I became a crime writer in my middle years, from a rather unlikely starting point, and I'm very glad I did. The reflections that follow deal with the life experiences that inform my writing, the challenges that crime writing presents and the wonderful things that it offers for writers and readers alike. The reflections are written from an entirely personal perspective, but I hope that reading them will nudge people to explore further the rich genre of crime fiction for themselves.

1. 'I always knew I wanted to be a writer'

I never cease to wonder when I hear others say: *I always knew I wanted to be a writer.* I'm struck by an image of them as newborns, their faces wrinkled with the effort of exposition; scribbling ideas on the trays of their highchairs; parading the premise of their latest story during show-and-tell. Their sense of vocation bowls me over. It wasn't like that for me. I grew up in a small Canadian town in which, at the time, the principal employer for men was the pulp mill and most married women stayed at home to mend and make do. My grandfather was a logger, my father a commercial fisherman. The idea of writing as a career simply didn't occur to me.

I adored reading, however, as did my mother. Mom concealed racy romances behind the furnace, and I hid my love of reading, because, among so many of our peers, reading was considered somewhat weird and not a little suspect.

In career terms, luck was on my side. I went to college, developed a passion for social science, and eventually, after moving to England, became a university professor. I wrote academic books and papers on a bulky old electric typewriter. I co-wrote a textbook which ran to four editions and earned a small fortune.

But until the 1990s, I never turned my hand to fiction. It was an encounter with a stalker (of which more later) that compelled me to have a go at writing a novel. To my astonishment, *Every Breath You Take* was snapped up by publishers in several countries, and I found myself with a new career.

Selling a first novel is a thrilling experience. But by then I was hooked on the writing itself. Writing turned out to be a challenge – and after years and years of teaching, a challenge was a welcome thing.

Writing became an escape. At the end of the day, I'd feel as if I'd been somewhere new, and had an adventure.

Writing freed me to have a new relationship with the world around me. As an academic, I tended to bury myself in my thoughts. Now, I've become expert at listening in to other people's conversations. I plunder the landscape for the materials for word pictures. I stare openly at people on the Underground. (*Yes, that was me. Sorry.*)

These are some of the pleasures that I've found through writing. Of course, there is a commercial interest, too. Books sell, sometimes for relatively little money, sometimes for a lot. That fact allows me to spend most, though not quite all, of my time in writing.

But beyond the prospect of money is the vast delight to be found in the act of writing itself. I've never had a talent for music, but I imagine that the rewards of playing an instrument are rather similar to those of writing. Writing involves playing with language. I get a huge buzz out of the rhythm and sound, the crash and hum and tinkle of words. What could be more delicious?

As the writer Anne Lamott says in *Bird by Bird*:

> *... publication is not all that it's cracked up to be. But writing is. Writing has so much to give, so much to teach, so many surprises. The thing that you had to force yourself to do – the actual act of writing – turns out to be the best part. It's like discovering that while you thought you needed the tea ceremony for the caffeine, what you really needed was the tea ceremony. The act of writing turns out to be its own reward.*

2. Reasons to write a crime novel

Do you remember that British slogan, *Go to work on an egg?* (Penned, as it happens, by an advertising team led by novelist Fay Weldon.) It's not a bad idea, but here's a better one: Go to work on a crime novel.

People are, generally speaking, keen on the idea. At parties, I often meet accountants or toy-model makers with fiendishly clever plot synopses in their waistcoat pockets; the book clubs I visit are bursting with dental nurses who are burrowing away at serial killer stories. When I run crime-writing workshops, lawyers turn out in droves. Even – but perhaps this is less surprising – prisoners are keen.

For those who have the urge to write a crime novel, there are dozens of reasons to do so. I have pared them down to the few that chime most closely with my own experience:

- **To lighten up**. While it is not infrequently the case that writers of, say, experimental fiction find an emotional release in their work, for crime novelists (who deal with the dark things that we push aside in order to get on with everyday life) the cathartic attraction of writing can be decisive. This was certainly the case for me.

  There was a time in my life when my sleep was punctured by nightmares. When I was constantly scanning for signs of danger. When I couldn't pass a dark doorway without stiffening in fear.

  Writing crime changed all that. I transferred my dark thoughts on to the page, and the nightmares receded. As long as I'm beavering away at a crime novel, I sleep like a lamb.

- **To satisfy the story-telling urge**. Items in the news, memories from the past, things that puzzle or fascinate or frighten you: once you begin to exercise your imaginative muscles, you'll find yourself, as I did, constantly bumping up against stories that demand to be told. They just keep coming, and they won't be denied.

- **For companionship**. It's an open secret that writers can be difficult people to know: gloomy, competitive and bitchy. Romantic novelists are reputed to be backstabbers to a woman – though it goes without saying that the few whom I know well are sweetness and light. But crime writers are a remarkably convivial and good-hearted lot. They work hard – the pressure to produce a book a year is no joke – but they pass up no opportunity for fun. Crime-writing conventions are just one such opportunity, exhausting, exhilarating and irresistible. (We'll give details at the end of the book.)

- **As an outlet for aggression**. It is widely mooted within the crime fraternity that crime writers are easy to hang out with precisely because they channel belligerent impulses into their writing, leaving them, in real life, meek and mild. I wouldn't like to confirm or deny that rumour. But I can tell you that a crime novel is a great place to park your rage. The prospect of giving vent to righteous anger in a safe form can be particularly attractive for women, who are taught, from an early age, that aggression is unfeminine. A sharp-tongued woman is subject to sanctions that rarely apply to a sharp-tongued man, and a woman who meets provocation with an outburst of rage – let alone a well-placed punch – is likely to be deemed a shrew and a slag.

  But draft a crime novel and all that's set aside. When I first came to write a scene where my private investigator was required to defend herself against a knife-wielding man, I drew on that submerged feeling of rage. Once I'd made the leap into my imagination, punches and kicks came surprisingly easily. More than that, I found that writing a fight scene was good clean fun. I suspect that I'm not the only one who derives from writing crime novels the pleasure of letting rip – entirely on the page.

- **For the thrill of research**. As someone who's done both, I can confirm that the research you do as a crime writer is every bit as satisfying as scholarly research – and it's far more diverse.

  Research has given me an entrée into worlds that I wouldn't otherwise know. It has taken me to see children, some as young as eleven, who had been locked up for murder, arson and rape. It's taken me to a refuge in Notting Hill to interview Filipina maids who've fled abusive British-based employers – TNTs, as the women are called in their own language. It's taken me to a formal tea with diplomats at an Arab embassy, while in the background a horse race thundered across the television screen.

  In the interests of research, I've breached security in Britain's tallest skyscraper, provoking an outburst from a security guard who was caught napping on the job. I've worked with a forensic artist as she reconstructed human features from a fleshless skull and magicked into being up-to-date 'photographs' of a child who'd vanished years before. I've posted notices in women's washrooms inviting prostitutes to interview; one of the conversations that followed was a poignant exchange with a teenager who begged me to find her a job as a call girl. Dilemmas about the ethics of research, you see, are not confined to scholars alone.

The central character in my series novels, Laura Principal, is a cool and likeable private investigator, so I am spared the need to master the intricacies of police work. But even so, I get a lot of help from the police, particularly from a high-ranking officer who once upon a time was my graduate student. The Inspector keeps me on the straight and narrow. She provides information on serious matters – like airport security and the condition of corpses – and on more frivolous matters, too. After she'd read a draft of one of my novels, I received a fax from police headquarters with a stern reprimand: *Female police officers do not, I repeat not, wear regulation underclothes.*

- **To foster humility – and freedom**. If you are determined to produce a really outstanding novel, but you want to avoid becoming swell-headed, then crime writing is for you. No matter how sparkling your prose, how penetrating your insights, how prolific your output, how ambitious your writing, you are unlikely to be ushered into the salons of the Literary Elite.

  Instead, you will be greeted by phrases like – 'What *do you do?* What *sort of books? Oh, I see, a* crime *writer.*'

  Or – *'D'you know, you're good enough to write a real book.'*

  Or by the smug declaration, 'I *don't read crime.'*

  Incidentally, when someone says to me, 'I don't read crime', I am pierced by a suspicion that the speaker's knowledge of crime fiction is trapped in the world of Agatha Christie.

FOR SOPHIE HANNAH on ...

the psychological depth of Christie's whodunits, see 'Tips and tales – guest contributors', p. 124.

I've got nothing against Christie; in fact, I defended her recently on BBC3's *Battle of the Books*. But I do consider her approach to the crime novel – the formulaic puzzler, the tricksy but not entirely credible plot, and the dearth of critical reflection about the world around – distinctly limited and definitely out of date. Crime fiction long ago moved beyond the generic bounds that reigned in Christie's time. There are still *whodunits*, but more prominent now are *whydunits* and *whowillbedones* and – the staple of the thriller – *willhedoits*. Some crime novels revel in pure action, and a very few concentrate on puzzle alone, but many more are engaged in an interrogation of psyche and society as acute as that on offer in so-called 'literary fiction'.

So when someone says to me: 'I don't read crime', I bite back the obvious response: *What? Don't read stories in which transgression or violence (or the consequences thereof) play an important part? Don't read who, then? J. M. Coetzee? Truman Capote? Peter Carey? Joyce Carol Oates? Ian McEwan? Harper Lee? Margaret Atwood? Dostoevsky? Dickens? Shakespeare?*

But don't be put off by the disdain of Literary Types; even this has its positive side. When you come out, so to speak, as a crime novelist, you no longer have to worry about whether or not your writing is 'avant-garde'. You are free to create a cracking good story, with vividly drawn characters and sharply etched locations. Free to dive into the darkest corners of the human heart. Free to surface again into a world enriched by the reflection (so central to the genre) on life and loss and death.

What's not to like?

3. The shadow of violence

I was fourteen years old, at high school in Canada, when I first came face to face with murder. An RCMP squad car pulled up in front of my school and Mounties broke the news to one of the boys in my year that his sister and her boyfriend had been brutally murdered. The killer was a man for whose children she used sometimes to babysit.

Not long after, a girl who'd been a close friend of mine came home from the cinema to find that her father had shot her mother, little brother and baby sister, and then turned the rifle on himself.

I grew up in the 1960s; like many of my contemporaries, I didn't want to live the corseted lives of earlier generations of women. I wanted, as it seemed at the time, something more: to have a career, to pursue causes I cared about, to travel, to have fun. And one thing was always clear to me: if it's adventure you're after, you mustn't think too long or too hard about violence. Worries about danger – about strangers who can't be trusted, about the risks you take when you're far from home – can stop an adventurous girl (or a boy, for that matter) dead in her tracks.

So I put those childhood murders out of my mind.

Except at night, when brutal nightmares were always with me. Afraid to go to sleep, I read novels late, late and later, and slept less and less.

During the day, I persuaded myself that violence was something that happened only to others. That I was safe.

Except that it wasn't and I wasn't.

I'd just finished university when, for the first time, I experienced stranger-violence that was aimed directly at me. I lived in Venice Beach, in southern California. At that time, the place was a haunt of Hell's Angels and drug addicts, with a scattering of elderly couples who played cards on the promenade and closed their eyes to much of what went on. Other people tended to avoid Venice Beach, which left me able to enjoy long stretches of golden sand in solitude. I felt at home there.

Until one day, after a morning by the sea, making my way home across the beach, I found myself surrounded by a group of men.

They were young, tall, strong and well-spoken, like a college basketball team on their way to a match. They formed a horseshoe around me and began to push and prod, rerouting me in the direction of Venice Pier. *Let's play under the pier,* they said, and I knew I was in serious trouble. Even when the Los Angeles sun blazed down, the space under the pier was darker than sin.

That walk across the sand lasted minutes; it felt like hours. I could see the apartment where I lived, with the blinds pulled down to cut out the midday sun. I could see the promenade in the distance, but the card players and the bikers were too far away to hear me if I screamed. I wept, and the proddings turned to punches.

Then, only a dozen yards short of the pier, we were accosted by an extraordinary-looking man. He was short and brown-skinned and muscular; he was dressed like Huckleberry Finn, in cut-off dungarees and a straw hat. He ignored the men and focused on me.

'What's your name?' he said. None of the others had asked me this.

I told him. What did I have to lose?

'Hey, brothers,' he said. He looked up and locked eyes with the six much larger men who surrounded me. 'This here's my friend, Michelle.'

There was a prolonged pause. Then, one by one, my captors mumbled their goodbyes, and jogged off towards the promenade, leaving me alone with Huckleberry. When the basketball team was out of earshot, I asked the obvious question: *Who are you?*

He showed me the contents of his wallet. It contained arrest warrants from different states, all in his name; the charges were armed robbery and murder, several times over.

'Who am I?' He smiled, a most engaging smile. 'Honey,' he said, spreading his arms expansively, 'I'm da King of da Beach.'

Looking back on this episode, what amazes me now is how coolly I took it. How easily Roberto became part of my life, dropping in every so often to visit, wrapping a mantle of protection around me. I was never hassled again on Venice Beach.

Roberto was not so lucky. He failed to pay a drugs debt and was dragged behind a motorbike until dead.

There have been other brushes with violence during my adult life. There was the occasion, also in Los Angeles, when a policeman leapt out of an alley and put a gun to my head. In England, there was the armed raid on a building society in which I was caught up, and the student who threatened to kill me and my family. I'll leave these aside for the moment. Enough, surely, is enough.

Why am I recounting the murders that spooked my schooldays? My close shave with a fate worse than death on Venice Beach? Because they explain, as nothing else can, why, partway through my adult life, I've taken to writing novels, and why I write the kind of novels that I do. I've met many men and women who enjoy reading books about the mafia, say, or about brutal underworlds. They find these stories exhilarating and perhaps, also, curiously consoling, because such stories validate the comforting view that violence takes place 'out there'. That it occurs to other people – criminal classes, low-lifes, gang members – in other places – the projects, the inner city, the East End – and that it won't much intrude into their safe little world.

My own life won't allow me that kind of comfort. Violence hovers at the edge of my vision, like the monster in a horror film.

It's because I can, and do, imagine the worst sort of events in the most mundane places that crime writing feels like coming home. I write about the kind of dangers that burst into the everyday lives of ordinary folk. I write about the nasty things beneath the scrubbed-clean surface.

I write to exorcise the ghosts of violence. I weave my fears into stories and I offer them to readers in the form of suspense. And once I've done that, the murders in my childhood and even the meeting with da King of da Beach seem to have taken place a long, long time ago.

4. Just when you thought it was safe to come out of the water ...

You know those occasions where people are honoured for their achievements? For scripting the best film, building the steadiest Millennium Bridge, or composing the funkiest military march? There's always that embarrassing moment when they become very solemn, and begin a sentimental speech of thanks to the mother, the co-writer, the agent, who made them what they are today.

Well, I recently had a curious thought. What I am today is a writer of crime novels. And the person who was most important in making me that? My family was supportive, and agents and editors offered wisdom and encouragement. But, strange as it seems, the person who deserves the greatest credit is the man who stalked me.

I taught for over twenty years at university. I came into contact with thousands of students, and watching them negotiate this delicate phase of their lives was, on the whole, a pleasure.

However, I also knew a student – only one, but one was enough – who made my life hell. He was a stalker. He had, in abundance, qualities that academics value highly: 'focus' and 'concentration' and 'commitment'. The problem was, his focus was on me.

It started when he was in his second year. I was working one evening in my office and noticed him hanging around outside. He was clinging to the walls in the corridor, clearly distressed. I did what any caring academic might have done. I spoke to him kindly. I sat him down in my office for a few minutes and listened to his confused and confusing story. I wrote letters to his tutors and to the counselling service, pointing out that he was in a bad way. That was all.

But that was all it took. From that moment, my stalker loved me.

He loved me so much that he rang me at home. It was once a day at first, then several times a day. Soon he was ringing during the night as well.

He loved me so much that he stood outside our family home for hours on end. He pressed up against the front door, as if trying to hear what we were doing inside. He didn't offer any violence, not explicitly so; but his hulking presence was always a threat. The knowledge that he was lurking in silence, only metres away from our bedrooms, kept all of us from sleep.

He loved me so much that he smashed floor-to-ceiling windows in the college, calling out my name. That moved the authorities to action. Stalking is one thing; destruction of property is another.

And, above all, he loved me so much that he threatened to kill my family. It was my husband and children, he claimed, who kept us apart. He issued an assurance: soon they'd be gone, and then he and I would be married.

He was committed to the local psychiatric hospital. From there, he sent a stream of confident messages, crowing about our forthcoming wedding. By chance, my daughter, who was only six at the time, saw one of these and was deeply upset. I asked for help from the hospital. Insisted that I wanted no more messages from him. The senior psychiatric nurse didn't laugh it off, but nor did she give any sign of understanding. *It can't be that bad,* she said; *at least he loves you.*

Things escalated. My stalker – let's call him Graham – was released after a few weeks in hospital, his condition 'stabilised' by drugs. He left a message for me. He'd made a wonderful new friend in hospital. I had to meet Nick. I would really like Nick. Nick was just my sort of guy.

Nick rang. His voice was a dreadful rasp; when I think of it now, I think of barbed wire. Perhaps it was Graham with his own voice disguised; a psychiatrist suggested that Graham posed as Nick in order to act out his most violent fantasies. But whoever he 'really' was, Nick upped the stakes. Nick threatened to do things to us that Graham never had. Things that I don't want to write about. Not now. Not ever.

I dialled 999 and told the police that someone was coming to kill us. And just as I ended the call, there was my stalker at the front door, howling through the letterbox. He had brought Nick, he said. They were coming in.

I locked myself in the bathroom with the children and a kitchen knife. The police didn't arrive for almost an hour. To drown out the sound of thuds and shouts from the front door, I led the children in the singing of nursery songs, over and over and over. I've never since been able to hear 'Wheels on the Bus' without a rising sense of panic.

The end finally came to our eighteen months of agony. My stalker was sectioned to a high-security psychiatric hospital – and I became a novelist.

On sabbatical, in California, possessed by an urge to do something fresh, I decided to try my hand at writing fiction. For a time, my mind remained stubbornly blank, but then suddenly the beginnings of a book flowed out of me, like automatic writing. *Every Breath You Take*, about a stalking, expressed my worst fears. Writing put me back in control; I could shape the story and its outcome. Writing brought, in that much-maligned but useful phrase, a degree of closure.

Graham has been long gone out of my life, but he left me with three legacies that continue to this day to affect the way I write.

First, he left me with a deep understanding of what it is like to be terrified, for yourself and for the people you love. I use all that stuff in my books. I also use the sense – always with me – that however ordinary a person's life, violence could be just around the corner.

Second, my experience with Graham dampened any tendency I might have had to a love affair with violence. I don't like (*can't want*, as my mother-in-law used to say) vivid and sustained violence, especially violence of a sadistic kind. Whether it's a newspaper account of a brutal murder, an Amnesty Report on torture, or a novelist's graphic description, I don't like to read detailed accounts of eyeballs gouged out or electrodes applied to genitals. I prefer suspense to slashing. In my own writing, I want to grip readers, to thrill them, to give them a serious case of the shivers, but not to leave them feeling sick.

Finally, the experience of being stalked helped me to understand how a decent person can be moved to kill.

When someone declares that however much they felt betrayed, or injured, or violated, they could never bring themselves to kill another human being, I suspect that they count on getting satisfaction or protection in other ways – on an effective police force, or an unbiased and efficient criminal justice system; on a means of rescue that doesn't involve violence. They believe that they can make themselves safe, or that they can get justice. But what if you cease to believe that?

My stalking occurred before such acts were deemed a crime in England and Wales, and the police told me that, until Graham attacked one of us, their hands were tied. My husband and I viewed ourselves as competent adults, accustomed to sorting problems out; we were astonished and outraged to find that in the face of this fearful threat, there was no one to turn to for help, and absolutely nothing we could do. I fantasised then about hiring a contract killer. Fortunately, my sisters made me see sense. But I remain acutely aware of how readily a decent, upstanding citizen (me!) can be moved to contemplate cold-blooded murder. And that awareness is vital for creating credible situations in which otherwise ordinary characters may be pushed to cross the line.

5. Psychopaths and everyday killers, OR: Ed Gein has a lot to answer for ...

Many novels, films and television dramas (*Psycho, Hallowe'en, Silence of the Lambs, Seven, The Mermaids Singing, Wire in the Blood*) deal with psychopaths in the colloquial sense – with monsters, those who are insane, who have a compulsion to kill and rape and torture.

Fictional images of killer-monsters tend to come from two different sources. On the one hand, there are analyses by specialists (such as *The Anatomy of Motive* by John Douglas and Mark Olshaker) which examine the background and the actions of violent criminals and draw out patterns common across different individuals and different forms of violence.

More widely known, however, are the 'psychopaths' created by novelists and screenwriters, who used the image of a single real-life killer as the raw material from which to fashion their own monster. In the 1950s, Ed Gein, from Plainfield, Wisconsin (who killed two women and robbed several graves) provided such an image – the effeminate, mother-fixated voyeur, who makes objects out of human skin, who wears a leather mask, and whose murders take place in the heart of a small town. Accounts of Gein's life exerted a huge influence on Robert Bloch, who wrote the story that Hitchcock turned into his remarkable movie *Psycho*. They also formed a basis for the two film versions of *Texas Chainsaw Massacre* and for Thomas Harris's novel *The Silence of the Lambs*. An image originally derived from a single killer has been recycled in fiction again and again, until it sometimes seems as if murderers who fit this description are everywhere.

The result is novels and films that grip, and characters – such as Norman Bates or Leatherface or *Silence of the Lambs*' Buffalo Bill – who resonate in our minds long after we first encounter them. There is something horribly thrilling about coming up against what appears to be pure evil.

I've enjoyed (if that's the right word) many of these fictional creations. But I'm not keen to re-create them in my own writing, and I'm a little uneasy at the extent to which such 'monsters' have become prevalent in fictional depictions of murder. Why?

On the one hand, the depiction of killer-monsters has become almost a stereotype, and one that doesn't necessarily help in understanding dreadful acts. Monsters are rarely just monsters. The man who stalked me for eighteen months was relentless and terrifying in his actions, but the little I knew about his background – his father's long-drawn-out death, his brother's psychiatric illness, his mother's inability to cope – convinced me that, though he did evil things, he should be an object of pity rather than hate.

When we writers turn killers into monsters, we obscure the fact that acts of numbing brutality can be, and are, performed by people who are in other respects vulnerable and human. Could part of the reason why fictional 'psychopaths' are so popular with readers be because they provide excitement in a comforting form? After all, they nourish the notion that savage violence is something confined to deranged individuals, people completely unlike you or me. And that is much less frightening than the truth: that many women will be raped in their lifetimes, not by a psychopath, but by someone they know. That the biggest threat to children comes not from predatory strangers, but from members of their own circle of relatives and carers. That murder, more often than not, begins at home. I wonder whether it is this unwelcome and terrifying truth that the portrayal of killer-monsters helps to cloak.

The killer-monster strikes again and again, triggered like a wind-up toy by the sight of a prostitute or a tattooed sailor. For me as a writer, there's no challenge in this. I'm more interested in unpacking the feelings of revenge, of helplessness, of betrayal, of fear, that sometimes motivate complex human beings – not monsters – to commit the ultimate crime.

6. The grim reaper

Death is the ultimate disappearing act, so it's been said, and also the ultimate liberation. But in Western society today we've been distanced from death. Death doesn't take place at home any more, or rarely; it is swept away behind impersonal hospital curtains. The coffin doesn't sit in the parlour inviting us to confront the nature of death and the meaning of a life. When we speak about death, we cloak it in euphemisms and clichés (*passing away; sorry for your loss*) so we can avoid the dreaded words: dead, died, dying. We delegate the management of death to doctors and undertakers, and maintain a respectful distance.

True, we see all too vivid images of death and dying, of wars and natural catastrophes, on the television news but the bodies are too many, and too anonymous, to instil in us anything more than a dull horror.

One of the appeals of crime fiction is the opportunity it gives readers to confront death in a deeper and more contemplative way. This is the invitation issued by the character Jack McEvoy, a crime reporter, in the opening passage of Michael Connelly's *The Poet*:

> *Death is my beat. I make my living from it. I forge my professional reputation on it. I treat it with the passion and precision of an undertaker – somber and sympathetic about it when I'm with the bereaved, a skilled craftsman with it when I'm alone. I've always thought the secret of dealing with death is to keep it at arm's length. That's the rule. Don't let it breathe in your face.*
>
> *But my rule didn't protect me.*

Crime fiction gives us a chance to explore the moment of death, and its consequences for the people left behind: it enables readers to sit quietly in the parlour with the corpse. The fictional detective re-creates the murder victim as a whole person, and so helps to remind us that there is meaning to the life that went before.

Which is not to suggest that all crime writers approach death in a similar way. On the contrary. Those who look at death through the microscope of forensic science break death down into the punctured lung, the paralysed airway, and the crushed frontal lobe. Other writers focus on the moment of death from the point of view of the victim, who fears, then anticipates, then succumbs to the fatal blow. And so forth.

My own first attempt to write about death came in *Every Breath You Take*, when Laura Principal, PI, goes to see Monica Harcourt, and instead finds Monica's body. Laura says:

> *I stood in Monica's studio for a long time, perhaps five minutes, before I could gaze upon her body. Until I had glanced through those French doors that evening, I had considered murder only in a detached, professional context. I had been at the edges of two murder investigations, both of the victims men who had made a living and found a death through illicit drugs. And though these deaths were shocking in their way, there is enough of the Puritan in me that I am somehow unsurprised when people who live by the sword die by the sword. Monica's death was different.*

What surprises me about this passage, when I read it now, is how vividly it reflects my own anxieties.

> **FOR N. J. COOPER on ...**
>
> the emotional foundation of a story, see 'Tips and tales – guest contributors', see p. 119.

The detective who stands in awe, uneasy about approaching so close to the subject of death, was (for that moment) me. This was my first crime novel, and the passage echoes my own concerns about how to write honourably and unsensationally about death.

Titillation of readers (and filmgoers) through close viewing of dead (and often naked or semi-clothed) female bodies is a staple in popular culture. It has become particularly associated with hard-boiled crime writing, and with the pulp magazines that built large readerships at least in part on the allure of the blonde in the bathtub. One of the challenges for crime writers today is to foreground the victims of violence as real people, and not merely as provocative ciphers to give a story some pizzazz.

In later books, my concerns about the portrayal of death shifted. In *Running for Shelter*, the body of a teenager is found among piles of garbage in an alley, by people queuing for the cinema. This scene focuses on the impact on those accidentally caught up in the discovery of the body.

They should have let the body be. The officers who interviewed them about their discovery found that they had watched enough police procedurals to know that. But a seventeen-year old in a pink duffle coat had suddenly gone wild. She was what used to be known, without irony, as a good girl – friendly and honest, a companion to her mum, a treasure to her dad. The discovery of a girl buried under garbage had turned her world upside down.

... She looked at the slender throat, the jutting collarbones, the tiny breasts, for the girl was naked. She saw the concave rim around the belly, so different from her own soft stomach. She saw the thin thighs and the blood-splashed legs and the beautiful toes. Nothing escaped her notice. Years later, when her husband had left her and she was struggling to bring up three children on her own, she would wake up in the night in a cold sweat, every detail of this body imaged in hard-edged clarity in her mind.

In *Standing in the Shadows*, a woman's body is found beneath a walnut tree. This time, the emphasis is on the way death is filtered through different people's accounts, until we no longer know what is 'true'.

Howard Flatt's description of the murder was flecked with hesitation; just the facts. Geraldine King had died, he told me, on the fourteenth of October.

He left out all the important things. ... I only learned later – from Becca Hunter – that blood from the head wounds and run-off from the evening rain had puddled around the body as it impressed slowly into the soft earth. That by the time Geraldine was found, her cardigan was as wet as sea moss, her skirt so drenched that the tea roses in the print showed scarcely at all. It was Becca who reported that, when she touched Geraldine, the plushy arms were surfaced with the chill of death.

'And next to her body, just a few feet away,' Howard explained, as if he had omitted nothing, 'was the tree. And partway up the tree, at the head of the ladder, was a platform. And that was where—.' He came to a halt, a frown on the scale of the Cheddar Gorge splitting his bony brows.

'It's all right,' I said quietly. 'I remember.'

The point I'm trying to make is that, when you embark on writing a crime novel, you cannot avoid touching on the delicate and important stuff of death and dying. Writers of comic crime may lighten the terror of death by hedging it around with unexpected and amusing observations. For all other crime writers, there's everything to be gained by taking it seriously – and many different ways of doing so.

Concluding reflections on crime writing: gloom, doom and woe is me?

Glancing back at the subheadings I've given to these reflections – 'The shadow of violence', 'The grim reaper' – I fear I may have given the impression that crime writing is a morose, funereal sort of occupation. And that crime writers themselves are gloomy, doomy people. Nothing could be further from the truth.

As I've said before, crime writers are, with a few exceptions, a cordial and sociable lot. Some start out like that. Others, stiff and bristling at the outset, mellow as they deflect their aggression on to the page. Some, like me, discover that sharing dreads and disquiets by writing dissipates the blacker thoughts, and leaves us feeling lighter.

But the best explanation for the cheer that emanates from the persons of crime writers (as opposed to their novels) is that advanced by the writer Laura Wilson. If you spend much of your working day wrestling with the darker side of the human psyche, she points out, you surface to the delightful discovery that the real world is actually a pretty wonderful place.

Try it, and you'll see.

Reflections II

by Laurie R. King: A life of crime (fiction)

I am a story-teller. I am the descendant of cave-dwellers and itinerant jongleurs, epic poets and tavern bards, mothers distracting a feverish child and Scheherazade spinning out stories to save her life. My people are those who have tried, over the millennia, to understand the world by telling a tale about it.

And maybe, just maybe, to change it a little.

> **FOR LEE CHILD on ...**
>
> *the* thrillers – the genre – in human evolution, see 'Tips and tales – guest contributors', p. 116.

My background is in academic theology. I turned from a life of God (studying about God, anyway) to a life of crime in my mid-thirties, when small children, combined with a husband who gazed longingly towards retirement, made it clear that spending the next ten or twelve years doing a PhD in Ugaritic and Near Eastern Studies was not a practical option. I was one of the lucky ones, who found a home in the publishing world in time to save my children from begging on the streets. My first book came out 'only' six years after I started writing. Five more years, and I was actually making a living at it. I won some lovely prizes, I edged up on the best-seller lists, I was named guest of honour at some great conferences. And yes, I felt the cold winds blowing through the publishing world, when a world recession linked with an explosion of technological distractions to threaten the future of the printed page.

It is impossible at this writing, in 2012, to predict where those winds will take the world of books. I believe that traditional publishing will find its resilience – some of the sharpest minds I know are in the industry – and that boom or bust, e-books or print, people hunger for stories, and the system of acquisition, editing and publication that we have known for a couple of centuries will draw new breath, and surge on.

No, the story-teller's art is not dying. The forms in which it is transmitted to its audience may be undergoing a radical shift, but the key element, the story itself, is as exuberant as ever.

Which means that telling the best story possible – the richest, most evocative tale concerning the most fully rounded characters in a thought-provoking setting, a story that sings on the lips and reverberates in the listener's ear – is more important than ever.

That is why this book came about.

Mysteries, greater and lesser

Once upon a time, in a world before children and earning a living, I spent a few years among people intending to enter the ministry. Some of them were fresh-faced, clear-eyed young things who had planned their careers since childhood, with nary a doubt that this was the life for them. Others were men and women with grey hair and thickening waistlines, who had spent two or three decades doing what they had trained for (law, teaching, therapy, business) and making a success of it, before giving in to the realisation that being a lawyer or therapist wasn't enough. But young or old, if you asked them why they were going into a job that paid little, had terrible hours and guaranteed stress, most of them couldn't give you a reason that would win the approval of a high-school careers counsellor.

They referred to it as a calling. Sometimes the person called would jump at the very thought of a life of service to a congregation, other times one got the sense that he or she was being dragged towards the ministry with heels dug in, but in either case, there was agreement: something intangible was pulling them into the ministry, which was simply the place they needed to be.

Let me hasten to say that no, I do not regard the writing of novels as a ministry, although (as Michelle says) there are definite therapeutic elements to fiction, and I have been honoured to know how many people use my writing as an escape from some truly grinding situations. The analogy is a limited one, focusing on the parallel of the intangible impulse – in this case, to write, and specifically, to write crime.

Making a crime writer

Just as there are a handful of people who know that they will be writers as adults, so there are a few writers who always knew they wanted to write crime fiction, who started producing mysteries before they were out of their teens. The vast majority of us come to crime, if not to writing itself, later in life, tentatively picking up pen or laptop after having spent years and years reading in the genre. Our skills are learned, largely, by absorption, like the person who has lived so long among foreigners he begins to speak the language without thinking.

That was how I came to crime fiction. I grew up with books, since we moved so often when I was young that making friends became far too much work compared to the easy companionship of a library. I was a dreamy child, immersed in the world of fiction that was both escape and education, and I can only wonder that it never occurred to me early on that I, too, could become a writer. I suppose I felt that the books on the library shelves must have been laid there by some divine hand, that mere mortals had nothing to do with them. Perhaps if I'd met an actual author as a child, I'd have begun writing a lot sooner.

FOR GEORGE PELECANOS on ...
the power of books, see 'Tips and tales – guest contributors', p. 142.

It wasn't until I hit my mid-thirties that I sat down to write a book. My first venture was a futuristic novel, which I set aside halfway through (I did eventually finish it) when I realised I had no idea how to write a novel. Three or four years later, when my children were old enough to be in school a few days a week, I sat down again.

This time, my defining sentence was, 'I was fifteen when I first met Sherlock Holmes, fifteen years old with my nose in a book as I walked the Sussex Downs, and nearly stepped on him.'

This time, I had a voice, a setting and a character that could carry me forward into the story.

This time, I finished the novel.

It took seven years to get it published, but *The Beekeeper's Apprentice* is still in print, it has sold hundreds of thousands of copies in numerous languages and formats, and I am one of those rare creatures who make a decent living out of making up stories and setting them on a page. I have more than twenty books in print and a number of shorter stories.

There are few greater joys than to be able to say, 'I lie for a living'.

The path to where I stand was convoluted – typical of crime writers, whose bios tend to read like a survey of colourful minimum-wage employment. Steve Jobs, giving a Stanford commencement speech that looked at his journey to Apple, talked about the steps: 'You can't connect the dots looking forward. You can only connect them looking backward. So you have to trust that the dots will somehow connect to your future.'

Each of us can trace a similar path in our lives. Elements of my varied background – my academic interests, my travels, my personal life – can all be found in the fiction I write.

Take, for example, my first standalone suspense novel, *A Darker Place* (*Birth of a New Moon* in the UK). It began with the figure of a woman I had dreamed, or perhaps envisioned, when I was seventeen: an older woman who walked with a cane and lived with a couple of dogs in a cabin in the woods. Just that: a mental picture of what the touchy-feely types might call a spirit guide, who then stood quietly in the back of my mind for two decades, until I decided that she would be the starting place for a book: dot one.

Dot two: as an undergraduate I did a course in alchemical symbols, the images used by medieval alchemists to describe the external transformation of lead into gold, and the internal transformation of their inner selves.

Dot three: in November 1978, at the annual joint meeting of the American Academy of Religion and Society for Biblical Literature in New Orleans, all that the theologians could talk about was the apparent mass suicide of a cult known as Jonestown, then blaring across the headlines. And fifteen years later, the Waco siege exploded, dominating television screens across the nation.

Dot four: graduate-level courses taken during the 1980s were mostly text-focused – my Master's was in Bible, not religious studies or ministry – but one underlying and inescapable thread was the process by which a radical offshoot of Judaism called Christianity came to rule an empire: How does a splinter religious group grow and become mainstream?

Dot five: during a 1995 combination book tour/spring break, my two children and I explored the Arizona high desert, including Sedona.

Dot six: being married to an Anglo-Indian with ties to England, I came to know the country fairly well. During one trip to Cornwall, I visited the 'lost' Heligan gardens.

In 1997, these six random ideas coalesced into a book: grey-haired Anne Waverley, who lives in solitude in the deep woods with a pair of dogs, and still uses a cane from an earlier run-in with religious fanaticism, investigates a potentially dangerous group that draws inspiration from alchemical imagery, a cult in the process of expanding from its high desert setting to a new centre in the midst of a hermetically sealed English garden.

I am an excellent recycler of material: the BA thesis I wrote on *The Holy Fool in Western Culture* flowered into the novel *To Play the Fool;* my series character Mary Russell, herself a student of theology (imagine that!), in one story gives informal tutorials on *Feminine Aspects of God in the Old Testament* (which by remarkable coincidence happens also to be my own MA thesis title) working with Hebrew and Greek (languages I also happened to study in grad school). In another story, she is given a first-century papyrus that could blow Christianity open – a letter with curious links to certain graduate courses on the Church Fathers and Mothers and on women and leadership in early Christianity ...

As for travel: *The Game* takes place in India, *O Jerusalem* in Israel, part of *The Language of Bees* is set in the Orkneys, 'The Salt Pond' in highland Papua New Guinea, *Garment of Shadows* in Morocco – need I say I have been to all those places?

And personal life? Characters in Mary Russell's 1906 San Francisco bear a remarkable resemblance to my own family, there at the time of the earthquake and fire. My kids claim that elements of the younger characters in various novels duplicate parts of their personalities and histories. And as for older husbands – well, with a husband thirty years my senior, I will merely say that nothing Mary Russell finds when she marries Sherlock Holmes would astonish me.

In none of these stories are the details heavily autobiographical. Rather, the adventures and experiences of the characters are infused with my own understanding and experiences. It is less a case of writing what I know than writing who I am.

(If you're interested, I talk more about the process of converting life into fiction in a lengthy autobiography written for *Contemporary Author*, on www.LaurieRKing.com.)

The dreamy child grew up to craft what John Gardner calls the 'vivid and continuous dream' of fiction. My childhood love of books, my intellectual interest in religion, the raising of children, the building of houses, and the travel I've done all merge into what I write. And my lack of formal education in the craft of writing no doubt contributes to *how* I write, which is basically: I get behind the wheel and set off.

Perhaps not only how, but *what* I choose to write, as well.

Because yes, the dots do connect.

The mystery of the mystery

Discussions regularly flare up about the relative merits of genre fiction – story-telling – versus proper literature; about how shoddy, garish, popularised novels steal all the niches on the *New York Times* best-seller list, while meticulous, navel-gazing, too-subtle-for-the-masses tomes hog all the good spots on the same newspaper's book review pages. Mostly this sound and fury is on the part of fans and reviewers, since those of us who write for a living are too busy for full-out combat.

I bring it up because of a question the two writers of this volume discussed early on: Would this be a book on Crime Writing, or on writing?

Granted, this book will focus on the Crime side of the fiction world, and certainly, there are specific needs and attitudes that the genre requires and mainstream fiction does not. However, those of us who are serious about what we do, who strive to write the very best sentence, and paragraph, and book that we can, think of ourselves as writers, not crime writers.

Personally, I'm more than happy here in my genre neighbourhood. I treasure the formal requirements of Crime, and I have never found myself chafing at its limitations. Crime, for me, has been a broad roof, with infinite possibilities for exploring the story-teller's craft.

So to answer the question: This is a book on writing, crime.

'Why do you write crime fiction?'

I am often asked this, in interviews or public events, often by those who politely withhold the second half of the sentence: '– when you're good enough to write real books?' The answer I give depends on my whim, and on who is asking, and why: *I started with mysteries because I knew nothing about writing and at least this genre had some rules.* Or: *I didn't know I was writing genre fiction, until it was categorised as such.* Or: *A mystery allows me to explore the Greater Mysteries of life, and death, and other Important Things.* Or even: *As a young mother, I had a* lot *of aggression to work off.*

The truth is, like a lot of crime writers, I more or less backed into the neighbourhood: I started writing, then discovered that what I was doing shared characteristics with things called mysteries. But once I realised that this was where I lived, and set out to explore my new home, I found that not only was I more than comfortable here, it was a serendipitous find – connecting dots I did not know were leading anywhere:

WHY THE MYSTERY?

(This essay was originally written for the Mystery Writers of America 1996 Edgar Awards programme. Part of it, amusingly enough, appeared – with neither permission nor acknowledgement – as the background typescript in a season trailer of the television series Castle*, apparently*

'borrowed' to represent a piece of writing by the eponymous character, a fictional writer of crime fiction.)

Why the mystery novel? The classic mystery, the Christie-esque whodunit, is built upon a crime and its resolution. However, since many non-mystery novels begin with a similar foundation, as an aid to the beleaguered bookseller who just wants to know where to shelve the things, the publishing world sweeps together an often mismatched lot of books and classifies them as 'Mysteries'. The childlike simplicity of the move leaves one gasping.

What do we do when an established mainstream writer such as, say, Jane Smiley, Michael Ondaatje or Michael Chabon produces something that in other hands would be shelved in the genre section? Do we call it simply a dark novel that happens to deal with a crime? Worse, what are we to think when a known multiple offender of crime fiction such as Josephine Tey or Peter Dickinson comes up with a perfect literary gem that has only the most tenuous dependence on the form?

The whole genre question is further complicated by the undeniable fact that much crime fiction is indeed pap, pre-digested and undemanding, suitable for the reader who either lacks the inner fortitude necessary for tackling something with fibre (moral or otherwise) or simply doesn't feel up to chewing his or her way through something substantial after a hard day's work. Many writers, good writers who ought to know better, focus so tightly on the structure demanded by a crime story that they lose track of the fact that they are writing a novel. Accusations of both sensationalism and trivialisation are, alas, often justified.

(Since we are concerned here with the mystery field, I shall politely refrain from pointing to the pap in mainstream fiction, those books where Nothing Happens apart from 300 pages of kvetching about a divorce. True, most mainstream pap gets thrown out before it sees print, whereas with a mystery, there's always the hope that someone will fall for a gaudy cover. The point I'm making is not who has the worse record, but the difficulties in categorising a book.)

A crime novel is about something; a mainstream story can be about anything. Knowing that a book is assigned to a genre makes the would-be reader feel snug or smug, depending on how that reader feels about the genre. To those who buy my books in order to curl up in the story, I can only say, thank you. To the smug deprecator of the mystery novel, I have to shake my head and say, *You're missing some fine writing.*

So why the mystery? Because it is a strong form that none the less allows me to do what I wish with it, possessing both rigid structure and immense freedom. On its bones I can hang a story about things that matter, about death and pain and the dark side of the human mind, about fear and triumph and joy and the price we pay for justice. A story about the full gamut of human response.

The mystery novel, because the form is as big as I need it to be, and as intimate.

The mystery, because it's human.

Why do I *read* crime fiction? It entertains me, yes, but it also teaches me about sides of life I will never see, and challenges me to think about my own actions.

The crime story is, at base, a tale of quest. Medieval romances such as the saga of King Arthur saw knights questing, most famously, for the Holy Grail. The knight departs, to be caught up in a dark and perilous journey in which he becomes lost – or rather, during which the fact that he is lost slowly becomes clear to him. The mythologist Joseph Campbell describes the journey as the hero setting out from his comfortable, everyday world into a place of terrible forces and wonder, where he finally achieves victory and returns to his world, bringing some boon for his fellows. Many of Campbell's elements are found in crime fiction: hesitation and an initial refusal of the call to adventure; some mentor who bestows a crucial gift;

a dark road with trials, temptation and acceptance; and an often reluctant return, to the land he left, and where he finds himself irrevocably changed by his journey.

That last, to me, is the most important element of crime fiction: the hero comes back changed. Because the role of the story-teller is to put the listener – the reader – into the hero's shoes for every step of the journey. And a writer wants, more than anything else, for the reader to come back from the story changed.

What I love about writing crime fiction is that this journey can wear all kinds of trappings: when it comes to the details of the story, I can do whatever I want. I can shape it into a frivolous romp or a serious exploration of the impulse to terrorism; I can be intellectual or snappy; I can revel in language while making words invisible; I can tell a story about the past that is a mirror to the present.

I can look at the dark side of a good man, and the good side of an evil one, never forgetting that the villain is the hero of his own story.

I can talk about things that matter while providing simple entertainment – and I can provide entertainment that is not simple, for people badly in need of distraction. Nothing makes me happier than being told that one of my books has let a reader forget for a while the hospital bed at whose side she was sitting, that reading a story aloud provided contact between two people.

The crime novel is of the world, and as such there are few limits to where it can be set, or to what people may inhabit it.

Still just writing haiku?

There's a fair amount of romance and self-glorification that goes on when talking about the act of putting words on a page – variations on the theme of, 'Writing is easy, you just sit at the typewriter and open a vein.' Anyone who has earned a living by cleaning motel rooms, digging holes or caring for small children is justified in thinking that the person glorifying the agonies of a writer never had to pay the rent by scrubbing toilets.

On the other hand, there is also a fair amount of belittlement when it comes to putting words on a page. Some years ago, I was in town for a conference and took my college-age daughter to dinner with some friends. One boy asked what I did, and when told I was a writer, said politely how nice that was for me. A couple of weeks later, he spotted a display of my books at the local bookstore, and came to my daughter in surprise. 'Your mom's a *writer*!' he exclaimed. She said yes, she knew, and in fact she had told him. 'Yeah, but when you said she's a "writer", I thought you meant haiku or something!'

Since this book is being written by people who are real writers, yet who have also spent time wielding scrub-brushes, you'll find a certain amount of perspective here when it comes to the relative importance of what we do.

Compared to creating world peace or finding a vaccine for AIDS, OK, this is small.

But when it comes to being a writer? When it comes to your right to claim enough time and freedom to put your words on a page? When it comes to the integrity and thoroughness of what you're writing? When it comes to the validity of genre fiction? To the nobility of story-telling? To the right for your work to be considered as work, and thus taken seriously?

There we're without mercy: it matters.

If you write, you are a writer. You walk in a noble tradition, and if your work in progress isn't *War and Peace*, or even *The Da Vinci Code*, so what? After all, your disapproving lawyer-sister ('Don't you think you've wasted enough time with your hobby?') is never going to be a Supreme Court Justice; your exasperated husband ('But I thought you'd be published by now!') should spend more time with the kids, anyway; your supercilious neighbour ('I don't read fiction.') is getting wrinkles from the facial expression caused by eating sour grapes.

Women especially find it hard to assert the validity of their writing. As Anne Tyler said, 'I was standing in a schoolyard waiting for a child when another mother came up to me. "Have you found work yet?" she asked, "or are you still just writing?"' Anne Tyler, who would become a best-selling author and winner of multiple awards, including the Pulitzer. Anne Tyler, who is still just writing.

Gilbert and Sullivan put people like Tyler on their list of eminently disposable individuals:

That singular anomaly, the lady novelist –
I don't think she'll be missed – I'm sure she'll not be missed!

If writers of crime fiction are given little respect by the literary lions of the age, the lady novelist is given less – and as for the lady *crime* novelist ... well, you can imagine. In 1987, a group of women crime writers founded Sisters in Crime in part to address the inequality of book reviews, of which women received about 15 per cent of the male writers' tally. As founder Sara Paretsky put it, 'I could accept that the men were twice as good as I was, but *seven* times as good?' After twenty-five years, the rate has gone up to – depending on the magazine or journal – 20 or 30 per cent. Fortunately, publishing houses and readers continue to buy books by women.

So I urge you, reading this now: do not worry about the lawyer-sister or the exasperated spouse. Instead, you will take your work seriously even when the rest of the world looks askance at your 'hobby'. You will be gently assertive of your right to carve out as much time for yourself as a busy life permits. And you will write.

Writing as an active verb

But surely, successful writers – those who make a living from words on a page – have a secret? Some surefire technique for success?

They do: they write.

FOR LAURA LIPPMAN on ...

showing up every day, see 'Tips and tales – guest contributors', p. 129.

When a writer like me answers the question, 'How many books have you written?' she often hears the response, 'Wow, you're really disciplined!' The polite reply is not a snort, but a demurral that it's not a discipline if you love doing it. Which is true – to some extent. What's truer is, it's not so much discipline as the powerful knowledge looming in the front of my mind, every day: If I'm not writing, I'm not a writer.

The primary characteristic of writers who sell enough to qualify for the title is that they put words on a page. Some of them clock in to forty-hour, five-day work-weeks; others nurture their fiction in the precious forty-eight hours of Saturdays and Sundays, while still others plunge into a first draft and spend every day there, to emerge, blinking, weeks later. Some enter the process with all the loathing of a colonoscopy (or so they claim), while others slide into a new book as if they were giving in to an illicit affair. One writer is most productive dictating, to secretary or software, while his brother attacks a yellow pad with a fountain pen.

But all produce words. If they don't, they're not writers, they're readers who dabble.

Now, considering the current state of publishing, and the ever more limited percentage of the average reader's income each writer is jostling to receive, I ought happily to say: if you don't feel like writing, by all means don't. Less competition for me, less headache for you. But if you've come this far into *Crime and Thriller Writing*, that may not be an option. You want to write, you *need* to write, but what you also need is an insider's look into how that is done.

Let's begin by assuming you have a life, one that doesn't leave you staring at the walls wondering how you're going to fill the next twelve hours. You already have a life that doesn't leave a lot of time for friends, much less for taking on a new part-time job.

On the other hand, maybe you've just quit (or, these days, more likely been downsized) and are deciding that it's now or never with the writing gig.

Either way, the answer's the same: you write.

A novel is anywhere from 50,000 words up; a page of typescript has in the neighbourhood of 250 words. Surely you can write 250 words a day?

If so, in seven months, you'll have a novel – the first draft of one, at any rate. Can't imagine where you'll fit it in? Michael Gilbert wrote dozens of novels and short stories, many of them penned on the train, morning and evening, while he commuted to his job in London.

So that's your Step One: ruthlessly carve a slice out of your day, and devote it to the written word, the whole written word, and nothing but the written word.

Then comes the question, what to write? There you are, sitting in your study/at the library/in the coffee shop with your laptop/legal pad/digital voice recorder, in the hour before the kids get up/on your bus home from work/with the entire day ahead of you, and the page is blank.

What do *you* love about this genre of crime? What keeps *you* up reading until far too late, makes you willing to shell out for a hardback on the day of publication, tell your friends about it, reread it until you can recite portions?

What is the thing that, if it's lacking in an otherwise fine book, might find you laying the book aside and forgetting to finish it?

This is not quite the same question as what category of crime fiction you like. You may find yourself reading a lot of thrillers, not necessarily for the breakneck pace and tension, but because that's where you've found the tight plotting you crave. You may look at the books on your shelves and notice that they're mostly gentle, pure mysteries – 'cosies' – not because you care one way or the other about their absence of graphic sex and violence, but because you adore the structure and mental gymnastics of the whodunit.

Take a look at the last book you really loved, and make a list of just what it was that excited you. It might look something like this:

- Dialogue (tight, specific to the character, and multi-purpose)
- Humour (often within the dialogue)
- Setting (in this case, a city I'm not crazy about, but the writer revels in it)
- Specifics (by this I mean research, but seamless to the story)

This list is based on a novel I read recently, the story of a pair of New York private investigators. If I looked at the last half dozen books I've enjoyed, I might come up with a few more characteristics, or I might not. But as I did my analysis, I would find myself with a fairly specific description of what I aim at with my own writing.

But will it sell? You've narrowed down what you like, but you're wondering if anyone will buy such a thing. If maybe you ought to take a closer look at the best-seller lists and see if you can figure out what's hot.

FOR SARA PARETSKY on ...

'brands' versus the truth that fiction bares, see 'Tips and tales – guest contributors', p. 138.

In fact, there is very little point in writing what's hot at the moment. By the time you hear the stampede of interest, it's already on its way past. There must be a thousand writers out there with vampire books in their computers, for every one currently selling. Unless you can 1) judge a trend before it breaks and 2) write a book and have it published in no time at all, don't bother.

Write what you love, and if you are lucky, others will love it too.

A community of stories

Writing has saved my life. A shy child whose best friends were between the pages of books has become a person at home in the world, whose real friends inhabit that same world of books.

The books I write have given me a community, of writers, publishers, booksellers. I am at home among people who find nothing the least bit unusual in sitting all day, every day, pounding words on to a screen. People who accept that as work. People who have no lack of opinions about the role of the adverb, the use of graphic sex in a novel, or the fictional death of old women. Men and women who can sit in a bar sharing casual anecdotes on the motivation of serial killers and commiserating on bad cover art. People who understand that when a deadline is looming, no you really can't go to the movies; who understand that when a first draft is burning through your brain, no you really can't be expected to talk like a human being.

My people.

But I have also found a community of readers, men and women who worship the story, and – this is still a peculiar sensation to me – worship those who write the story. Men and women who listen to my words, who share my pleasures, who treat my work far more solemnly than I do myself, and who know far more about it. People who come out and see me on a cold night in Seattle or a baking day in Phoenix; who 'friend' me and 'comment' on me and pass me on to 'friend' and friend alike, who are there to help me when I forget a character's name or hair colour. People with demanding lives who give me endless hours of their limited free time, first to read the words I put on the page, then to support me and make my life easier. Who talk to each other, online and in person, and grow a community around the characters I have written.

Who think that perhaps a writer like me might have advice worth listening to.

People who believe in me.

Ways of writing

Because so much of what is said throughout the book rests on how two very different writers go about doing their jobs, Michelle and Laurie talk here about how the world looks from a pair of vastly different perspectives.

Michelle Spring: The Orderly School of Writing

My way of writing crime novels has been hammered out, gradually, by trial and error. The first draft of *Every Breath You Take* almost wrote itself – spilling out on to the page, as some first novels do. It felt on occasion as if an electric current were running from some switched-on part of my brain to my fingertips – as if the part of me that normally plans, and considers, and decides had been completely by-passed. In that state of high excitement, over a period of months, in between giving lectures, and looking after two small children, I wrote 150 pages.

When the 150 pages were finished, I weighed the manuscript against other novels on my bookshelf, and realised that it wasn't nearly substantial enough. More like a novella, or a long story, than a novel. So I devised an interconnecting subplot, and then wrote it up, weaving it around the existing story as I went. It felt as if I were taking two fine strands of hair, and braiding them together until I had a sturdy plait.

It's often said that the second novel is harder than the first one. It certainly was for me. Not quite a novice any more, I knew far more about the challenges ahead, and I felt self-conscious and uncertain. Three months passed in which I learned the meaning of writer's block. I started, wrote for half an hour, read the pages over, and ripped them up. I had a coffee, started again, and stopped again. Soon even a pile of dirty laundry looked more attractive to me than the prospect of writing. The electricity had been well and truly switched off.

That's when I finally came up with the approach that has served me well ever since. For the first time, I planned before I wrote – and writer's block was banished.

Roughly, after I have the germ of an idea for a story, my process of planning (or plotting) works in two stages. First, I turn this idea into two or three scenarios, each a paragraph or so in length. Then I select the most promising scenario and develop it into a detailed outline that tracks the action through (at the least) the first and final portions of the book.

Simple! But of course it's not simple at all. And since many potentially excellent writers are stumped by the challenges of plotting, I've included in this volume a detailed breakdown of the process. (See the chapter 'Getting Ready' below.)

Creating that outline for my second novel was one of the toughest things I've done in my adult life, and also one of the most useful. It helped me to understand how stories develop. How to achieve simplicity and economy – how, for example, one character can be made to do the work of two, in ways that benefit the story. It enabled me to predict problems with pace or progression, and nail these right away.

Writers who outline are sometimes dismissed as people who lack imagination, as cowards who hide their creativity behind a rigid plan of work. But that's not how it feels. When I sit down with a morning's work in front of me, what I feel is excitement. The outline gives me my marching orders: *produce a scene at a May Ball at St John's College, Cambridge; introduce a pretty young guest; by the end of the scene, have her disappear.* Far from feeling fettered by instructions such as these, I find them exhilarating. I'm free to experiment, to approach the scene any way I like. I can begin, say, with the girl dressing for the ball, or with the committee supervising the decorations, or with a roadie testing the sound system. I can approach it as an omniscient observer, or from the perspective of the girl or one of the other guests. (As it happens, I couldn't resist the urge to begin with the feeling of anticipation that permeates the centre of Cambridge as the evening draws near ....).

For me, writing with an outline means the freedom to deploy language as I choose, and to shape a scene I like, but with the comfortable awareness that, yes: this scene will mesh well with those that follow, and it will play its part in creating a coherent narrative.

This Orderly approach is not how everyone writes, but it is what works for me. The alternative (see Laurie's description of 'The Organic Way' below) is to a produce a delightfully fast and furious first draft, and then to uncover the plot in the course of several rewrites, abandoning the irrelevant parts of the first draft as you go.

In the end, perhaps the choice comes down to this: would you rather write purposefully and then use your rewrite to polish and perfect? Or write feverishly without much thought for the story, and then do extensive, painstaking rewrites? I'm a purposeful writer, every time.

Laurie R. King: The Organic Way

I have little formal training in the crafting of fiction. I was taught writing basics – indeed, I am probably of the last generation tutored in the art of diagramming a sentence – but for the most part, I learned technique by osmosis.

This goes far to explain my system of writing – or lack thereof.

I am a writer of the old school. I average a book a year; I have had two editors in my life; I am always under contract for one or more books. Every book I have written is still in print. All of which means that much of what is talked about in this volume does not currently apply to me.

On the other hand, every book is a new world, and I enter it as I did when I began, half a lifetime ago.

Earlier, I talked about the apparently random dots that connect and give rise to a book. At other times, the elements that shape a book are sought out deliberately, as a plant's roots seek nutrients.

In the beginning is a seed. It is always a small seed, a mere speck of potential. Often it is a question: 'What would Rembrandt look like if he were a woman?' (*A Grave Talent*); 'What would a holy fool look like in modern San Francisco?' (*To Play the Fool*); 'Whatever happened to Kipling's Kim?' (*The Game*). It may be a phrase that catches my imagination, such as, 'The First Blast of a Trumpet Against *A Monstrous Regiment of Women*' (the glorious if long-winded title of a John Knox treatise). It may take the form of a challenge to myself: Can I write a book from a man's point of view? (*Keeping Watch*). Could I make the most competent and stable of individuals into an unreliable narrator? (*Locked Rooms*). The standalone *Folly* started with the wish to write a book that didn't require weeks of research, and I already knew about house-building (although inevitably, in the end there was as much research involved as any other book).

But in each of these, the initial seed – the embryonic idea – was only a wisp. In each case, once that seed was planted, roots greedily spread out, searching for ways to feed the idea, to build on it, to make it grow.

Perhaps a better analogy is that of a pearl: the book begins with a piece of grit, sitting in my mind, irritating me, collecting material to itself, layer upon layer.

Take that question, *Whatever happened to Kim?* A quick review of *Kim* and its author tells me that, yes, I could use it as the basis for a story in my series that is currently set in 1924. And because the book will be part of a series, I already have my main characters. Plus that, I've been to India – and my Anglo-Indian husband can help me with details.

So I cast out the first threadlike roots, absorbing the elements from which the book will be made. I read *A Passage to India*, yes, but also Forster's memoir of his time as private secretary to a maharaja, *The Hill of Devi*. And looking at 1924, I come across the accounts of a government census-taker, with a wealth of detail about life on the road, moving through rural villages across the north. Then there's the book I'd read some time before, Tahir Shah's bizarre and ridiculous account of his apprenticeship to a travelling magician in India, *Sorcerer's Apprentice*. Add to that a 1923 tome by Robert Baden-Powell (yes, the Boy Scouts founder) on the art of pig-sticking, and my growing story has put down a tap root.

My protagonists would sail to India to find the missing Kim, now a middle-aged man. They leave an England where the freshly elected Labour Party is threatening to turn the country Bolshevik, travelling to India – where the Russians are similarly moving behind the borders.

And because that part of the world is still in the headlines, still facing the same international issues, I begin to feel the present-day reverberations that good historical fiction calls for.

At this point, an Orderly writer would be constructing a detailed outline.

I, on the other hand, find myself at that tipping point where uncertainty gives way to impatience.

So I start to write.

Trust and the Organic system

Writing is the ultimate faith-based initiative. How can my editor be sure that I'm going to give her the book she's already paid me a big chunk of money for? How can I take money for something that's nothing more than a vague idea? How can I possibly believe that launching myself off into a story with no more preparation than some pages of notes is a good idea?

For one thing, both my editor and I have done it before.

For another, crime fiction has the singular advantage of a basic structure. Crime fiction in general, and the mystery in particular, have a system of internal design not found in more mainstream fiction. This is the source of much criticism, as though a writer of sonnets and sestinas has less to say about the world than a practitioner of free verse. We will go into crime fiction's specific subgenres in a little while, but all share the requirement of a tight structure: a plot.

Even if what I write tends to be more suspense than whodunit, there are requirements I must meet: a crime, a puzzle, a protagonist surrounded by uncertainty and threat, who must solve the crime in order to restore order. There are bones to build before the story can move under its own power, and although I might flesh them out in a hundred different ways, knowing that the bones must be there gives crime writing a structure that mainstream fiction, or genres such as science fiction, lack.

And although for a writer like Michelle, the 'automatic writing' style is a one-time affair, for me – a proponent of what we are calling the Organic School of Writing – that basic knowledge is enough to begin me on my way.

I sit down; I give myself permission to write crap, locking the door on all impulses towards self-criticism; and I sink into that 'vivid and continuous dream' of the story. I keep notes of where my research is thin (more about research later, too) but I don't stop to hunt down that information unless the plot threatens to sail off a cliff without it. I put in subplots that I'm not sure about and allow my characters to move across a landscape (physical, social and political) that is only faintly sketched in. I introduce characters who don't quite fit, add scenes that go nowhere, permit actions that aren't clearly motivated. I spend two or three months, writing from one to three thousand words a day, and end up with 300 pages of shining chaos.

As a first draft, it is beyond rough. It is a hodge-podge of poorly related characters and events, partial storylines, inadequate plotting. It is utterly unpublishable: bad, senseless, untidy, incomplete – unlike many, perhaps even most writers, my first drafts are thin and incomplete, with much of the story left out rather than having everything dumped in. What I have in my hands at the end of three months of work is little more than a 300-page outline of the book I will write.

But it has one great, gleaming and singular virtue: it exists. Three months earlier, all I had was an idea.

Now it has a basic plot, waiting to be developed. The characters, too, are there, albeit in glimpses and behind curtains. Short bits of it excite me. But most of all, it gives me raw material to work with.

Because for writers like me, the meat of the matter with a book is not in the writing, but in the rewrite.

When I am finished with the rough (oh, so very rough!) first draft, the only person I show it to is my editor, excellent woman, who has the astonishing ability to see a diamond caked with mud. She and I talk, and generally we agree on what the book needs.

Then, and only then, do I allow my Inner Critic back out of the closet where she has been locked for the past three months, raging in frustration while the editorial pencil has gone unwielded, the slipshod pages have accumulated, the library reference books gathered dust.

The Critic descends on the manuscript in a fury. No page – no paragraph – goes unassaulted. If a rare sentence squeaks past unchanged, it is sure to be a short one. Clean typescript is buried under pencil, as the main plot is hammered into place, the characters given flesh, the subplots teased into place, the research filled in.

It takes four or five months for my 300-page outline to become a 450-page manuscript that I am willing to show another human being. And even then, the manuscript goes through the editor's close scrutiny, then to a copyeditor, and maybe a couple of friends with good eyes for mistakes, before it is sent to the typesetter.

But let us not forget: Laurie R. King lies for a living. And she is lying about this, to you and to herself.

The truth of the matter is, by the time I start a book, Someone in the Back of My Head has a pretty clear idea where the story is going and how to get there. I simply do not put the plan to paper. And I certainly don't ask that Someone to tell me, for fear that if I know how everything turns out, my writing will go instantly dull. Transferring the plot to words on a page, even electronic words on a screen, threatens to bore me to tears, or into a state of terminal writer's block.

I, personally, need to feel the sensation of living on the edge while I am writing a first draft, to feel that anything could happen. Or far worse: nothing.

If I don't know what happens next to my characters, they surely can't know.

This is not a comfortable situation. I do not particularly recommend that you become a student of the Organic School and toss out all attempts at outlining. There are a lot of very bad books that come from the Organic School (and from the Orderly School as well, but those tend to be bad in a different way). And even when the book is good, the author has sometimes had to spend a truly idiotic amount of time fiddling with recalcitrant plot points that the Someone in the Back of Her Head overlooked.

As Tony Hillerman put it, to speak in favour of writing without an outline is like a fellow lacking a right arm trying to convince people about the superiority of left-handed bowling. It's simply the way some of us are made. And it is the way that works for me.

Not everyone feels this way. The co-author of this present book does not feel this way (which disagreement, I feel, improves the book no end). There are many superb writers who look with scorn, if not outright horror, on the Organic School of Writing, regarding the idea of a self-propelling story as amateurish and self-indulgent. And many of those Orderly writers, despite beginning their project with a detailed outline, do manage to capture a sense of spontaneity.

I am very happy for these members of the Orderly School. But I am not one of them, any more than William Faulkner, Thornton Wilder, Stephen King, Donald Westlake – well, you get the idea. The list is long.

I describe my style of writing because it may be yours. If you have never been able to outline a school project before writing it, if you get three scenes into planning your next book before the tedium of writing overwhelms you, then you may be a seat-of-the-pantser, a left-handed bowler, a devotee of the Organic School of Writing.

Coda

(For the use of a coda in crime fiction, see Part Three below ...)

We are story-tellers, you and I. We are the descendants of epic poets and tavern bards, mothers and myth-makers. We seek to understand the world by explaining it, through the medium of a story.

And maybe changing the world, just a little, as we go.

The world of crime

The roots of the matter: a history of crime fiction, by Laurie

Story-telling is as old as humanity. Stories are the way we make sense of the world, the way we pass down hard-learned wisdom, the way we celebrate triumphs, remember heroes, commemorate sacrifices.

We tend to credit Edgar Allan Poe with being the father of crime fiction, but what is *Hamlet* if not a murder mystery, or *Oedipus Rex* if not a thriller? A thousand years before Poe's C. Auguste Dupin was applying his 'ratiocinative' powers in the Rue Morgue, Scheherazade filled her thousand and one nights with puzzles and whodunits; a millennium before her, Daniel was playing detective to save lovely Susanna.

'Susanna and the Elders' belongs to the Apocrypha, a wild collection of stories and writings that were considered too esoteric ('*apokruphos*' means 'hidden') or in some way too problematical to be included in the canonical Bible. In the tale, a beautiful young married woman named Susanna is bathing in her garden when two lust-filled elders see her, want her, and attempt to blackmail her into submission by threatening to accuse her of adultery. She refuses, they accuse, and on their testimony she is sentenced to death – until young Daniel stands up and demands that he be allowed to question the two old men. Separately. One of the questions he asks each is, 'Under what kind of tree did Susanna meet her lover?' One says oak, the other says mastic, and since there is no mistaking one tree for the other, their lie is laid bare, and they are condemned instead.

Susanna and the Elders became one of the most popular stories performed in the medieval mystery plays. For centuries, mystery plays acted out a vital blend of entertainment and moral instruction, with the occasional, well-hidden dash of subversive political criticism, for the masses of Europe.

In the twenty-first century, the mystery play has a myriad of descendants, from the tale of an octogenarian amateur sleuth who lives in a small village and solves whimsical murders in between rose pruning and knitting, to a graphic, blood-drenched saga of a sexually motivated serial killer.

The nineteenth century saw the explosion of crime fiction, from Poe to Dickens, Collins to Doyle. In the era of Victoria, sensational titillation went hand in hand with the expectation of orderly behaviour, and dangerously changing social mores required moral warnings and a clear sense that Wrong will be Punished. In the early twentieth century, one gets the impression (not entirely true) that the ladies took over from the men, as Mary Roberts Rinehart seized the best-seller lists, followed by Agatha Christie, Dorothy L. Sayers, Ngaio Marsh and Josephine Tey.

But if women ruled the Golden Age, the men came on strong with the hard-boiled detective stories of the 1930s and 1940s, led by Hammett, Cain and Chandler, giving crime, as Chandler says, 'back to the kind of people that commit it for reasons, not just to provide a corpse'.

Of course, the development of crime fiction was nowhere near this tidy. The Victorian age had its fair share of bloodthirsty sex, and men could write Puzzle Age Mysteries as well as the ladies. But in all these, over all the eras, one finds the same elements that the medieval plays had – entertainment, moral instruction and a trace of political criticism – aimed at the everyday reader, not the capital-L Literary sort.

What *is* crime?

'Crime' is one of those words that have been around so long, their roots become obscured. The Greek *krima* refers to an offence or mistake that isn't necessarily a moral wrongdoing. Latin roots of decision and judgment overlay the Greek, so that *crimen* can mean either a charge of wrongdoing or a *cry* of distress – although that last etymology feels a bit stretched.

As a form of fiction, crime is considered a genre like science fiction, romance, horror, and the once-popular western. One of the synonyms occasionally given to genre fiction is formula fiction, an indication that predictability occasionally elbows aside a story's other elements.

One of the primary uses of a 'crime fiction' definition is to give the bookseller an idea where to put it on the shelves. It may be silly to shelve a novel about bored aristocrats figuring out a murder alongside an epic about the effect of an untimely death on the victim's family, but that's the way the publishing industry works.

FOR IAN RANKIN on ...
embracing the crime novel, see 'Tips and tales – guest contributors', p. 144.

For the most part, a crime novel has a death at its core. In some, the corpses are heaped high, while in others, the body in question is little more than an academic exercise. In thrillers, the corpse count tends to be high but largely theoretical – a looming threat – while a few excellent murder mysteries turn out to have no murder at all. Even in today's free and easy publishing world, mysteries for children and young adults tend to have few murders, and none at all for the younger market.

Murder or not, the crime around which the story is built has to matter. It must have sufficient weight and importance to keep a bookful of characters working hard to figure it out. Theoretically, 'any man's death diminishes me', but even John Donne might have found it tough to write a rousing novel about hunting down the perpetrator of an accidental, rainy-night, hit-and-run death of a smelly and disagreeable John Doe. The crime has to matter, to the writer and to the reader.

Because, as Michael Connelly has said, it's not so much the characters working on the crime as it is the crime working on the characters. A crime novel is about a crime because crime diminishes us, and writing about that process allows us, the readers, to fight against being diminished.

The crime spectrum, gentle to thriller

FOR S. J. ROZAN on ...
the soaring ur-story of genre fiction, see 'Tips and tales – guest contributors', p. 150.

Whether you love or loathe the overall categorisation of crime, it's hard to ignore it. Anyone who intends to sell a book needs to be aware of how the market works, and where within the machinery of publishing your particular niche – or, would-be niche – lies. You may choose to write a bloody and brutal story for teenagers or build a heart-pounding thriller around a dog-napping ring, but when it comes time to sell that story, you ought to know the uphill battle before you.

(Do we need to go into the disdain within the genre – the scorn of thriller readers for the lovers of cosies, the thinly veiled contempt with which the fan of detective fiction looks at the fuzzy-minded, rule-flouting suspense reader? Surely there's enough disapproval from outside this genre without permitting judgment from within.)

Crime fiction has a spectrum, with overlaps. Actually, it's mostly overlaps, since few novels fit perfectly into one slot. And in fact, titles we treat as synonymous here really aren't, since there is some difference between, say, a 'mystery' and a 'detective story'. To complicate matters further, something one person calls a 'PI novel' might also be called 'suspense' or even 'thriller'. However, since we are merely trying to point out some of the distinctive characteristics of different kinds of crime fiction, we will permit a certain amount of border-crossing.

To put the spectrum at its simplest: mysteries are rational, thrillers emotional. The pure detective story is a puzzle for the mind, with little interference from the heart (Dorothy Sayers, proponent of the classic mystery, apologised for the romantic elements she permitted to creep into *Busman's Honeymoon*, giving it the subtitle *A Love Story with Detective Interruptions*). The central problem is not urgent or immediate to the protagonist, the solution is intellectually satisfying, and the reader spends the book looking over the investigator's shoulder at unfolding events.

Suspense and thriller novels, on the other hand, are just that: stories that, while they may engage the mind, must elevate the pulse. The key problem involves a pressing and personal threat to the hero, the solution is cathartic, and the reader spends the whole book looking out of the protagonist's eyes – or, sitting on his shoulder, looking ahead at where greater trouble looms. We shall speak more about *how* both are written later; first, some definitions.

The mystery

Also called a detective story, a whodunit, or in its slightly pejorative form, a 'cosy', the classic mystery follows a clear pattern: a murder; an investigator; clues; suspects; red herrings; a clear solution. (In America, 'mystery' is the overall definition, so that 'Mystery Writers of America' includes thriller writers and whodunit authors alike.) An amateur investigator, often brought into the investigation by friendship or family connections, is typical of the cosy mysteries, but professionals are also found in intellectual crime fiction.

The intellectual game of the classic mystery begged for tongue-in-cheek solemnisation by those who had been through English public schools and universities. One such, Ronald Knox, in 1929 engraved the basic rules in stone:

FATHER KNOX'S DECALOGUE FOR CRIME FICTION

I. The criminal must be someone mentioned in the early part of the story, but must not be anyone whose thoughts the reader has been allowed to follow. [A rule clearly aimed at closing the barn door to would-be imitators of Christie's *Murder of Roger Ackroyd*.]

II. All supernatural or preternatural agencies are ruled out as a matter of course.

III. Not more than one secret room or passage is allowable.

IV. No hitherto undiscovered poisons may be used, nor any appliance which will need a long scientific explanation at the end.

V. No Chinaman must figure in the story. [These being the days of the arch-villain, Fu Manchu.]

VI. No accident must ever help the detective, nor must he ever have an unaccountable intuition which proves to be right.

VII. The detective must not himself commit the crime.

VIII. The detective must not light on any clues which are not instantly produced for the inspection of the reader.
IX. The stupid friend of the detective, the Watson, must not conceal any thoughts which pass through his mind; his intelligence must be slightly, but very slightly, below that of the average reader.
X. Twin brothers, and doubles generally, must not appear unless we have been duly prepared for them.

The rules are arch and silly, deliberately so. However, they point out two characteristics of early crime fiction: 1) cliché elements arrived early and 2) the mystery story's absolute foundation is: **one must play fair with the reader**. Readers must be given enough information that they could (if only they were attentive enough and clever enough) solve the mystery for themselves.

The PI novel

The private investigator, or private eye novel proudly claims roots in the 'pulp' era, when cheap novels printed on rough paper brought an air of hard-streets realism to readers accustomed to the drawing-room crime of the Golden Age. As Ed McBain says, 'All you had to do was talk out of the side of your mouth and get in trouble with the cops. ... If it weren't for the cops, the PI could solve a murder – any murder – in ten seconds flat.'

The PI is a lone wolf, working against the villains, the cops, and often against his own client as well. There were novels about female private investigators, confronting less two-fisted enemies, back in the mid-nineteenth century, but the private eye novel was thought of as a male world until Paretsky, Muller and Grafton crashed the club in the 1970s, bringing a female grittiness to the genre.

In the classic PI novel, the morality of the situation is not black and white, but drawn in shades of grey. The hero is a person of honour confronted with the possibility of a dishonourable solution.

The caper novel

The heist, the caper, the perfect crime, its details finessed to the nth degree, every second of the schedule plotted out, the position of each member of the team choreographed, the whole machinery of the crime dependent on the expertise of a number of individuals: what could go wrong?

Put that way, it is obvious why so many great comic crime novels have been based around all the things that can go wrong with a meticulously plotted heist. But when a heist is treated seriously, it becomes a thriller.

Police procedural

Basically, a crime novel with more or less realistic cops. Often these novels wrap together more than one ongoing investigation, and often they are less of a 'whodunit' than a 'how-to-prosecute-it', but the more effective procedurals explore the dichotomy between the individual cop and his or her larger police community.

After all, who wants to read a book with an entire community as the protagonist? We want an individual, we want conflict, we want good guys who might not be. The police procedural requires a lot of detail to get it right – many crime readers know police departments very well indeed – but enables the writer to approach a serious crime, or a series of them, in a far more realistic manner than when writing an amateur sleuth or private investigator.

Suspense

All crime has suspense, but not all crime *is* suspense. Basically, 'suspense' is the name given a crime novel that doesn't stay inside the precise murder/clues/investigator structure of the mystery novel, but which isn't as tightly wound as a thriller. 'Romantic suspense' is a variation in which the female protagonist struggles to save herself and her own future, while at the same time making steps towards a romantic liaison. Romantic suspense is generally condemned to that dreadful unliterary hinterland of 'women's fiction', unlike its male equivalent –

The male romance novel

The male romance is a category described by Elaine Viets in a 2005 post in the blog *Lipstick Chronicles*:

> *You've read them. You just didn't realize it. That's because the critics call these books 'gritty realism,' 'hard-boiled,' or 'scathing social satire' ... In these highly acclaimed mysteries, the hero is a broken-down forty-five-year-old man with no job and a drinking problem ... The hero is too noble to actually torture and kill anyone. Good thing he's got a wacko best friend to do it for him. Then the hero can disapprove but still get the bad guys dead.*
>
> *There are lots of guns and gore in the male romance novels, but they're as sentimental as a royal wedding.*

Hard-boiled

The more hard-boiled a novel, the less moved the protagonist is by violence, emotional ties or sex. He (very occasionally she) is tough, cool and impervious to the softer things in life: the hero may bleed, but he does not hurt. Hard-boiled is the farthest a reader can get from sentimentality – although see 'The male romance novel' above. Often these are PI novels, but 'hard-boiled' may also describe police procedurals, espionage novels and thrillers.

Espionage

When the Cold War ended, talk was of the end of spy novels, and speculation was rife as to what John le Carré would do. In the decades since, spies have continued to find work, certainly in fiction. Spy stories are most often thrillers, with the current focus tending towards confronting terrorists, but the thriller format may also be deliberately shunned in favour of grey, emotionless spycraft – making the novel all the more realistic.

Thriller

A thriller, like a mystery, can be about pretty much anything – political turmoil, a complex legal case, a bomb that will kill hundreds, a plague that will wipe out the world – but primarily, it has to thrill. The mystery is built on an intellectual challenge, but in a thriller, every element serves to tighten the emotional screws: even if the characters pause to make jokes or have sex, the reader must be aware of building menace.

The stakes are death, for the protagonist, or for some innocent who matters to him. There is an enemy, whose identity is often known from the start, who plans something terrible that must be thwarted. There is a protagonist, who may be an Everyman far out of his depth or a larger-than-life hero trained for an impossible task – either way, his enemy is powerful: to all indications, more powerful than the protagonist. There is a clock, and it is ticking. And there is the very real possibility of failure.

If the protagonist fails and dies, the book is called noir.

Overlapping worlds

Crime blended with other genres makes for some fascinating effects. We've mentioned romantic suspense, and writers like Dean Koontz or S. J. Bolton who combine crime and horror take on the atmospheric label of 'gothic'.

FOR S. J. BOLTON on ...

dark and creepy crime, see 'Tips and tales – guest contributors', p. 111.

Even straight thrillers often verge on horror; China Miéville's *The City & the City* is a police procedural set precisely down in a sci-fi world (or – is it?); John Connolly's Charlie Parker series finds the paranormal woven through a PI story – which is, in fact, where crime began, in the pulp magazines' fascination with the macabre.

We've come a long way since Daniel rescued Susanna.

Getting ready

Reading like a writer

For writers, regular reading isn't an add-on; it is essential. Reading imprints the rhythm of language, the crash bang hum of words, in your brain, and stretches your ability to create sentences that flow and paragraphs that sizzle. Reading increases your vocabulary and familiarises you with the way that language can be used for effect. Reading helps you recognise what a story is, and how it works.

Reading any decent fiction will help to mould you as a fiction writer, but you'll have to read substantially in crime or thriller sections, too, if this is the kind of book you aim to write.

If you're lucky, you've been immersed in the genre since you were knee-high to a grasshopper. You may have begun reading crime intended for children, and graduated to Meg Gardiner or George Pelecanos. You may have sampled a wide range of crime fiction and thrillers, so that you know precisely the sort of book you want to write. If so, hooray for you! The pleasures of reading will help to propel you straight into the pleasures of writing.

On the other hand, like many people with an urge to write, your reading in the genre may be more limited. Were you once an avid reader, but have been too busy in recent decades for books? Does your familiarity with characters such as Lisbeth Salander, Kurt Wallander or Lincoln Rhyme come primarily from the screen? Could it be that you don't even much like thrillers or crime novels, but have settled on the genre because crime novels sell like Starbucks lattes, and you want to earn a bundle and spend a summer idling around Peru?

If you've answered 'yes' to any of the preceding questions, there's a job to tackle before you begin to write: enter the realm of crime fiction through reading, and make yourself at home there.

- **Read widely**: be adventurous in what you read, stepping outside your comfort zone. If you're a committed fan of historical suspense novels, and lap up every Andrew Taylor or C. J. Sansom that comes along, great, but why not throw some Dreda Say Mitchell gangster stories or Sara Paretsky PI novels into the mix? Unless you've read extensively across the range of subtypes, from the gentlest of genteel novels to the noirest of noir (see above, 'The crime spectrum, gentle to thriller') how will you know what possibilities are out there for plot and tone and theme?

- **Read outside the genre**. Not only mainstream fiction, but biographies, history and poetry: biographies for insight into how interesting people look and act; history for the relationship between person and society; poetry for a lesson in the concentration of image and emotion, and in the suppleness of language.
- **Read old and new**. You may be a Christie devotee, but be unaware of how both the crime novel and its readers have evolved since the 1940s. Or perhaps your reading only began more recently – say, when Stieg Larsson's *The Girl with the Dragon Tattoo* exploded on to the scene – and so you have passed by the sometimes subtler delights of earlier writers. Crime is a spectrum over time, as well, and you should understand its evolution.
- **Read critically**. Go deeper than *I like Laura Lippman* or *I don't care much for James Ellroy*: figure out why. Let's say that you are entranced by the opening paragraph of Guy Saville's *Afrika Reich*, or thrill to the vivid London Blitz in Laura Wilson's *The Lover*. These passages can teach you a great deal about how to make an effective opening to a novel, and how to create descriptions that burn into a reader's brain. Take note of them, their pace, vocabulary, dialogue. With a little effort, the stories you read for pleasure will provide a bank of resources to sharpen up your own writing.
- **Note the negatives, too**. Pay attention to the chapter in a much-hyped thriller that is so dull it has you reaching for the television remote, to the clunky language that mars an otherwise intriguing passage, to the character whose actions simply don't ring true. You're learning what to avoid as well as what to aim for.
- One of the joys of reading as a writer is that your eye becomes educated: yes, you may become more critical and abandon a higher percentage of

novels halfway through, but when a writer gets it really right, the pleasure and admiration can be all the more intense.

- On the other hand, many writers find that reading a book too close in topic or flavour to the one they're working on can be dangerous. If you read a crime novel during the time your first draft is hot in your mind and find yourself obsessing on a comparison, or if you discover that you are imitating the other novel as you write, maybe this would be a good time to catch up on your sci-fi or mainstream fiction.

Won't reading critically take the pleasure out of reading?

Not if you don't let it! Read with a notebook nearby; when a passage strikes you as particularly effective (or particularly amateurish), don't stop to analyse. Simply make a note of the page number, and carry on reading. After you've reached the satisfying (or not?) conclusion, flick back to the sections you marked and ask yourself: *Why? What was it about that description that brought the Blitz so vividly home? Why was I bored by that stretch of dialogue?* Thinking about questions such as these is one of the best ways of training yourself to write in a way that is engaging and persuasive – as all the best writers do.

EXERCISE: READING LIKE A WRITER

Think back to a thriller or crime novel that you've read recently. Try to recall what struck you as strengths and weaknesses, and note them down.

What did you find memorable? Exciting? Chilling? Intriguing? Thought-provoking? Moving?

What, on the other hand, was unconvincing? Tedious? Melodramatic? Preachy? Dull?

What lessons does this suggest for your own writing?

P.S. If you can't think of a crime novel that you've recently read, your local bookshop awaits you – or, we talk about 'Recommended Reading' at the end.

Ideas

Write what you *really* know, by Laurie

The new writer is often told, 'Write what you know,' only to reflect that the market surely has to be limited for books on grad school, office work and caring for small children. It is true: imagination is of far greater importance in a novel than experiences.

Instead of writing what you already know, write what you *want* to know. Often a writer who comes new to a place or a situation sees it with inspired eyes, and can bring to bear a fresh and fascinated viewpoint. The goal here is making those descriptions, whether they are of a Boston neighbourhood, a beat cop's day or standing before a jury, feel fascinating for the reader, yet everyday for the characters. (We talk about how to write 'Descriptions' in Part Three.)

Write what you *really* know. This can be tough. Sue Grafton's bitter divorce and Michelle Spring's stalker gave emotional weight to their early novels. David Corbett writes feelingly about loss and abandonment, because his own loss is raw. Your protagonist may be, like you, a stay-at-home mother, but if you are being honest, you are also writing about your own frustration with rearing small children, the grinding boredom and the sense that the adult world is leaving you behind. You are writing what you know, but deeply so, not just in the surface sense of skills and information.

Michelle says: When it comes to the emotional life of your characters, you can often be well served by going inside yourself on imaginative journeys. As an undergraduate, my friend Ellen fell under the spell of another student who managed to manipulate her into doing things Ellen came to regret. Many years later, Ellen still experiences a rush of shame and anger when she remembers this time in her life. She is writing a novel now, using that emotion to fuel the story of a poisonous woman whose malicious influence sours relationships and leads people astray.

If you can find a germ of emotion that you share with your character, you may be able to 'what-if' it into your story. For instance, when I was getting to know the stalker in my sixth novel, *The Night Lawyer*, trying to get a grip on his motivation, I recalled being ashamed in high school over a small lie I'd told; I felt again the intensity of that shame and the way it had lodged in the pit of my stomach. I could imagine how that feeling might grow and grow; I pictured myself without other means of self-esteem to act as a counterbalance. I could envisage how the fire might rage, and spread, and eventually lead to stalking, and to murder. In a sense – and this was the first time I realised it – a writer is like a method actor, building a character out of a few strands of emotional information.

Where do you get your ideas? by Michelle

As a child, I thought that ideas were things to be avoided. Whenever my mother heard of girls behaving in unseemly ways, she would wag a fierce finger and declare: 'Now, Michelle, don't you go getting ideas.'

But for a writer, ideas are precisely what's needed. An idea doesn't make a novel; a novel is forged in the fire of imagination and application and craft. Ideas are the spark that sets the blaze alight.

FOR GAYLE LYNDS on ...

twenty years of living with an exciting idea, see 'Tips and tales – guest contributors', p. 130.

I sometimes come across the notion that there is a particular challenge in coming up with 'ideas' where crime novels are concerned. Ed – a tall, edgy-looking man with a canvas bag full of newly purchased hardbacks – took me aside at one mystery convention and asked for my help. 'I want to write a crime novel,' he said. 'I've got great characters. I have a spectacular setting where the crime will be staged. What stumps me is the method of murder. I haven't been able to locate a new poison that doesn't leave a trace; they've all been used by writers before!'

As Ed told me more about his project, I could see that he was on to a good thing. His story might just work. But I tried to convince him to abandon the search for a unique murder method. Brain-teasers of this kind often cropped up in traditional detective stories, but on its own an ingenious killing device won't keep a contemporary crime story afloat. The most satisfying crime novels today derive their appeal not from tricksy crimes, but from stories about people who are caught up in some kind of moral dilemma, people who are confronting a personal challenge, or people who are dealing with a painful, puzzling or frightening experience. Such stories fascinate because they draw readers into a world where difficult decisions have to be made and the consequences confronted. In this respect, the 'ideas' that inspire thrillers and crime novels are not that far from the ideas that underlie mainstream or 'literary' fiction.

So in your hunt for 'ideas', put aside the search for exotic weapons or ingenious alibis. You want a situation – there must be zillions of them – which presents a struggle that is challenging for the characters and intriguing for the readers. You want a predicament that characters have to grapple their way out of. The predicament could be physical: how to escape from the top floor of a burning building? It could be emotional: a Sophie's choice about which child to sacrifice. It could be social (how to deal with the prospect of public humiliation?) or moral (love, or duty?) The situation need not necessarily be murderous or even criminal; but it must raise urgent questions about what characters can do to resolve their dilemma. Such situations become the trigger that sets a story-bullet in motion.

And where do you find such ideas? You find them here, there and everywhere – everywhere that men and women face the challenges of living.

You may find your 'idea' in an incident from your own life, in a situation that gripped you in the past, as Ellen did, above. But what if your life has been relatively uneventful – or filled with incidents that you don't wish to share with the reading public? Must you simply wait for the muse to strike – which could, let's face it, take years? No. When ideas don't drop into your lap, any prospective writer must become a hunter.

Go on the prowl.

Check out casual conversations (your own, or those you 'just happen' to overhear). Perhaps a friend tells you about a seemingly intractable problem he's having with an erratic colleague; you may begin to ponder on the possibilities of a murder based in an office.

Consider the things that frighten you; your own deepest fears may be a source of an idea. The (largely irrational) fear that my own children might be abducted lay behind *In the Midnight Hour*, the story of what happens to a family when a child disappears without trace – and how they cope, years later, with the arrival of a young man who may (or may not) be their son.

Make a habit of scanning news reports and magazines for likely situations, such as these:

- A Bangladeshi shopkeeper in Devon opened his front door every morning for several weeks running to find a large turd on the pavement outside. Was the motive revenge? Was it a racist insult? He didn't know – and neither did the police.
- A woman wins the lottery, invests all her money in a luxurious Spanish estate, and then gradually discovers that Spanish village life isn't to her liking.
- A European couple, marrying while on holiday in the Maldives, realise that the person whom they thought was conducting a marriage ceremony in the local language was actually taunting them with insults.

FOR ALAFAIR BURKE on ...

the 'what if' of growing a story, see 'Tips and tales – guest contributors', p. 114.

Sketchy but suggestive incidents like these can, with a little speculation on your part, blossom into fully fledged ideas. Robert Goddard's best-selling historical thriller *Sea Change* began with an unanswered historical question, a mention of the missing accounts of the South Sea Company.

Historical material can also spark ideas for stories set in the here-and-now. Local rumours of a notorious Spinning House, where until the late nineteenth century Cambridge University officials imprisoned women of dubious reputation, helped to trigger my novel, *Nights in White Satin*; the Spinning House made an appearance, and complemented the core of the story about prostitution today.

These examples should give a flavour of the wide range of external sources that you can trawl for 'ideas'. But as you become more used to collecting ideas, you may well find that many of the most engaging emerge out of everyday life. One of the skills you will hone on your way to becoming a writer – or a better writer – is to keep your eyes and your mind open to possibilities for 'ideas'. Observe the people around you. Ask yourself questions about what they're doing, and why.

One example may show you what I mean. Recently, in the centre of Cambridge, I saw two men running along the pavement, dressed in jackets and ties. What, I wondered, is going on? Are they involved in a desperate chase, and if so, why? Is one man leading the other to an emergency situation? At the least, I've stored away in my mind the visual basis for an action scene in a future novel.

Harvesting ideas

Just as the command 'Write what you know!' has little to do with humdrum daily life, so the question 'Where do you get your ideas from?' has less to do with a day's constant stream of events and thoughts than with the jolt of one in particular. An idea that can grow into a book is an idea that makes you go, '*Yes!*' It is an idea that grabs your mind and your heart, that refuses to go away, that grows and takes over.

FOR DANA STABENOW on ...

being hit by Eureka! see 'Tips and tales – guest contributors', p. 157.

Once you've recognised a *Yes!* idea, you have to harvest it, to make sure it stays with you. Carry a notebook, everywhere you go, so you can write the idea down when it comes to you. Keep a file – electronic or physical – collecting incidents or situations that capture your attention. Come back to them from time to time to see if any of them catch your imagination. Set them next to other ideas, play with them like pieces of a puzzle. Some will be duds. Others are merely information, to be transferred into your notes under 'Flowers blooming in London in March' or 'Contents of a police officer's duty belt'. But if you don't harvest them now, they won't be there later, when you need them.

Laurie says: An idea notebook, physical or virtual, can be a valuable resource when it comes to building your characters and your plot. Torn-out magazine pictures of your protagonist's home or the kind of wristwatch your villain would wear, links to photographs of the setting, a phrase that seems to catch a certain attitude, a gesture you noticed on the subway, ideas that occur to you while you're drifting off to sleep. My 'notebook' for *O Jerusalem* included a slim beeswax votive candle I had liberated from a monastery outside Jerusalem, with a rich honey odour that instantly took me back there.

Some ideas are just ideas, others are IDEAS! The difference is the excitement you feel when you come across an IDEA! and the way you can't get your mind off it.

TOP TIP

Actual crimes are not necessarily the best starting point for crime novels. The idea behind crime novels – the trigger that sets the story-bullet flying – is often a relatively innocuous sequence of events ... which grows.

But it is of course possible to get ideas from reports of real crimes, which you, the writer, can then fictionalise and develop. The 1964 Kitty Genovese murder in New York, where a young woman was attacked and killed outside her apartment building while her neighbours did nothing, sparked a number of fictionalisations, including Ryan David Jahn's *Acts of Violence* and Dorothy Uhnak's *Victims*.

One thing to bear in mind about novels that take their idea from real-life crimes: if you are writing crime *fiction* (as opposed to true crime), the actual details of the event are unimportant, except in so far as they catch your interest and get you thinking. What writers of fiction need is a germ of a story that they can develop for themselves. Yes, Ryan David Jahn's *Acts of Violence* drew extensively on reports of the 1964 Kitty Genovese murder, but his novel takes us on an imaginary journey inside the minds of the victim and the bystanders, making his readers feel as if they too are witness to this dreadful event. The result is not a documentary, but a fascinating and powerful novel.

EXERCISE: ON THE PROWL FOR IDEAS

On each of the next seven days, capture and harvest one situation that might become the starting point for a novel. At least one of these should come from news sources, and another from your own experience or those of your friends.

Testing your ideas

Let's say you've been collecting ideas for some time now. You have at least a dozen possibilities in the notes on your Smartphone or battered ideas book. How do you choose between them? How do you decide which one to work with, and which to set aside?

There are two crucial tests of a *Yes!* idea:

- **Test 1: a *Yes!* idea is an idea that you care about**. One that will hold your interest through months (at least) of planning and writing. It doesn't matter how exciting your tale of dodgy husbands and vulnerable wives is in the abstract, or how gripping an idea about explosions in a nuclear reactor could be: if it bores you, it's not a good idea *for you*. If you can say, *Oh, boy, that's a story I'd love to read*, then probably the idea is one that will sustain you through the writing.

- **Test 2: a good idea is one that can be developed in interesting directions.** And the only way to discover whether this is possible is to have a go at converting your nifty idea into a workable scenario. (See the section on 'Plotting: The Orderly Approach'.)

Getting rid of ideas, by Laurie

One of the temptations in writing a novel is to scoop up everything in sight and try hard to work it all in: revenging yourself on an ex-husband plus your affection for the local coffee house and the interesting relationships in your amateur theatre group, and then there's the neighbour's bizarre night-time habits and your son's dog and the need to raise awareness of the hungry children in West Africa and ...

Stop.

This is one of those places where fiction needs to be *less* realistic than life. Yes, people can be complicated and daily life is a constant barrage of mismatched elements. A novel that messy would be unreadable.

At some point – either in the outline, if you're doing one, or in the rewrite, if you're writing Organically – you need to pare things down. Pick one of those six exciting ideas as the central one – say, revenging yourself on an ex-spouse. (Hey, it worked for Sue Grafton, who wrote *A is for Alibi* to work out murderous fantasies about her ex.) If it's a thriller you're after, you could support the central idea with the African element, involving your protagonist, or her ex, in a UN programme – or if you'd like to try your hand at romantic suspense, the local coffee house might play a large supporting role. A serial killer? What better than the bizarre neighbour? (Just make sure you disguise him in your novel!)

You need to keep your eye on the goal. First: I'm telling a story about a woman seeking revenge on her evil ex-husband. Second: ... who is using his position in UNICEF to steal funds and take bribes. Or: ... who seems to be paying far too much attention to the barista at Beans to You, the local coffee house. Or: ... who has developed an odd fascination for the creepy neighbour. *Or*, not *and*.

As a third element, a minor subplot, your neighbour's bizarre habits could provide humour, while the introduction of your son's dog could add pathos – or build tension, depending on the dog's fate.

EXERCISE: GETTING RID OF IDEAS

- Revenging yourself on an ex-husband
- Affection for the local coffee house
- The interesting relationships in your amateur theatre group
- The neighbour's bizarre night-time habits
- Your son's dog
- Raising awareness of the hungry children in West Africa

Take three items from those listed above – or make up half a dozen potential topics of your own, and choose three from them.

Decide which item will be central, which supporting, and which will add dimension. Write a paragraph describing the story that might result.

Try reordering your three items, choosing a different one as central, and so on. See how your thoughts about the book shift as you change the elements.

At a certain point along your journey to being a writer, you may find yourself abandoning your ideas notebook. This may not be a bad thing. Your growing writerly habits mean that *Yes!* ideas tend to identify themselves earlier. Your mind has decided that frankly, if an idea can be forgotten, perhaps it should be.

Early decisions

Point of view, by Laurie

The first sentence of your book requires a decision: who is telling this story? Will it be told in the first person, as if it were a memoir? Is it a third-person limited, with the camera locked on to one character the entire time? Or third-person omniscient, that godlike view of events and inner thoughts that treats villain and hero alike? (We won't consider the second-person point of view, since the constant assertion of 'you' in a piece of prose tends to be wearing, and best saved for the literary experiments of adolescents.)

First-person is where story-telling begins, and there's no doubt that the immediacy of the narrator's personal voice, the intensity of action and reaction, grabs the reader's interest from the outset.

There are drawbacks to first-person narrative (apart from the polite sneers of those who regard it as the mark of the amateur). One of those is a simple, practical consideration: if my protagonist is telling the story, how do I let the reader know what is happening to my other characters? Pausing for long catch-up narrations can bog down a story's momentum, but there are a couple of ways round that: put it into dialogue, which maintains the narrator's viewpoint while the faster pace of speech keeps the story moving, or just bite the bullet and stick in bits of third-person among the first-person POV. This can be awkward – I was forced to use it in one novel (*The God of the Hive*) when I had half a dozen major characters all going their separate ways for large parts of the story, and playing catch-up on that scale would have been tedious beyond measure. I just pretended my memoirist had assembled the story that way, and ploughed on.

There are more subtle drawbacks of the first-person POV. At first glance, it would appear to offer the greatest chance for intimacy with the character – and it's true, when every scene takes place within that person's skin, the reader gets to know her quite well. However, first-person narration can be paradoxically distancing from the character, since the reader has no chance to witness those unconscious gestures and tics that reveal what a person is *really* thinking, no alternative viewpoint to offer a sense of dimension. There is also no way to know if the narrator is being entirely honest with herself – and thus with the reader. This drawback can be worked to magnificent effect if the reader is made to suspect a degree of self-delusion, hearing the off-notes of an unreliable narrator (I aimed for this in *Locked Rooms*). Tricky, but very effective.

Third-person, while it imposes a certain distance between protagonist and reader, at the same time permits a greater view of the surroundings. Within the third-person point of view, there are degrees of intimacy that the writer must take care to preserve.

If the narration is tightly limited to the protagonist, if the goal is to preserve the closeness of a first-person POV while permitting the revelatory gestures and tics, the writer must take great care to keep that viewpoint throughout. When everything is seen through a protagonist's eyes, the farther the writer strays, the greater the danger of jarring the reader. For example, if you want to give a physical description of your central character, having him glance into a mirror and notice the brown hair, cleft chin and titanium-framed glasses jolts the reader out of the intimacy. Having your character glance at that same mirror and be irritated because he's missed the tuft of hair in that damned chin cleft again and that those expensive glasses his ex-girlfriend talked him into buying are still riding crooked on his face, gives information without pulling the reader too far out of the dream.

A single point of view, be it first- or third-, is best used if you are writing a mystery in which the investigator is unravelling a puzzle. Multiple points of view are well suited to the suspense story.

The widest point of view is that of the **multiple third-person**. This is sometimes called the omniscient POV, although true omniscience shifts around the interior thoughts of all the characters, creating the sensation of a godlike narrator who is at a distance from them all. Multiple third-person, on the other hand, allows you to play on each character's own limited point of view and the knowledge each one holds, permitting the reader to see things coming that the protagonist does not, and encouraging the reader to build the overall narrative in her own mind. A great way to build suspense.

With third-person narration, when alternating characters, take care to establish clearly whose point of view is being followed. The simplest way of marking the change is to open a new chapter, but even then, the reader must be in no doubt whose eyes are watching the scenery now. A shift in POV needs to be a shift in the scene as a whole. For example, feel what happens as you read the following:

When Bella walked in, the smell of death washed over her, bringing the usual visceral memories, the usual futile attempt to shove them down. As she squatted, her right elbow automatically twitching the baton on her duty belt out of the way, her left hand hesitated, held back by the body-memory of lifting up the blanket from a homeless man. Her face, more interesting than pretty, twisted into a grimace of anticipation.

More interesting than pretty? Where did that come from? One minute we are inside the uniform of an on-duty cop looking at a body, our elbow moving automatically to keep the butt end of the baton from jabbing us in the belly, when suddenly there's an intruder in the scene commenting on her looks.

Try out the first- and third-points of view with the beginning of a novel: should I write: *I was fifteen when I first met Sherlock Holmes*, or, *She was fifteen when she first met Sherlock Holmes ...*? And there isn't a federal law that says you must stick to one POV for the entire life of the series: Lee Child has been known to alternate, when he decided that a book was best suited to first- or third-.

Setting, by Michelle

A strong sense of place gives an extra dimension to any story. Where would *Wuthering Heights* be without the wind-scoured moor? *Great Expectations* without London? *To Kill a Mockingbird* without the small community of Maycomb? Strongly realised settings – whether the fog-shrouded London of the Sherlock Holmes stories, the silent forest of David Guterson's *Snow Falling on Cedars* or David Simon's unruly Baltimore – linger in the mind's eye long after you finish reading. A vivid setting invigorates a novel: readers feel as if they've visited a foreign land and come home refreshed.

Crime fiction – perhaps even more than other novels – puts a premium on location. This is partly because crime novelists often write in series, rooting their stories to a specific location which may become over time as familiar to readers, and as fondly regarded, as the protagonist. Good writers, James Lee Burke says, can find universal stories within one small area; they examine 'a grain of sand and find the nature of the coastline'.

The early detective novels tended to be set either in a sprawling metropolis (Margery Allingham's *Tiger in the Smoke*) or in an idealised English village (Agatha Christie's St Mary Mead), where the horror of murder is heightened by contrast with an ordered and decorous way of life. Today's crime novel tends to be regional, and built around variations in social concerns as well as topography: in Britain alone, we can explore Anne Cleeves's Shetland Islands, Denise Mina's Glasgow, N. J. Cooper's Isle of Wight, Colin Dexter's Oxford – and dozens more.

Exotic settings – Lindsey Davis's Roman Empire, Barbara Nadel's Istanbul or Donna Leon's Venice – have the power to sweep readers out of their own world. But a setting doesn't have to be exotic to be effective. Ian Rankin reanimated the rather staid popular image of Edinburgh by setting his Inspector Rebus series there. Colin Dexter's Inspector Morse novels attract almost as many visitors to Oxford as the colleges themselves. Chris Simm's *Outside the White Lines* – that rare and wonderful thing, a novel pulled out of the slush pile – took as its unusual setting a motorway, and brought it creepily alive. Simms's success demonstrates beyond a doubt that it is not a glimpse of the extraordinary or the exotic that makes a setting memorable, it is the vividness with which that setting is conveyed.

And how do you do that? How, as a writer, do you make setting come alive?

Whatever setting you select, it is always worthwhile using characters that arise out of the setting itself. I chose to set my standalone novel (*The Night Lawyer*) in a part of the East End of London known as the Isle of Dogs. One hundred and fifty years ago, the island (it's really an isthmus, projecting into the Thames) was an important centre of commerce and industry – ships from the empire unloaded their cargoes there, and the waterside was thronged with factories and processing plants. Since the decline of the docks, the Isle of Dogs has undergone a dramatic change. At one end is Canary Wharf, England's mini-Manhattan, bristling with skyscrapers and washed with a brash affluence. At the opposite end are the remnants of a traditional working-class community with its roots in the docks.

I spent a lot of time in the Isle of Dogs, and it gave life in my imagination to two characters. The first, Ellie Porter, is a lawyer who works in Canary Wharf. Her job is pressured and lonely, and Ellie has to pretend to a confidence she doesn't really feel. The second character comes from a long line of dockers; working now as a security technician, supervised by a graduate half his age, Carl Hewitt feels like a failure. He deeply resents the decline of the traditional island community, and he is implacably hostile to Canary Wharf. From the moment Carl sets eyes on Ellie, he is convinced that their fates are bound up together; through the book, Carl's obsession, and Ellie's terror, grow. By rooting characters in the social and physical landscape of your novel, you can exploit your setting for the fullest effect.

FOR YRSA SIGURÐRDÓTTIR on ...

location, see 'Tips and tales – guest contributors', p. 155.

If your setting is a city or a particular landscape, do not try to convey the place through maplike description; if a building, perhaps a college or a monastery, do not try to pen the word-equivalent of an architectural plan.

That level of detail quickly becomes tedious, and it unnecessarily limits plot development. Aim for a few judiciously deployed details. Give readers a hint, a telling detail or two or three, and then let them put their imaginations to work. Give them insight, not description. I once heard a writer say that her research was so exacting that she was able to cite the precise number of post boxes in the town where she set her novels. I ask you: is that the sign of a conscientious writer, or of someone with OCD? Who would know whether or not she'd counted correctly? More importantly, who would care?

Veer away from iconic images of the kind that are endlessly reproduced on picture postcards. Don't rely on the Eiffel Tower or the Golden Gate Bridge, the Piazza San Marco or the Acropolis, to inform your readers that you are in Paris or San Francisco, Venice or Athens. There are far too many mysteries that rely on double-decker buses and Big Ben to convey an image of London, and they are unconvincing and deadly dull. By contrast, Nora Kelly, in her 1990s thriller *Hot Pursuit*, gave us a contemporary London transformed by deregulation, a London that came alive on the page. The job of any writer is to look at a setting with fresh eyes and convey it in original terms to the reader. (Also see 'Description' in Part Three.)

As well as the physical topography of a setting – the streets and the short-cuts and the red-light district – crime novels may also convey a moral climate. Alongside gondolas and vaporettos, Donna Leon brings home to readers the frustrations of dealing with Venetian bureaucratic muddle. Henning Mankel's Ystad illustrates the erosion of the certainties of Swedish social democracy. James Ellroy leads us through a twentieth-century Los Angeles that glitters with swank and corruption. These writers take the moral temperature of a city, and share it with their readers.

Setting is not just the place itself, it is everything that a world of literature, gossip and news reports has attached to that place. New Orleans is not just a port city in the Gulf of Mexico, it's the Big Easy, it's catastrophic destruction, it's the spirit of Mardi Gras emerging from the mud. Rural England is not just temperate farmland, it's Agatha Christie, it's kings and commoners, civil wars and cathedral spires, Shakespeare and fox hunting. But to avoid the iconic and expected, it's also a busy school playground in

New Orleans, it's walking up a bucolic English hillside to look down at a furious six-lane motorway.

Are some settings better for crime novels than others? Traditional detective stories were often built around a closed and secluded setting, where only a finite group of suspects could have committed the crime. In the 1930s, for example, Mary Roberts Rinehart (*The Wall*) used an island. Agatha Christie (*Murder on the Orient Express*) made memorable use of a train. T. H. White (*Darkness at Pemberley*) described serial murder in a Cambridge college. Isolated villages, monasteries and convents, stately homes, ocean liners, and – of course – locked rooms, have all been used to good effect. Some secluded settings crop up to the present day: see for instance, P. D. James's *The Lighthouse* or *Death in Holy Orders*, which take place on an island and a remote theological college, respectively, while Jim Kelly, in *Death Wore White*, gives a cool modern twist to the locked-room mystery.

FOR JIM KELLY on ...

the locked room and the *possible*, see 'Tips and tales – guest contributors', p. 127.

A remote setting has its advantages, but the setting should also be one in which it is possible to keep secrets. Rumour has it that when the best-selling Irish author John Connolly was asked why he'd set his long-running Charlie Parker series in the US, he replied: 'Because in Ireland everybody would've known who done it within days.'

Raymond Chandler was famously impatient with crime stories set in genteel English villages and stately homes; the disparaging term he used in his essay, 'The Simple Art of Murder' was 'Cheesecake Manor'. The only setting that gained his approval was the mean streets of the city, as opened up by writers such as Dashiell Hammett. Chandler has a point; Dreda Say Mitchell, George Pelecanos and other contemporary writers forge exciting and thought-provoking stories in the mean streets of today. But when it comes to setting, the other possibility is contrast. Mean streets hold a sense of menace; but rough, tough neighbourhoods sitting alongside smugly affluent streets offer even more opportunities for trouble in all its guises.

Consider how closely you want to adhere to the details of your setting. On the one hand, many keen fans of crime enjoy reading about places they know well, or places they have visited. A commitment to the actual topography (a river here, a race course there), if skilfully done, can enhance authenticity. On the other hand, being a stickler for detail may unnecessarily limit your options when it comes to plot. Sometimes it may be better to blur the details in order to make a car chase or a hidden body plausible. The truth about a location lies in its ringing true, not in the accumulation of detail. And the story always comes first. In *In the Midnight Hour*, Timmy Cable disappears from a beach beneath sweeping cliffs at the end of a lane in Weybourne; but the story required that those cliffs be readily accessible from a village with a windmill, and Cley next the Sea was the obvious choice. So I invented the fictional village of Cleybourne, and acknowledged this at the front of the book:

> *Cleybourne has been formed by merging Cley next the Sea with Weybourne; the four or so miles of coastline that separate the two villages have been magically compressed. My apologies go to the people of Salthouse who have been swept away in the process.*

There is also a question of sensitivity here. How much do you want the nasty happenings in your book to taint the people and places you describe? Colin Dexter, author of the Inspector Morse series, applied a clear policy. The descriptions of Oxford in his novels are highly accurate – with one important exception. Where, for the sake of the plot, Dexter attributes something negative to a specific place he will give it a different name in his novel. A hotel where Morse has had cause to complain about the food will not have the same name as the original. Lonsdale College, in *Death is*

Now My Neighbour, takes the place of Brasenose College. And Canal Reach, the site of a murder in *Dead in Jericho,* is renamed Coombe Reach in the book – Dexter didn't want residents to hold him responsible for lowering the value of their houses.

EXERCISE 1

Close your eyes, and think of a town, or village, or a landscape, that you know reasonably well. Take your time. Conjure up a strong visual image. Now, select two or three telling details that you feel will convey most succinctly the atmosphere of that place, or what it feels like to be there. Write a paragraph using these details to give a vivid impression of your setting.

EXERCISE 2

Choose two characters who relate to your setting in different ways, or have different experiences of it. One could be a homeless person, say, and the other an estate agent [a real-estate agent]. Describe the setting again, as one character might see it, and then as the other might see it.

Period, by Laurie

Historical mysteries, once a relative rarity, have spread out to cover the ages, from ancient Greece to the day before yesterday. They tie in, naturally enough, with where the story takes place: a story set along Hadrian's Wall will be a different thing in the year 500 than it would be two centuries earlier, when the Romans were in place; Berlin needs little explanation, once the reader knows it is 1938.

FOR LAURA WILSON on ...

not zipping your flies in 1940, see 'Tips and tales – guest contributors', p. 163.

Generally speaking, people who write historical mysteries do so because they were interested in the period to begin with: Jason Goodwin wrote about Byzantine history before he began his crime series set in nineteenth-century Istanbul; medievalist Sharan Newman specialised in twelfth-century France long before she started to write about a twelfth-century novice nun. The writer knows the time, and the place, well enough to know where to find an interesting niche for his characters, what the possibilities were when it came to solving crimes and meeting danger.

Others, however, more or less stumble into their period, when they come across an event or historical personage that catches their imagination (such as the current writer, who decided to write about a girl who met a retired Sherlock Holmes, and found herself in 1915).

Either way, there is research involved, since being an expert in a given period, unless that expertise is archaeological, rarely qualifies a person to write about the minutiae of daily life. (We will discuss 'Research' in more detail shortly.)

Some periods are more popular than others when it comes to crime fiction, and there tends to be an ebb and flow in what is hot. Regency England seems to have endless potential for backstabbing and other colourful relationships, as does ancient Rome, while the Victorian age, thanks to Dickens, permits a strong sense of the grittiness of life outside the gates. Elizabethan England has flowered in crime fiction in recent years, as has the First World War and the 1920s. Sue Grafton, writing a series set in the 1980s (which didn't begin as period crime!) makes full use of the limitations imposed in that pre-Internet, pre-cell phone, pre-DNA era.

By and large, historical novels tend to be nearer the soft-boiled end of the crime spectrum, although that reflects their character as series novels more than it does their period – the historical standalones of David Liss and Caleb Carr (admittedly, *The Alienist* did have a sequel) are more thriller than whodunit, and nobody would call Umberto Eco's *The Name of the Rose* cosy.

When choosing a period for setting a crime novel, the primary consideration is your own fascination with the time. Do you love it enough to spend months, even years there in your research? If not, maybe you'd rather pick a time closer to home. But if so, take a while to decide just what is it you love about the period. The convoluted politics? The ornate fashion? The formality of social interaction? The class turmoil?

Historical crime works best when its period is already rife with tension, before your plot gets going. This doesn't mean open warfare, although it may – in Ellis Peters's Brother Cadfael series, civil war is building in the background of the early books.

Series or standalone?

The publishing world goes in and out on this question, with one generation of writers informed that they absolutely have to write a series if they want to sell, then a decade later new writers finding that the standalone is the gold standard. Dick Francis wrote what might be called a series of standalones, each book being tied to the world of horseracing.

FOR VAL McDERMID on ...

the series and the standalone, see 'Tips and tales – guest contributors', p. 133.

The advantage of the series is, you capture readers who want to continue with the adventures of your characters. Once they're hooked, they tend to stay hooked, considering themselves part of the family. The downside of this is, there will be readers who pick up your new book, see that it's number eight in a series, and put it down again. If book one is not sitting beside it, you may never catch that reader – although today's ease of e-book conversion makes it easier to use your backlist to hook new readers. A cheap first-in-a-series e-book can be a gateway drug into a writer's work.

The advantage of the standalone is, every book is a new beginning, fresh and frightening as the first page ever written. The reader who lives with an entirely new set of people for every book lives in little danger of boredom. Standalones tend, very generally speaking, to be 'bigger' books not only in the number of pages, but in their scope. When a novel is the entire universe of that set of characters, it tends to be more closely written, more intensely researched, more tightly plotted. There is little room for the kinds of digression into a slightly peripheral subplot that series novels encourage.

'Subplots', 'themes' and 'author's voice'

These three elements are grouped together here because, to some extent, none of them exists.

Laurie says: **Subplot** may be a misnomer. What the reader takes to be a tangential storyline, stuck in to provide character development or a change of pace, is a valuable way to reinforce the book's central concern. All subplots lead back to the primary storyline: in Dorothy Sayers's *Busman's Honeymoon*, the brilliant slapstick scene of cleaning the chimneys makes the reader completely overlook the cold, hard clue at its heart. In *Justice Hall*, two plotlines that seem to have little to do with each other – one man trapped into doing his duty; the death of another – link together in a woman with green eyes.

Subplots may also be red herrings, driving the reader to follow intently a line of inquiry whose main purpose is to deceive. Even here, it is best if the peripheral storyline still performs more than one function: use it to tell us something about the characters or the relationship dynamic that we wouldn't have discovered without it.

If the subplot doesn't lead back to the central storyline, it probably should be cut.

Theme is the underlying concern of the story, the thread that ties the elements together and, in the end, ventures a comment on the human condition. Theme is the message or the moral, without the self-consciousness those words bring. A story is about people (characters) in a place (setting) who do things (the plot): theme is the reason why. The theme of *Huckleberry Finn* can be seen as freedom; Dan Brown's 2003 potboiler *The Da Vinci Code* was hugely popular in no small part because of its underlying theme of the betrayal of the faithful by their spiritual authorities.

Laurie says: Different readers may see different themes in a book. To me, the theme of *Touchstone* is the roots of terrorism; others have seen it as a book about the damages of war, the evils of government or the complexities of love. Depending on the reader's viewpoint, *Huckleberry Finn* may be about a child's sense of morality, race as a determining factor of personality, or the deep need for family.

Theme may be more useful as an analytical tool rather than a planning one. You write a story because it moves you; it may only be on a rereading that you come to understand why you are so caught up in what your characters are doing.

It may be only later, when you read through the completed draft, that you realise that at the root of your story is the theme of 'revenge', or 'over-reaching ambition', or 'the frailties of human nature'. At that point, you may decide to pick out a few places in the draft where you can bring your theme to the surface – by a comment, a sharply drawn incident, or an image.

The central issue that runs through your novel can be underscored by the occasional image or example that touches on the same theme in an oblique way. For example, Robert Traver's *Anatomy of a Murder* (first published in 1958) tells the story of a trial, the outcome of which is dependent on establishing the sexual character of an alleged victim of rape. Scattered throughout the book are phrases that evoke the image of deceitful and promiscuous women:

The vast, glittering, heaving lake, the world's largest inland sea, as treacherous and deceitful as a spurned woman ...

'What's a four-letter word describing a woman of ill-repute?' the reporter Grover Gleason said, emerging absently from his puzzle, thoughtfully fluttering his eyes and pursing his lips.

'H-o-r-e,' I spelled. 'Didn't you know? In the Upper Peninsula, Grover, invariably it's hore.'

Author's voice is a concept many new writers fret over, since the one thing they hear about why editors buy books is that the buyer is caught up in the author's voice, and they want to know how they should build it. 'Voice' is an intangible, a complex blend of syntax and ideas that creates a distinct impression of the personality behind the words. A writer can find 'voice', but not create it. But lest you think all lost, hear this: a writer can fake 'voice'.

FOR DREDA SAY MITCHELL on ...

the author's voice and where it comes from, see 'Tips and tales – guest contributors', p. 136.

What an editor means by voice is, basically, assuredness. Solid, strong prose with nothing flashy or hesitant about it, that steps forward and gets the job done. At the end of this book, in the section 'When to start the promotion wagon rolling?', we talk about presenting a confident face to the public even when you're quivering inside. This is equally true for a writer's 'voice': the assumption of confidence is all it takes.

Thus: a subplot is a thread of the central plot that only appears to be separate; a book's theme exists in the eye of the beholder; an author's voice is heard only in the ear of the reader. We never said this writing stuff was simple, did we?

Plotting: how (and when) to do it

Plotting is a supremely individual process. No two writers do it in precisely the same way. Many writers do it differently from one book to another. Diana Gabaldon writes scenes – hundreds of scenes that excite her – and then creates the novel by stitching them together. Another author uses dozens of bits of paper, laid out on the floor of his study, to help visualise the way the book will take shape (one hopes he works with the window shut!) Others use a tree diagram, spreadsheet, or 'mindmap' – free software for these is even available online.

FOR ANDREW TAYLOR on ...

discovering a book's plot, see 'Tips and tales – guest contributors', p. 159.

The goal is to allow the mind to feel sure about the journey it is about to begin, several months on the road with a novel. Or, sure enough to set off.

Both Laurie and Michelle talked about their writing styles in their 'Reflections', by way of introduction. Here, we explore more fully both the 'Organic' and 'Orderly' Schools of writing, to give a closer idea of the options and to help you figure out which works best for you, and for the book you are setting out to write.

Neither is wrong. Both have their strengths and weaknesses. Both contain the potential for crafting fine novels.

The Organic approach

For writers who follow an Organic approach, the outline is a largely unconscious awareness of the plot rather than an actual document. Many of them find the outline to be not a planning device, but an analytical tool, that helps to strengthen the final draft by pointing out plot flaws. This can make for a very draughty first draft, with gaps and holes in the plot that require a lot of filling in, and Orderly writers may be frankly horrified at the lack of structure. E. L. Doctorow (whose oft-quoted remark also appears in Andrew Taylor's piece – see 'Tips and tales – guest contributors', p. 159) summed up this seat-of-the-pants approach when he said: 'Writing is like driving in the dark with only your headlights to guide you. You can only see a few feet ahead, but you can make the entire journey this way.' Orderly writers would demand a clear map.

Booker Prize winner Pat Barker also works in the organic way. Barker begins with an idea and simply dives in, writing steadily and regularly, not even rereading what she has written, until she has accumulated tens of thousands of words. Only then does she read her nascent manuscript, and delete the chunks (sometimes as much as two-thirds) that point least successfully in the direction of a story. Two more periods of writing and editing follow, until finally, she holds up a finished manuscript. And is made a CBE for her efforts.

There is no doubt that Barker's technique would leave – has left – a good many writers with nothing but a teetering stack of unpublishable typescript.

Michelle says: I have tried the Organic approach, and wasted months in doing so. With my third novel, impressed by a writer friend who leaned in the Organic direction, I sat down with an idea – a ten-year-old boy who is locked up for killing his foster mother, and the quest to discover 'why'. I began to write. It was a highly pleasurable process – at first. My imagination scampered free, and I churned out scene after scene, without regard to how they might fit together. At the end of three months – by which time I had become increasingly anxious, suspecting disaster – I had 64,000 words.

After a week's break, I read the manuscript through from cover to cover. I listed inconsistencies and anomalies, issues left dangling, subplots that petered out, problems that weren't resolved, characters who were unconvincing – and placed the entire draft into the bottom drawer of my filing cabinet, where it has languished ever since. Perhaps the manuscript could have been rescued by a very persistent editing process, but I didn't have the heart for it.

After a brief period of mourning, regretting the story that would go forever unread, I went back to my original idea and began work afresh. I outlined, and the book – *Standing in the Shadows*, later shortlisted for a top crime-writing award – began to take shape.

Many highly successful crime writers manage quite nicely, plotting in the Organic way. Peter Robinson, for one, starts with a scenario and his characters, and writes. When he gets to the end of his first draft, he reads through, identifies weaknesses and inconsistencies, pinpoints plot problems and happily rewrites. And anyone who has read the Inspector Banks series will know that he does it very well. If this approach inflicts on you a creeping sense of panic, then you may be too Orderly for it. If it seems eminently sensible to you, then you may be of the Organic school.

However, even card-carrying Organics freely admit it isn't for everyone, and would go further and say, if in doubt, be Orderly. No one wants to throw away half a book. And no one wants to be responsible for causing another to throw away half a book. If you think you might be Orderly, read on.

The Orderly approach, by Michelle

There's no doubt about it: outlining is hard work. It's not half as much fun as writing. But I've learned that it suits me. When I have an outline, I can fling myself into writing with the confidence that one chapter will follow another in a sensible sequence, that my characters will retain their identity throughout, and that the flaws that remain at the end of the first draft will be readily repaired. Having ploughed my way through the cold lamb chops and Brussels sprouts that is outlining, I tuck with delight into the sticky toffee pudding of writing.

How does an Orderly writer construct an outline? The answer is: step by step. Break the task down into stages: idea to scenario, then scenario to outline.

From idea to scenario

THE IDEA

A normally quiet neighbourhood is shaken by a violent murder. In her husband's coat pocket, Joanne finds a scrap of paper. On it is the phone number of Francesca, the woman who was killed.

This idea grabs you. You're intrigued by the notion of marriage to someone whom you don't entirely trust. But is the idea feasible as well as appealing? Is it strong enough to carry a novel? Think about the situation, and describe a direction in which the idea might develop. You needn't introduce a murder, but sketch out two or three incidents or actions that might follow – things that the central character might do, or that might happen to her. Here are three such scenarios.

SCENARIO 1

Let's say that the wife – Joanne – feels ashamed because she was snooping when she found the scrap of paper, and she is reluctant to have her husband think that she doesn't trust him. (Because she does – wholeheartedly. Still, it's very odd, she thinks ...) So Joanne begins to investigate. She finds out as much as she can about the victim Francesca, even going so far as to strike up a friendship with Harry, the widower. Harry comes to trust Joanne and he reveals the painful fact that his late wife had been having an affair. Harry has some clues as to the identity of the lover. Joanne is shocked to discover that these clues point to her own husband – as the lover of the murdered woman, and perhaps the killer, too.

Developed in this way, your idea could easily evolve into a tense psychological thriller, with Joanne at the centre, torn between her love for her husband and her increasing suspicion of him, and torn, too, by her growing feelings for Harry. Readers will suspect even before Joanne does that she herself might be in danger: has her husband the heart of a murderer? Could he, would he, kill to keep Joanne quiet? Or has Harry invented the story about his wife's lover in order to divert suspicion away from himself? Etc. etc. Twists and turns galore.

But if you're intent on working up an idea, don't stop with one scenario. Ask whether there are other ways that Joanne's story could go. It is equally possible that ...

SCENARIO 2

Finding the scrap of paper in Declan's pocket, Joanne concludes that he's the murderer, but determines to protect him. (She loves him with a passion; Francesca was a tramp who brought it on herself; etc. etc.) Joanne destroys the scrap of paper, and gives false information to the police to throw them off the scent. Further on, Joanne herself is suspected of murdering Francesca out of jealousy, and her lies are used against her.

SCENARIO 3

Joanne finds the scrap of paper, and – after much apparent heart-searching – tells the police. But in the end, it turns out that she's been playing a dangerous double game; actually, Joanne and the 'grieving' widower are madly in love. Together, they murdered Francesca, and framed Joanne's husband for the killing – intending to rid themselves of two superfluous spouses in one fell swoop.

As you can see, any starting idea (in this case, Joanne finding the phone number of a murder victim in her husband's jacket pocket) can give rise to a number of scenarios. Some scenarios will be more promising than others, but it's only after you've put some thought into developing them, that you will be in a position to choose the best of the lot.

QUESTION

Which of the three above would you most like to work with? And why?

EXERCISE: FROM IDEA TO SCENARIO

The idea: Sylvie lands a coveted job at a local radio station. Her boss starts coming on to her. She applies for a job elsewhere in an attempt to escape his attentions, but he tells her that he will write her a bad reference unless she complies.

Take the idea described above – or if you'd rather, choose one of the ideas in your notebook. Use your imagination to outline one direction in which the story might develop. You needn't introduce a murder, but think of two or three incidents or actions that could follow from the situation. Write these up in such a way as to move the story on.

Develop a second scenario that takes the idea in a different direction.

Place the two scenarios side by side, and compare their strengths and weaknesses. What do you think of each of the stories you have created so far? Which one is more plausible? More intriguing? More likely to capture a reader's attention? Are they capable of being developed further? Or, on the other hand, are they dull or repetitive or melodramatic? Are the situations clichéd – one you've read about many times before? Or are they fresh? Which one is the most promising and, above all, which one appeals to you the most?

From scenario to outline

A good scenario is a splendid thing. Scenarios make for excitement. Here you are with a great scenario featuring Sylvie and her randy boss, and you're eager to begin the thrilling task of writing up.

Rein in that enthusiasm. You're hot to trot, but before you light the candle in your garret and begin piling up the pages, you have to tackle the thorny issue of plotting. If you're an Orderly writer, that means transforming your promising scenario into a compelling plot outline – one that tracks the action from one chapter to the next.

Let's try to transform one of the scenarios concerning Joanne and her possibly murderous husband into an outline. First, construct a table that looks something like this:

PART I			
sequence	*event*	*character(s)*	*status*
repeat for PART II, PART III and WHERE?			

Using your scenario as a guide, jot down all the points (the events/incidents/actions/ideas) that you, the writer, will have to 'deliver' to the reader to get your story across. Each point gets a separate line in the table.

Where it's obvious, position the event in Part I (the early part of the book), Part II or Part III. Otherwise, pop it into the final part of the table, labelled WHERE.

Soon, your table may look something like this:

PART I			
sequence	*event*	*character(s)*	*status*
	news of the murder circulates through the neighbourhood		
	introduce Joanne	Joanne	
	introduce Joanne's husband	Declan	

	introduce Harry, whose wife has been murdered	Harry	
	Joanne hears of the murder	Joanne	
	Joanne finds the scrap of paper in Declan's pocket	Joanne	
	Joanne figures out that the phone number on the paper belongs to Francesca, the murdered woman	Joanne	
	Joanne considers whether to ask Declan about the phone number, but decides to leave it for now; she doesn't want to admit that she's been snooping	Joanne	
	Joanne tries to learn as much as she can about Francesca. She reads different reports of the case, and finds the obituary	Joanne	
	Joanne raises questions about the victim at the coffee morning. Gets conflicting reports of Francesca's character	Joanne and neighbours	
	over breakfast, Declan tells Joanne that he will be in meetings all day		
	Joanne asks Declan whether or not he knew Francesca; he says no		
	Joanne is moved by the sight of Harry, Francesca's widower, crying his eyes out		
	Joanne attends Francesca's funeral service, even though she wasn't a friend. She is surprised to see Declan there, since he'd said he'd be in meetings all day. Joanne ponders whether or not she can trust Declan	Joanne, Declan, other mourners	
	set the scene: emphasise quiet suburban neighbourhood, nothing ever happens here. Houses shielded from view by hedges		

	Joanne notices a police detective who is working on the case, and becomes anxious to know whom the police suspect		
	introduce Joanne's friend Connie, who doesn't like Declan	Connie	
	Connie criticises Declan for his behaviour towards Joanne (what, specifically?) and Joanne feels compelled to defend him		
PART II			
sequence	*event*	*character(s)*	*status*
	Joanne watches a Hitchcock movie on television, in which the husband intends to kill the wife		
	Joanne confronts Declan and asks him whether he had an affair with Francesca. Declan is furious at first at the suggestion, but then goes all sweet and reassures Joanne he could never be unfaithful. Joanne is won over		
	the police detective visits Joanne. Joanne wavers, but doesn't tell him about the scrap of paper. He asks her difficult questions		
	Joanne meets Harry at the gym. She feels sorry for him, and starts a conversation		
	Joanne learns (from whom?) that the police suspect Harry of having killed his wife		
	Joanne and Harry meet again. Harry tells her that the police are hounding him. Why do they suspect you? She asks. He says it is because the police believe that		

sequence	event	character(s)	status
	Francesca was having an affair, and that Harry killed her out of jealousy. Harry tells her that the police have evidence of Francesca meeting a man on Kings Cross Station; he shows her a grainy CCTV still – and Joanne recognises the man's shoes as identical to ones belonging to Declan		
	something happens to make Joanne wonder whether Harry was telling the truth about the CCTV picture		
PART III			
sequence	*event*	*character(s)*	*status*
	Harry goes away for a few days, and Joanne realises how much she misses him	Joanne	
	without Harry around, Joanne becomes increasingly edgy about Declan. Could he have been Francesca's lover? Could he have killed her?		
	Connie could help Joanne, but Joanne is still reluctant to voice her fears to Connie, who has never liked Declan		

This is a beginning, but only a beginning. Put the beginning outline away for a day or two. Get some distance. Come back to it with a fresh and critical mind.

Check that you've put the events in the Part where they belong; if not, move them. (For example, you might well think that *Something happens to make Joanne wonder whether Harry was telling the truth about the CCTV picture*, currently in the middle section, would work better in the dénouement; if Joanne reaches the point in Part III of trusting Harry, and being frightened of Declan, a sudden revelation that throws Harry's trustworthiness into doubt would provide a good twist.)

Go through each Part, item by item. Decide which events would come early in that Part, and which later. (For instance, introducing readers to the settled nature of the neighbourhood should come much earlier in Part I than its present position.) Put the events in sequence. And as you write a scene or make notes for it, record that in the 'status' column.

Once your items are more or less in order, you will be forcibly struck by what's missing. Wouldn't Joanne have a mother or a brother to whom she might confide at least some of her fears? Insert an item to that effect. Might Joanne do a more thorough search of Declan's things, hoping to find something that could answer her questions one way or another? (If Declan came home unexpectedly and caught her, this would produce a nice heightening of pace.) And so on. Keep going, patiently and stubbornly, until you have a fuller list of the things that will happen in the book, in the order they're likely to happen.

Is the story starting to emerge? Are there any 'events' that get in the way, or distract from the main plot? Can they be modified or cut?

You have your events/items/incidents/points in a sensible sequence, but it would be folly to try and create a scene based around each and every item. Instead, see whether any can be combined in a single scene in order to make the telling less fragmented. (In Part II, there are three events that could readily form part of the same scene: Joanne seeing Harry in tears; Joanne going to the funeral and noticing Declan there; Joanne spotting a police officer who is working on the case. It would be economical and elegant to combine these three events into a single scene that takes place at Francesca's funeral.)

Think of each scene as potentially delivering three 'events': something about one of the characters, perhaps, plus a clue, plus an incident or action that moves the story along. Bracket these together.

By this meticulous and painstaking process, you can eventually arrive at a skeleton outline which will carry you through the writing of an entire book.

A variation. I build my scenes out of points or events or items that fall at a similar point in the sequence of events, and group together well. There are other Orderly writers who do it the opposite way; they begin by envisaging whole scenes, complete with points to deliver, and characters, and setting. (It's said, for instance, that before he set himself to write, Robert B. Parker, creator of the Spenser series, made outlines of each chapter so detailed they were almost synopses.) They note the details of each scene on record cards. When they've amassed a stack of cards, or scenes, they arrange them in sequence.

Whether you proceed event-by-event or scene-by-scene, the advantages of the Orderly approach are crystal clear. Once you begin writing, there will be little need for pause. You can throw yourself into the act of writing, secure in the knowledge that your outline will carry you through. You will never be side-swiped, having written the first fifty thousand words of your novel, by that most horrible of feelings – that you haven't got the faintest idea what's coming next, and that what you've already written is about as plausible as a *News of the World* headline. For writers like me, the Orderly route gives a confidence about structure that makes it possible to lose yourself in the writing, to make the words come alive, to make the story trot along.

One of the writers who works wonders with the Orderly approach is Val McDermid. Another is Jeffrey Deaver. Both have developed the discipline and the skill that allows them to plan each novel in meticulous detail before they settle in to write. The result is formidable productivity and novels that combine intricate plotting with powerful emotion.

What if a whole scene pops into your mind?

Imaginations, once set in motion, often have a force of their own. Sometimes you may become so overwhelmed by the vision of a scene that you feel compelled to write it out in full. Go ahead. It's sure to be exhilarating, and may be useful later. But bear in mind, a scene that doesn't fit with the others will have to be junked later – and all writers find it hard to abandon their babies. If you're an Orderly writer, your emphasis at the plotting stage should not be on drafting scenes, but on devising a skeleton which will later support the body of your draft.

Middle ground: the Orderly Organics

Just because we speak of two schools of writing doesn't mean there aren't three, or a hundred. Even the most committed members stay flexible.

Michelle's outline is always most complete, most comprehensive, most prescriptive, where it deals with the early part of the novel. The first third of the book sets the whole story up; it is the most difficult, and yet the most important, to get right. She works out the key revelations and the climactic action that will come at the end of the book, and decides whether it will end on an optimistic note or a tragic one. Knowing the ending gives a direction to the writing, something to work towards, and it helps to keep the tone of the draft consistent.

But she may leave great swathes of the middle of the book only loosely plotted, because by the time she has the early outline and the ending in mind, the story is so alive, so pressing, that she cannot wait any longer to begin writing. She has learned that once she starts writing, the events in the middle part of the story will come, and can be inserted effortlessly into the outline.

Similarly, even the loosest Organic type sometimes sketches an outline before she dives in. When Laurie is looking forward at a particularly tricky bit of plot – five people, three cities, two chronologies – she will figure it out on paper first. Just because she prefers to drive cross-country by her headlights alone, doesn't mean she wants to set off with flickering bulbs.

For more on plot, see 'When you're "finished": the rewrite', in Part Three.

Research

What you need to know in order to write, by Michelle

I was lunching recently at a Cambridge college with a friend from the Margery Allingham Society, when a professor, having learned that I was a crime writer, leaned forward and said, 'That means you write about murder, yes?'

I was immediately on my guard. Scepticism was dripping off his every syllable.

'Well,' I replied, trying not to panic, 'I write about many things – sexual violence, missing persons, stalking – but, yes, of course, also about murder.'

'I thought so,' he said. He made a gesture that took in the entire table. 'The first rule of writing,' he declared, 'is to write what you know. Yet we have a glut of crime writers who've never walked a mean street in their lives. Don't you wonder whether any of them has ever been personally involved with a stalking, say? Or a murder? Tell me,' he demanded, skewering me on the end of a piercing gaze, 'I don't suppose you've ever come across a multiple murderer?'

Well. He should have heeded that old barristers' warning: Never ask a question to which you do not know the answer.

'As a matter of fact,' I said, 'I've come across several.' I tried not to look too smug. 'I've been friends with one multiple murderer; known two others fairly well; and had a passing acquaintance through prison visits with another two or three.'

So, as you can see, the professor was out of luck when he tried to expose me as a crime writer without suitably sinister connections. But he made another, far bigger, mistake when he assumed that rubbing shoulders with things and people criminous is a *precondition* for writing effective crime fiction. Even though my experience of being stalked permeates two of my novels – *Every Breath You Take* and *The Night Lawyer* – I would insist that there are many compelling reasons to reject the instruction to write what you know.

Let's deal with just one: writing is a demanding business. It takes commitment and discipline to sit down at your desk every day – to ignore the unpaid bills, the inviting novel, the friend with a bottle of wine in hand – and churn out several hundred words. In order to generate this kind of commitment, it is desirable to write not about what you know, but about something that moves you. The energy that enables you to keep on with the story from the beginning to the end comes from passion.

This presents writers with a dilemma. On the one hand, you want to focus your writing on things you feel passionate about; on the other, you can only write about things you know and understand. This is where research comes in. Research is the bridge that conveys you from what you care about to what you know.

When I began to work on the novel *In the Midnight Hour* – the story of a Grantchester family whose little boy goes missing from a Norfolk beach – I knew nothing about the extraordinary complexities of missing persons cases. I had no idea, for instance, what might happen when a skeleton, long decomposed, turns up on a Scottish mountainside. I learned through research that that's when the forensic artist for the National Missing Persons Helpline (Di Cullington, at the time) would be called in. She'd analyse the body for evidence of the year of death. She'd link the shreds of information with missing person reports from that period. She'd clean the skull and mount it on a platform in her studio, and then, using a material like putty and matchsticks to gauge the depth of the flesh, give the skull a face that someone might recognise. That is the fascinating sort of thing you can learn from research.

A warning, however. From the questions that come my way, it seems that many readers imagine that crime writers spend all their time accompanying police on midnight raids, or boiling up human heads to see how quickly they dissolve. This is a misconception. Technical detail is the staple of writers like Patricia Cornwell or Kathy Reichs, or of thrillers packed with information about explosives and firearms. But most writers of crime fiction make only the most delicate of incursions into territory like this. Most crime novels are not full of bodies with the larvae of exotic moths in their mouths; most are about people, believable people, facing human challenges. In most cases, the main interest is not in the physiology of death, but in the person who inhabited the body, and in the motive of the people who killed them.

Forensics is not the key; the key is character.

Research in stages, by Laurie

I tend to do my research in two stages. The first is before I start writing, when I'm thinking about possibilities. Often this part stretches for years, with articles torn out of magazines, photographs that evoke a certain specific story element, books that one day feel as if they might contribute to a novel. If, for example, I'm going to be writing about Morocco in 1924, I'll need to read up on the time and place, because it wouldn't help to get halfway into writing the book before discovering that there was a rebellion going on.

But I am an academic, by training and by nature. A few Wikipedia articles aren't going to do the job. So I hunt down and print off reams of material on everything from the rebellion's leaders to a 1926 article written by an American engineer about Moroccan iron deposits, and I make a trip into my local research library to bring a barrow-load of books home. I read some, skim others, slap a million sticky flags into places that have telling details about the place, the people, the time. I make copious notes. I study maps. I hunt down newsreel videos, and locate first-hand accounts from people who travelled there during the 1920s (since my usual requirement for historical settings, a guidebook, is sorely lacking for 1924 Morocco) until I have a sense for the place.

And then I put everything away except some photographs and the map. Books stay on the shelf (*my* shelf, not the library's!) and notes in a file, while I write the novel.

I do this precisely because research is so very tempting for me. More than once, I have found myself twisting the plot to follow some delicious piece of information I've come across, and then another one, and a third, until I've lost any control of the story and the book starts to read like a glued-together series of 3x5 cards.

Now again, we come up against the question of preference. There are writers who seem to have no problem controlling their research, who assemble all (or most of) the information they need and happily weave it all in. And if some of them read like well-organised filing cabinets, who am I to criticise? One such (A. S. Byatt's *The Children's Book*) was shortlisted for the Booker, a prize for which none of my books will ever – *ever* – be nominated.

But for me, a writer who cannot afford to spend three or four years joyfully immersed in research, it works better to limit myself to a shallow first pass in the world of research, while keeping a close eye on places where I am uncertain, and then returning to the more detailed and specific hunting down of facts once the first draft stands on its own.

Then, I get to work.

Research for me has several goals. First, to make the reader feel that they are there. Concrete details are the lifeblood of any fiction, and more so for the kind of story built on clues, but the research needs to be invisible – a landscape composed of smooth Chinese brush strokes rather than laboured detail.

This means leaving stuff out. A lot of stuff, some of it really great. To the point that it hurts.

Say you have a scene where your Victorian protagonist is leaving the house in the morning. As she gets dressed, do you need a complete inventory of garments and how each is donned? As she eats breakfast, do we need to survey the complex household machinery of butlers and maids, place-settings and warming trays, the recipes for kedgeree and the variety of meats to choose from? As she leaves the house, need we know the details of the crossing-sweeper and the dress of the hansom-driver and ...

Which is not to say that *you* should not know all those things, just that you need to consider how much of it to inflict upon your reader.

Much better to treat your research as casually as this Victorian lady would treat the minutiae of her day, with the storyline prevailing while the occasional telling detail lends its flavour. Nine out of ten readers will miss most of these throwaway tidbits anyway, leaving your hard work and genius unappreciated. However, think of the person who really knows their hansom cabs or Victorian cookery or women's garments – how impressed that one reader is going to be, how convinced that you really know your stuff!

A sense of place, by Michelle

For my standalone novel, *The Night Lawyer*, I spent days in the British Library, poring over memoirs of childhood, studying old photographs and maps, trying to absorb what it would have been like for someone like my stalker-character, Carl, who grew up in East London, on the Isle of Dogs, forty years ago. To re-create some of the stories Carl's grandfather might have told him, I devoured guidebooks, architectural commentaries, histories. I learned about the West India Docks, once the point of arrival for cinnamon and spices, tea and molasses, timber and precious metals, from all over the empire. (On certain kinds of days, you can still smell cinnamon and sugar in the former warehouses that are now posh shops and restaurants.) I walked around the perimeter of the island, and back and forth through the foot tunnel that runs beneath the Thames. I persuaded writer N. J. Cooper to join up with me for a pub crawl. (Anything for our art!)

Right now, for a novel that focuses on a dark episode in Cambridge history, I've been immersing myself in the 1970s. Old catalogues and newspapers provide detail that help to capture the period, as do friends' recollections of lifestyles and fashions. *Kelly's Directory*, available in the public library, lists every shop on every street in Cambridge in 1974, making it possible for me to re-create that world in which there were few restaurants, no wine bars, no gyms, no 'boutiques', and a butcher's shop on almost every corner.

FOR CHARLES TODD on ...

the richness of setting, real and imagined, see 'Tips and tales – guest contributors', p. 161.

Above all, researching a crime novel – any novel – involves asking questions. I do this routinely – asking people about their jobs, for example, just on spec. (Most of us have very limited knowledge of jobs beyond those of our own circle of friends – and you can't fill all your novels with teachers, doctors and carpenters.) It's wise to maintain a database of useful contacts, who often emerge in chance encounters; I met a Home Office firearms expert on the train one day, and an arson investigator in the interval at a theatre. Living in Cambridge is a bonus: the city is chock-a-block with experts.

And people are usually happy to help. While I was doing research in the Isle of Dogs, I was invited to speak to a women's networking group. I mentioned that I'd been going through official channels for a month, without success, trying to get access to a CCTV monitoring centre. Two women stepped up to the plate. The next morning, I was ushered through a muddy field into the Portakabins that housed the Tower Hamlets CCTV Monitoring Centre.

Sometimes, people can be too eager to help. A couple of years ago, coming out of a friend's home after midnight, I flagged down a taxi, and asked to be taken home. The driver took an unexpected route, and ended up, in spite of my protests, in a leafy deserted side road. Blast, I thought, just my luck to flag down the only serial-killing cab driver in Cambridge. But no ... 'Sorry,' he said, seeing the alarm on my face. 'You are Michelle Spring, aren't you? I just wanted to show you the King's Ditch ... Perfect place for a body, don't you think?'

So, to take us back to where this discussion started: crime novelists do not necessarily require a close personal acquaintance with the underworld, nor to immerse themselves in the mechanics of death or firearms. Research for crime novels involves forensic science, from time to time. But more often, it involves reading, looking and listening, and asking questions. Anne Lamott put it beautifully (in *Bird by Bird*) when she said that research sources are all around us, and that a writer has to learn to live 'like a ship's rat, veined ears trembling'.

A sense of place, by Laurie

Once a writer sets foot outside her home town, dangers arise. Not dangers to her person, necessarily, but to her reliability – particularly if the new setting is intended to be home base for one of the characters.

The larger the portion of your story set in a foreign place, the greater your need to go there, to see the people, to smell the air, to watch the sky and absorb all the telling details that will permeate your writing. It's tough to write about a place with any degree of authority and intimacy if you haven't spent some time there.

But not impossible. H. R. F. Keating wrote a number of his Inspector Ghote novels before setting foot in Bombay (now Mumbai), including the Gold Dagger-winner, *The Perfect Murder*. And in those books, there is never the slightest doubt that the reader is in India:

> *It was called the Perfect Murder right from the start. First the Bombay papers plastered it all the way across their pages. And then it was taken up by papers all over India.*
>
> *The Perfect Murder: Police at House.*
>
> *The Perfect Murder: New Police Moves.*
>
> *The Perfect Murder: Police Baffled.*
>
> *Every time Inspector Ghote saw the words he felt the sweat spring up all along the top of his shoulders. It was as if every one of India's four hundred million people were looking at him, challenging him to break it. The Perfect Murder.*

Keating sets us firmly in Bombay not through a list of characteristics, but largely though the rhythm of his writing, short, choppy sentences that capture the rhythm of subcontinental speech.

But whether the writer knows every inch of the city or hasn't even flown over it, the most effective way to describe any place is not to do so. Instead of spending half a page focusing on the appearance of a street in a tropical country – dusty road, large trees, horse-drawn carts, shuttered buildings – focus on the character making her way down the street, how she dodges from one patch of shadow to the next, how she is forced to pause in the beating sun for a lethargic horse to amble past, bones working beneath its skin, how a beggar has drawn his bare toes back from the sharp edge of sunlight. Even then, those events are background to her purpose, things dimly glimpsed while she is thinking about where she is going, whom she is about to see.

We'll talk more about making use of setting in Part Three, but as far as research goes, if you can possibly get to a place for your writing, do so. (Remember, travel expenses can be tax-deductible!) And if you can't, photographs, videos, memoirs and films will have to do.

Google Earth can also be enormously helpful for studying those parts of the world you don't know well, or whose details you have forgotten. The street-view function can take you there, if you're writing about a developed country that has been sufficiently mapped, and even if you're sticking to satellite view, it's worth a re-view of your story's ground.

Library vs Internet, by Laurie

As the Internet expands, more and more research material comes available. Even a few years ago, online research tended to be more of a frustration than a tool, useful primarily to locate people who might know something.

Google books is making historical and out-of-print books available to people who live far from a research library, although it will be a long time before the computer replaces a library – and a librarian. A good research librarian can be your very best friend – *The Game* is dedicated: 'For the librarians everywhere, who spend their lives in battle against the forces of darkness.' Even a good local library often has an Interlibrary Loan arrangement for those hard-to-find books (although you should ask how much it costs them before you decide you must have that volume). Most universities will let you use all the books in their stacks without question, and permit you to check them out for a small fee. The more demanding privileges, like ILL, may be out of reach unless you're an alumnus, but the wealth of material available on the shelves of any university library should keep you busy for quite a while.

Newspapers, personal diaries and novels of the period (*not* modern historical novels) can offer a wealth of information on daily life – better than memoirs, which tend to gloss over details in favour of larger events. Actual newspapers and magazines, with their advertisements and personals, give the writer a tactile sense of the reading experience (remember black fingers after reading a paper; the smell of newsprint?) and a myriad of everyday details that add vitality to a story. (We have included more suggestions in the 'Resources' section.)

The expert, by Laurie

One of the things to keep in mind as you do your research is that people are astonishingly willing to help. When I first started writing, I tended to apologise for my questions by saying that I was only writing a piece of fiction but I'd been having problems figuring out ... And almost without fail, the person I was asking, whether the director of a tiny Dartmoor museum or a San Francisco police captain, would push up his metaphorical sleeves and shower me with his expertise.

A twofold caveat here: beware of putting too much weight on one person's opinion, and, beware the difference between opinion and knowledge. Yes, this is fiction we're constructing here, but the world is full of real experts, and they often read in their areas of interest. Anachronisms, misunderstandings of firearms or vehicles, geographic impossibilities, and social *faux pas* act on the reader like the substitution of salt for baking soda in a recipe: they may look right, but the change can spoil the recipe, or the read.

The world is full of charlatans and pseudo experts: so how do you know if the self-proclaimed expert you've located actually is one?

First off, simply listen to what he has to say, read what he's read. If it sounds too good to be true, it probably is. Read his articles with a critical eye – even if you don't know the field, fuzzy thinking tends to stand out. Do a background check: does he have specific training in the area where he claims expertise? If not, he may be riding a hobby-horse; take care not to join him on it. Finally, check his relations. Does he refer to the work of others in his field? Do others refer to him? And, *how* do they refer to him?

Specific tools of research are in the 'Resources' section at the end of this book.

Taking control of your research

Most writers have a love/hate relationship with research. Research is notoriously greedy. It longs to displace your writing self. The worst scenario? A filing cabinet full of facts, and the story scarcely written. Or, great unappetising dollops of research, clogging up your manuscript, like the lumps in badly mashed potatoes.

Keep your research under strict control. Let it know who's boss. Research is a necessary part of the verisimilitude of crime fiction – you wouldn't want to show your police officer smoking at a crime scene unless scorn for the rules is a deliberate part of his character – but it is far more important to keep readers from being jarred out of the flow of the story by a discordant fact than it is to Get Everything Right.

Yes, there are crime writers who have built their reputation on technical and forensic detail. However, crime fiction can flourish without it. To write convincingly and powerfully about crime and its causes and consequences, you don't need to be an expert in the decomposition of severed heads or the mental state of serial killers. To write convincingly and powerfully about crime, you need to be a writer with a feel for narrative. You need characters poised to leap off the page, and a story to tell, and the capacity to carry readers with you to the end.

If, however, you are writing a scene that is in some way technical, be sure you understand the ground under your feet (P. D. James famously had a motorcycle reversing up a lane, overlooking the problem that motorcycles have no reverse gear. She still hears about that, from readers.) You should assemble a research library of your own, with the kinds of information you tend to use, whether about historical firearms, slang of the 1920s, or modern police forensics. Use it; know it; check it. We have included reading material in the 'Resources' section.

FOR ALEX McBRIDE on ...

the dangers of evidence, see 'Tips and tales – guest contributors', see p. 131.

If you find that the pleasure of learning every last detail about explosives, or the Cuban mafia, or the Atlas Mountains, is taking over your life, there is a simple technique that will help you to stay in control:

THE RESEARCH TABLE

Allow a limited period of time for background research during the planning process – and stick to it. Then construct a table with four columns to use while you're engaged in the process of writing.

When factual questions that require research pop up while you're writing (How long does it take to drive overland from London to Istanbul? When was high tide in Aldeburgh on 13 March 1999? What kind of emollient do ballet dancers use to ease their aching muscles?) *do not go rushing off in search of answers. Instead, simply record each question on a separate line of column 1 of your table.*

In column 2, record the page in your draft on which an answer to this question is needed.

Use column 3 to note down sources (people, books, etc.) that might provide an answer, as and when they occur to you.

Monitor your attempts to get answers, and record the answer you finally come up with, in column 4.

With a table like this, you won't be constantly tempted to abandon writing and take up research again. The answers to your questions can be dealt with, often only in a day or two, after the first draft is complete. But the biggest benefit is that, because your research question arises out of the specifics of your story, you will have a narrow range of knowledge to explore. For example, you may know nothing whatsoever about guns, and plan on writing a novel in which a shooting takes place. To try and learn all about firearms could take months; to find an answer to the question *What kind of handgun, capable of killing a person at twenty paces, would fit into a woman's handbag?* might be answered in a matter of minutes.

Now, is the time when our guest speakers come in, bringing fresh air and a new perspective. In Part Three, Michelle and Laurie will return with the nuts-and-bolts craft of 'Getting Your Story Across'.

Part 2:

Tips and tales – guest contributors

Tips and tales – guest contributors

Mark Billingham: How to create suspense

Mark Billingham was born in Birmingham, England, and worked as an actor, television writer and stand-up comic before turning to crime in 2001, with the bestselling *Sleepyhead*.

I am often asked at events and creative writing workshops – as I know many other crime writers are – how you go about creating suspense. There was a period when, in answer to this question, I would talk about the tricks of the trade. I would bang on about the cliff-hanger, the twist and the 'reveal'. Such things are still important, of course, but I have come to realise that the answer actually lies in something far more basic, something that should be central to the writing of any piece of fiction: the creation of character.

The techniques mentioned above are of course all vital pieces of the mystery writer's armoury and, as such, are components of the genre that readers of crime novels have come to expect. They are part of the package; the buttons that a writer has to push every so often. When a crime writer thinks up a delicious twist, it is a great moment. Time to relax and take the rest of the day off. I do think that it can be overdone, however. There are a number of writers who believe it is their duty to throw as many curveballs at the reader as possible. To twist and twist again. These are the Chubby Checkers of crime fiction and while I admire the craft, I do think that it can actually work against the creation of genuine suspense. Put simply, I find it hard to engage with any book that is no more than a demonstration of technique. A character dies, but why should I give a hoot when I know that writer's stock in trade means that the character is almost certainly not dead at all? The cop has caught the killer, but is that the end of it? No, of course not, because there are still three chapters left and I know very well that the police have got the wrong man.

Make no mistake, this kind of intricate plotting can be hugely important and the success of writers who give their readers a corkscrew ride is testament to its popularity. But I don't believe that in terms of creating suspense, it is necessarily the best way to go.

The 'reveal' is an effective technique, and one with which I am very familiar from my time as a stand-up comedian. It may sound surprising, but a joke and a crime novel work in very much the same way. The comedian/writer leads their audience along the garden path. The audience knows what's coming, or at least they *think* they do until they get hit from a direction they were not expecting. The best example I can think of from the world of crime fiction is in the wonderful Thomas Harris novel, *The Silence of the Lambs*. The SWAT team have the killer cornered and are approaching his house. At the same time, Clarice Starling has been dispatched to a small town many miles away to tie up a few loose ends. A member of the SWAT teams ring the killer's doorbell. We 'cut' to the killer's ghastly cellar where he hears the doorbell ring. This is the moment when the dummy is sold and the reader buys it completely. The reader stays with the killer as he slowly climbs the stairs, butterflies flitting ominously around him in the semi-darkness ... we know he has a gun ... we know what he is capable of ... he opens the door, and ...

It's Clarice Starling! The SWAT team are at the wrong house, she is at the right house and she doesn't know it. It's the perfect reveal and it happens at the precise moment that the reader turns the page. The best crime fiction is full of heart-stopping moments such as this. They are punchlines, pure and simple, albeit very dark ones.

The reason that Harris's reveal works so wonderfully, however, is not just because of the sublime timing. It works because of the character of Clarice Starling, a young woman the reader has come to know well and to empathise with. Ultimately, *this* is where I believe that the key to genuine suspense is to be found.

The Damascus moment happened several years ago when I was reading a novel called *The Turnaround* by the wonderful American writer

George Pelecanos. Pelecanos is happy enough to call himself a 'crime writer', but he is not overly concerned with the sort of tricks already described. There is usually shocking violence and there is often an element of investigation in its aftermath, but his books are not traditional mysteries by any means. What he *does* do as well as any writer I know, however, is to create characters that live and breathe on the page and, as I read, I realised I had come to know some of these people so well that the idea that something bad was going to happen to them – and I knew it would – had become almost unbearable. I was turning each page with a sense of dread and it dawned on me that here was the best and most satisfying way to create suspense.

These are crime novels, after all. The reader has seen the jacket, read the blurb and knows very well what they are in for. Yes, there may be redemption and resolution of a sort, but there will also be suffering and pain, grief and dreadful loss. You know it's coming, but not when or to whom.

The tension is real and terrible, because you *care*.

So, by all means throw in a thrilling twist every now and again, but not so often that they lose their power to shock. Time those 'reveals' to perfection so as to give your reader a punchline they will remember for a long time.

But above all, give your readers characters they genuinely care about, that have the power to move them, and you will have suspense from page one.

S. J. Bolton: Contemporary crime in the Gothic tradition

S. J. Bolton was born in Lancashire, and had a successful career in business administration before writing crime, beginning with *Sacrifice* in 2008.

No novel pretending to be Gothic is complete without a legend or two. For *Blood Harvest*, I unearthed loads of agricultural and rural traditions, many of which appear (occasionally embellished) in the book. I had a lot of fun, and at the same time ran the risk of writing a story that few would take seriously. To guard against this, the modern Gothic writer has to establish credibility with strong contemporary themes.

The central theme of *Blood Harvest* is that of young children in danger and the grief of adults who lose them. I spent as much time researching the psychology of grief and the treatment of bereaved parents as I did rural folklore. Much less fun but, together with the considerable forensic detail I wove into the novel, it made for a book that has not, so far, been dismissed as a bit of Gothic nonsense. Folklore and forensics, I've found, balance each other surprisingly well.

To be a Gothic writer, you have to be a descriptive writer because a Gothic novel is heavy on atmosphere. Not as easy as it sounds, because description in a contemporary thriller is all about balance: too little and you wave goodbye to atmosphere of any kind; too much and the pace begins to flag.

Originality is key, and yet tricky when it all seems to have been done before. Giving a new twist to a description of autumn in *Blood Harvest* proved a challenge, until I tried it from a child's point of view and spun it around food.

> *October was when the trees started to look like toffee apples and the ploughed fields turned the colour of dark chocolate. Tom liked the way the air tasted on his tongue, fresh and sharp like a polo mint.*

So, you've created a picture in your reader's head and now you want to turn it dark. Try introducing the one tiny detail that's wrong. The opening scene of *Now You See Me* is a city park at night. I talk about monochrome colours, silhouettes of old trees, nearby buildings, tall and empty, and the sound that is totally out of place: that of a knife being sharpened against stone.

Another good trick is to break the rules. *Blood Harvest* is set on the moors in Lancashire. The moors are massive rock formations, as solid and unchanging as time. So introduce the idea that they move, that they creep closer when the sun goes down. Show that from the point of view of a young child and the book immediately takes a dark turn.

In my second novel, *Awakening*, I wanted to depict an isolated village absolutely teeming with life. I talked about vegetation covering everything, cloaking sound, trees towering in a massive green canopy, and everywhere the trickle of water that fed the plants. The mood I was aiming for was almost that of the vegetation coming to life, Triffid style; so when the snakes start wriggling out of the undergrowth, the reader is almost expecting them.

No Gothic novel is complete without a big fright or two and the double bluff is a great trick. I pulled it out of the bag in *Sacrifice* – bloodstained package, dark cellar, strawberries (you have to read the book!) – and may have to wait another decade before I can risk it again. Used well, though, it can't be beaten. Set your reader up to expect something very nasty, lead them to it step by slow step, get them holding the book at arm's length, only to find nothing happens at all. Huge relief, massive anti-climax, just starting to breathe again when – wham! – something they were never expecting. It's a great Gothic trick.

All my life, I've loved a creepy, dark tale. At the same time, even the best ghost stories can be rather frustrating, never properly resolved because – hey – the ghost did it. Crime readers won't buy this, and even a modern Gothic writer can't get away with it. Every scene that hints at the paranormal has to be viewable on two levels, the weird and the worldly. My books might masquerade as ghost or horror stories, but, by the end, everything is explained logically and scientifically. Far from easy but, ultimately, it's this blend of the deeply spooky and the unquestionably scientific that makes modern Gothic such a pleasure to write.

Alafair Burke: Watching the world with empathy

Alafair Burke, criminal prosecutor and law professor, is the author of two best-selling, award-winning series featuring NYPD Detective Ellie Hatcher and Portland Deputy DA Samantha Kincaid.

I've heard many writers talk about the 'what if' process. You read a newspaper article or stumble upon a little nugget of a thought and start to think, *What if X had happened instead of A? And then what if because of X, Y occurred? And then what if Z knew about the link between X and Y but couldn't tell anyone because of W?* Before you know it, you have a plot that's quite unrecognisable from its inspiration.

Ideas also come from characters. For me at least, characters come from watching the world with empathy. I try not to wonder, 'What would I do in situation X, Y or Z?' Instead, I watch people in the world and wonder how they'd react, how they'd speak, and how they became the people they are today.

Last autumn, for example, I came across a news story about an Orange County woman who drove for months with the body of a dead homeless woman in her car. According to media coverage, the fifty-seven-year-old former real-estate agent 'befriended' the homeless woman at a neighbourhood park in December and allowed her to sleep in the car overnight. When she found the woman dead, the car owner was too scared to call the police, so simply continued to use the car while the body sat covered in clothes in the passenger seat. By the time police intervened, the woman had placed a box of baking soda on the dashboard to mask the smell, even though she had gotten 'used to it'.

Comments posted online about the story tended to focus on the yuck-factor, or to joke about the driver's desperation to use California carpool lanes.

But yucks aside, this is the kind of story that should trigger empathetic imagination in a writer. What if the driver were lying? What if she and the other woman weren't just casual acquaintances from the neighbourhood but co-conspirators? What were they planning? And what went wrong?

But perhaps even more interestingly, let's assume the driver was telling the truth. Why did she offer her car to the other woman for sleep? Might it be related to the fact that she, according to the article, was a 'former' real-estate agent who 'once' lived in Corona del Mar, an affluent Newport Beach neighbourhood, but was now experiencing 'difficult financial times' and 'staying with a friend' while driving a 1997 Mercury Grand Marquis registered to her sick father?

And why was she so afraid to call the police? Did she do something she's trying to hide, or is there something about her that makes her fear police generally?

And who was the poor dead homeless woman? How did she come to be homeless in a park? How did the two women become friendly? How did she die? Did she know it was happening?

I never know where these kinds of ruminations will take me. My sixth novel, *212*, was about women living dangerous double lives in New York City. Many readers thought it was inspired by the so-called Craig's List Killer case, where the victim was a New York woman who, unbeknownst to her friends and family, was using Craig's List to book private massage sessions.

But I turned in the manuscript for *212* two weeks before that case occurred. If I had to guess where the idea came from, I'd trace it back to a winter morning more than five years earlier. I had just moved to the city and was staring out my little window in the east village, marvelling that my Wichita-raised self was living in great big important Manhattan.

I noticed an attractive younger woman walking on Mercer. She was tall, thin, well-dressed, gorgeous. I wondered what it was like to be her. She probably shopped at Barney's, I figured. Dated investment bankers. Whizzed past the red velvet ropes outside the hot clubs she frequented long after the likes of me had fallen asleep.

And then she stopped at the corner trashcan and looked in all four directions before pulling out a discarded pastry and eating it.

My fictional image of her life suddenly changed. The 'character' I had momentarily created in my head was no longer cliché.

So if your friends and family ever find you daydreaming – paying too much attention to people you don't know, staring into space wondering 'What if?' and 'What must it be like?' – tell them you are busy writing.

Lee Child: The evolutionary purpose of the thriller

Lee Child was born in Coventry and worked at Granada Television until he was fired during restructuring. He sat down to write *Killing Floor*, the first in the worldwide best-selling Jack Reacher series.

The Hall of Human Origins in the American Museum of Natural History shows how, over five million years, proto-human species emerged and changed and co-existed and competed and died out, eventually leaving just two survivors: Homo Sapiens – ourselves – and Neanderthal people. A couple of hundred thousand years ago – a blink of an eye, in geological terms – we were both around at the same time, maybe even in the same places, like dogs and cats might share the same city street, or rats and squirrels the same city park. Neanderthals probably had the upper hand. They were heavier and stronger and faster. They were superb tool makers. They were much better equipped to survive the brutal conditions of prehistory.

But they didn't survive. We did. Why?

Because Homo Sapiens developed language. Many primitive species could communicate by making sounds – and many still do: prairie dogs make distinctive noises if a predator is spotted – one noise for a ground predator, and another for an airborne predator. But Homo Sapiens went beyond two words. After a random mutation our brains grew large and the new capacity was colonised by language, with a theoretically infinite number of available words, and more importantly with *syntax*, such that as well as reporting we could plan and speculate. Not just: *a predator is coming*, but also: *a predator will come*, or *might come*. Not just reaction, but also prediction: *if we do this, we'll be OK*, or *if we do that, we'll be in trouble*.

And we needed all the help we could get. We were puny, few in number, often defenceless against ravening beasts. Alone, or in small disorganised groups, we were easy prey. But a coordinated crowd of two hundred Homo Sapiens was the most powerful animal on earth. The heaviest, the strongest, the hardest to kill. Thus, grunting Neanderthals slowly died out, despite their strength and speed, and talking humans marched on towards the present, despite our slender limbs and fragile skulls. Language guaranteed our survival, but more specifically *language in the service of truth.* Truth was the whole deal. There wasn't anything else. It would have made no sense to say, 'Watch out! There's a sabre-toothed tiger behind that bush!' if there wasn't. It would have made no sense to say to a group of departing hunters, 'I saw the woolly mammoths in the next valley,' if you hadn't. So language was about telling the truth, to help the tribe to survive.

But then something strange happened. We invented fiction. We started talking about things that hadn't happened to people that didn't exist.

When? It's hard to say, but we can guess. We know that representative art was around roughly fifty thousand years ago – there are cave paintings as evidence. We know that music was made around the same time – we have found bone flutes dating back to the same era. It's reasonable to assume that story-telling might have happened earlier. Art and music require technological intervention – mixed pigments, crude sticks or brushes for applying them, musical instruments of one kind or another. Story-telling requires only words and voices, and we had developed them already. All that was required was the change of use. So story-telling might be a hundred thousand years old.

The more interesting question is: why? Why tell stories? To relieve boredom? For fun? No, those are not possible answers. A hundred thousand years ago, we were still evolving, both physically and in terms of behaviours. Put simply, no new behaviour could possibly become established unless, at least to some slight degree, *it made it more likely that we would still be alive in the morning.* It was that simple.

So how could story-telling keep us alive? How could fiction help us get up in the morning more energetic, firmer in resolve, surer in ourselves? By *managing our fear*, I think. Imagine yourself one of a band of perhaps twenty people, in the late evening, huddled in your cave, with a smoky fire burning in the cave mouth, hearing the howls of the night predators outside. Intelligence brings imagination, and you might have been imagining your likely fate. 'It will be OK,' someone might have said. Eventually – after a thousand years, or ten thousand – that simple *It will be OK* might have expanded to a parable, about a member of the clan who found himself in the open late at night and was chased by a bear, but escaped, but woke a tiger, but escaped again, and made it back to the cave in safety. That parable might have evolved into a full-blown story, with the clear message: *Things happen to people like you, but they're survivable*. In other words – *don't worry. Things turn out OK*. Eventually, some empowering human heroism might have been edited in. Now maybe the guy slew the bear, and the tiger, and thereby not only escaped his fate but made the whole place a little safer for everyone.

We still tell stories exactly like that. The modern serial killer stories are direct linear descendants of those cave-based scenarios. Terrorism stories, too. The huddled twenty-strong cave-dwelling clan has changed to a terrified modern community – a nation, a town, or a suburb – and the lone club-wielder has changed to the CIA or the FBI, but the message is the same ... yes, there are monsters out there, but we can slay them and live happily ever after. Stories manage our fear, by showing us the precipice and telling us that we don't always fall off.

So, as a thriller writer, I smile to myself when critics imply that popular fiction is a recent and trashy invention. No, I think, so-called *literature* is the recent invention. And it was invented only because my story-telling ancestors helped the species stick around long enough to invent it. Thriller fiction is *the* genre. The original form, the essential form, the vital form, the boat on which other genres ride like barnacles. That's why readers enjoy it so much.

N. J. Cooper: Creating criminal characters

N. J. Cooper (also known as Natasha Cooper) is a lifelong Londoner who writes for a variety of newspapers and journals and was shortlisted for CWA's Dagger in the Library Award.

In the Golden Age of British crime writing many novelists avoided giving their characters fully developed personalities because in those days the puzzle was the all-important aspect of the genre. Readers were supposed to be able to suspect every single one of the characters in turn. Too much realism would have made that impossible.

The demands on writers have changed a lot. Although there is still pressure on us to provide more than a single suspect, along with a few shocks, a twist or two, and an unexpected dénouement, we are no longer required to make possible villains out of all the players in our plots. But we are expected to make them all psychologically coherent and credible as people.

Every writer develops his or her own methods. I have talked to some who go to extraordinary lengths to draw up biographies for each of their characters so that they know precisely how they were educated, what their favourite foods and music are, where they were geographically at every stage of their lives. For me that would be much too laborious, and I'm not sure it would work. I know I would lose the charts, get the dates wrong, and flounder in a mass of unwanted fact.

My own technique is to find an emotion that interests me and then wait while my subconscious creates a set of characters around that particular feeling. I have learned over the years not to start writing my synopsis – still less the book – for months after I've felt the first impulse. The important thing is to trust my subconscious, which knows far more about all this than my conscious mind would ever admit, and wait. Sometimes I write notes. Memory can let me down. But if the story is powerful enough to work it will stay in my mind.

And the characters develop. Sometimes I mine the published work of forensic psychologists and consult experts of all kinds as I get to know my villains and the people who have made them what they are, but I also look to my own emotions.

For *No Escape*, the first in my Isle of Wight series, I drew on memories of the six months I spent engaged to a charming, vulnerable man many years ago. As well as the charm and the vulnerability – and the extraordinary lies he told – he could be seriously scary. One evening he came down from his flat to let me in at the building's street door, carrying an enormous knife. I often found myself fantasising about a serious accident removing him from my life; worse, I kept having ideas about the best way to kill him. Eventually I realised that I didn't have to go ahead with the wedding, committing myself to a lifetime of rage and misery and him to even more damage than his childhood had caused. I broke off the engagement. He told me not to worry about him because he would kill himself. He didn't, although quite recently, long, long after we'd last met, he did die.

I gave those awful impulses, and a lot of the guilt I felt, to my series character Karen Taylor. Unlike me, she did go through with her marriage (at the age of eighteen). The discovery of her feelings led her to embark on a career as a forensic psychologist, whereas mine took me into crime writing. The men in question were completely different in every respect, just as I am quite different from Karen. But the feelings are shared.

Joan Littlewood is said to have made a young actor strip on stage and then act as though he were fully clothed because she believed that if actors were not prepared to expose their most private selves they would never succeed in the theatre. My view of writers – of crime fiction or of anything else – is much the same. We have to be prepared to lay ourselves open on the page, to explore the darkest and the most pathetic aspects of our personalities, if our work is to live.

This does not mean writing our own emotional biographies every time we embark on a novel. That would produce only the deadening fiction-as-therapy, which always bores readers even though it may satisfy its writer. But we have to use our own nightmares, secret shames and unachievable desires without fear or concealment, particularly when creating our villains.

At some stage in our lives every one of us will have had a moment of wanting someone else to be dead. A playground spat, a difficult moment in a serious relationship, bullying in the office, neighbours who play horrible music loudly all night, an endlessly crying baby, dangerous drivers, unsympathetic tax officials, corrupt politicians, cruel teachers, the burglar who stole a cherished family heirloom ... The list of situations and potential victims could go on for pages.

Because we're writers, civilised, aware, decent, truthful and law-abiding, we ourselves have never attacked anyone else. But I'll bet all of us have felt the impulse at one time or another. All we have to do when getting to know our fictional murderers is put ourselves back in the situation that made us think, 'I could've killed him/her', and then build on what we find out about ourselves.

As you write, your characters will develop. Each situation into which you put them will make aspects of their personalities seem more or less convincing. You may have to change quite fundamental things about them. But if you keep listening to your own subconscious as you work, you shouldn't go too far wrong.

And when a reader or a dear friend is shocked by what you have revealed, pride yourself on the fact that you've done your job and refused to hide.

Meg Gardiner: Why write thrillers?

Edgar Award winner Meg Gardiner was raised in southern California, graduated from Stanford, practised law, and writes what Stephen King calls 'simply put, the finest crime-suspense series I've come across in the last twenty years'.

People ask me why I write thrillers. What, they wonder, provokes me to tell stories of crime and suspense and deadly adventure?

Sometimes, the question they really want to ask is left unsaid: 'How can you write that stuff? You don't seem overtly bloodthirsty,' or 'You were such an innocuous child – what happened to you?'

The implication is that I must love violence, or want to see people suffer. Hardly.

I write thrillers because they get to the heart of the human condition. Thrillers, like all crime fiction, are about people facing severe danger, or confronting an evil that has invaded their world. A thriller tells the story of characters who must tackle the most critical problem of their lives. They must do it under huge pressure, often with their survival and the survival of their families, friends or community at stake. The heroes must find the resources to fight back – *now.* They must muster the courage to act against seemingly overwhelming opposition – *now.* They must rise to the challenge. Or not. Or die trying.

Writing thrillers is also fun. I get to slingshot readers into situations they would hate to face in real life. A kid in danger? Bring it on. Sadistic killers? Here, have another helping. My book gave you nightmares? Thank you, that's wonderful.

(And now I sense you backing away, thinking, *What did she say about not being bloodthirsty? Sure ...*)

It's wonderful because it means my story held the reader spellbound. The fun doesn't come from simply scaring readers. It comes from taking them on a convincing journey. It comes when readers believe, and fear, and hold their breath with worry for the characters. For readers, that's the thrill and appeal of crime fiction: sharing vicariously in the characters' struggles – physical, emotional and moral – as they face their greatest test.

So create sympathetic characters and put them in jeopardy. And take readers for the ride of their lives.

Tess Gerritsen: A tense situation

Tess Gerritsen began to write romantic suspense while on maternity leave from her job as physician, later turning to medical thrillers. Her series featuring homicide detective Jane Rizzoli and medical examiner Maura Isles are best-sellers worldwide.

Imagine you are sitting in a coffee shop. Imagine that you can hear the two women at the next table having a conversation and it goes like this:

'Lovely weather we're having, isn't it?'

'Yes, just delightful. So much better than yesterday.'

'And I hear it will be nice all week.'

How soon before you'd tune out and stop listening? Five seconds, ten? The point is you *would* tune out, wouldn't you, because what they're saying is so darn boring.

Now imagine their conversation went like this instead:

'Did you really have an affair with Rick?'

'Who told you? How did you find out?'

Would you still tune out? Or would you listen in, waiting anxiously to hear what's said next, what other secrets will be revealed?

That, in a nutshell, is the secret of story tension, and it's tension that makes us want to keep listening in or turning the pages. Tension doesn't have to involve action or danger or gunfire. In fact, I find that action scenes can sometimes be boring. *Tension*, on the other hand, is what happens before the action explodes. It's a sense of uneasiness or conflict in the air, a feeling of being off-balance. A sense that something *just isn't right*.

In our real lives, we encounter little micro-bursts of tension all the time. Think about the last unpleasant encounter you had with someone. Maybe it left you stewing for hours. I have one particular memory of being pulled out of an airline boarding line because I had a plastic bag with a bottle of water that I'd just purchased in the airport shop. 'That's a third carry-on!' the gate agent announced loudly. 'You're only allowed two!' Red-faced, I quickly stuffed the bottle in my purse, and she grudgingly let me board. I fumed about the unpleasantness for the rest of the flight. Conflicts like these, whether major or minor, fully engage us – and they engage us in fiction as well.

My novel *The Silent Girl* starts off with medical examiner Maura Isles testifying at the trial of a police officer who's accused of killing a prisoner. Maura knows that if she declares the prisoner's death a homicide, the whole police department will consider her the enemy. Nevertheless she gives her honest opinion, sending the officer to prison, and for the rest of the novel, Maura must face the cold stares and silence of Boston PD. The result is tension in every scene between Maura and the police. The conflict isn't overt; no one insults her or argues with her. But the cops' silent hostility leaves Maura feeling off-balance and on edge, and that makes her scenes more interesting. Throughout the Jane Rizzoli and Maura Isles crime series, I've tried to keep my main characters fresh and interesting by continually introducing conflict-ridden situations. In the course of nine books, Maura has fallen in and out of love several times – sometimes with stunningly unsuitable men. Jane's divorcing parents have forced her to play referee. Jane's partner Barry Frost has watched his marriage fall apart. Life gets complicated for all of them – just as it does for you and me.

Add the fact that they're also hunting for killers, and it's easy to introduce tension on every page. It may come from something as minor as a husband's dismissive remark to his wife. It may be as major as a killer confronting his doomed victim. But that tension *must* be there, in every scene.

Or the reader may give up and close the book.

Sophie Hannah: In defence of the puzzle

Sophie Hannah is the award-winning author of six internationally best-selling psychological thrillers, five collections of poetry, and a short-story anthology.

I recently took part in a panel discussion about the English Golden Age crime novel, of the sort written by Agatha Christie, Ngaio Marsh and others – was that sort of crime fiction obsolete now, hopelessly outdated, or was there still a place for it? I didn't expect there to be much disagreement among the authors on the panel; Agatha Christie, whatever her limitations, is one of the greatest crime writers who ever lived, and even if she isn't to one's personal taste, I reasoned, it would be a bit much to try to strike her from the record as having been irrelevant or an entirely negative influence. I was amazed to hear a well-respected male crime writer say vehemently that Christie was the opposite of a good writer: her characters were wooden and lifeless, as was her prose, and – the greatest sin of all – her novels were merely 'puzzles'. The only thing she was good at was plot, he argued, making no mention of *how* good at it she was.

As I waited for him to finish his rant, silently planning my defence of poor old Agatha, I became aware of something I hadn't realised before: how often I have heard one crime writer or another – in panel sessions, in bookshops and libraries, at literary festivals – deride the puzzle element of crime fiction. The contemporary orthodoxy seems to be that too much emphasis on puzzle and plot is somehow shallow, reducing both the writer and the reader to the status of crossword- or Sudoku-obsessed anorak-wearing geeks who care little for the deep concerns of humanity. On the flip side of the coin are the much-esteemed grails of contemporary crime fiction: psychological depth, caring more about character than plot (I've heard some crime writers boast that they don't care about plot *at all* and barely give it a thought), socio-political commentary and painstaking realism.

Well, I value realism and psychological depth as much as the next person, but to my mind, the puzzle aspect of crime fiction isn't something separate, to be disparaged and discarded. In fact, thinking about this issue made me realise that it's the puzzle factor which, more than anything else, drives me to write, and I'm not talking about puzzles as a feature of crime novels – I mean the puzzle as a feature of life.

The reason I've always loved mystery stories, and probably the reason, also, that I became a crime writer, is because, in my real life, I've always been obsessed with the need to know, a need that so often goes unquenched. There are so many unknowns in our day-to-day existence, so many unfathomable mysteries – not associated with murders usually, but fascinating none the less. When everything is known, life is, let's face it, boring. But when you yearn for information that is either deliberately withheld from you or for some other reason not available, you can't bear the thought that this burning question might never be resolved. The comfort of crime fiction is that, except for in the most experimental of mystery novels, the puzzle always is resolved.

Throughout my life, I've been painfully aware of all the things I don't know, will probably never find out, but would desperately love to know the answer to. When I lead crime or mystery fiction workshops, I sometimes start by asking participants to list some of the mysteries they've encountered in their lives so far. Here are a couple of mine:

1) Why did my dad's friend Harold, during a cricket Test match they attended together, suddenly turn frosty and withdrawn and, after that

Test match, sever all ties with my dad even though, ostensibly, nothing had happened – no row or falling out, no obvious incident. They'd been friends since they were five.

2) Someone I know started a romantic relationship some years ago with the widowed husband of her deceased best friend. Obviously people noticed this, and the two of them claimed that the notion that they might get together after the friend/wife died didn't once cross either of their minds while she was ill in hospital; they merely grew close (rather quickly) after her death, united by their grief. Is that really true? Or might there have been a modicum of impatience involved – *How much longer do we have to wait?* – that sort of thing?

These are true stories, and I'm sure everyone has niggles in their minds of a similar sort relating to people in their lives – why did so-and-so do this or that? – but I was recently made aware that my need to know the truth, however bad or recalcitrant it might be, is unusually high. A few months back, I was on the point of confiding in my sister (who has always been my primary confidante) about something that I wanted to keep private, just between me and her. She asked if this was a secret she could share with her husband. 'No,' I said. 'Of course not.'

'Then I don't want to know,' she said. It astonished me to discover that my sister was able to turn down the chance to acquire some quite possibly crucial information. I couldn't have said to her, or to anyone, what she said to me; I'm too interested in the workings of people's minds and their weird behaviours to be able to say, 'I'd rather not know.'

Puzzles arise in life *because* of psychological depth, because people have hidden worlds in their heads that they can't admit to having. Solving the puzzles that are individual people, and the even bigger puzzle of all those people trying to exist in the world together and what happens when the mystery of one person clashes or enmeshes with the mystery of another, is the single most useful activity you can engage in if your aim is to arrive at a deeper understanding of the world. I would argue that puzzles are absolutely essential, not only in crime fiction but in any fiction or drama.

By the way, I'm in need of a new primary confidante now that my sister has resigned from the post – applications on a postcard, please.

Jim Kelly: A modern key to the locked room mystery

Jim Kelly began writing on the 6:45 train out of King's Cross every night and has continued with two successful series, both set in East Anglia. He also rings church bells, a hobby inspired by Dorothy Sayers's *The Nine Tailors.*

There's nothing fiendish about the concept of the *locked room mystery*. At its heart is a puzzle. We are presented with a seemingly impossible crime in which – classically – a murder victim is found within a room with no windows and one door which is locked and bolted on the inside. How did the killer get in, then get out? This simple premise can appear in many forms. In my own attempt – *Death Wore White* – the victim is found at the wheel of a car surrounded by untrampled snow. A reader interested in unlocking this mystery, and indeed any like it, can do no better than read Chapter XVII of John Dickson Carr's 1935 classic *The Hollow Man* for a lecture on the various solutions available. Carr's analysis is often described as a textbook for crime writers. It is.

The problem for the modern audience is that the classic locked room mystery is essentially unreal – stagey, cosy, if not downright tricksy. Dickson Carr himself said that the solution to such a mystery had only to be *possible* – not probable. As a result the Golden Age of crime fiction ends up being as far away from gritty realism as C. S. Lewis's Narnia is from Stieg Larsson's Sweden. Two examples illustrate the point. In Conan Doyle's 'The Speckled Band' the killer strikes using a snake, trained to enter a bedroom and – at a given signal – bite the victim and exit. In Edgar Allan Poe's 'Murders in the Rue Morgue' the victims are killed in their fourth-floor locked room by an escaped orang-utan who swings in through the open window. You get the picture: biddable snakes, runaway circus animals, smoke and mirrors. This isn't crime fiction to us – it's children's party magic. It's certainly not *The Killing*, is it?

But is there life in the locked room mystery yet? I was encouraged on two fronts – first, I found an example that actually happened. Laetitia Toureaux died on 16 May 1937 on the Paris Metro. She was a police informant who had infiltrated a right-wing terror group called – rather wonderfully – The Hood. She didn't know that day that her cover had been blown and her death sentence passed. She got on a train at Parc de Vincennes and was the only passenger in the first-class compartment. Just forty-five seconds later the train arrived at the next station – Porte Dorée – and the first passengers to enter the carriage found Laetitia was already dying – a nine-inch dagger protruding from her neck. How had the killer struck? The crime is still unsolved – although if the police had taken the trouble to read Dickson Carr's lecture they might have got closer to the truth. (I'd have reinterviewed the witness who found the body.)

I was also encouraged by the fact that not all such mysteries of the Golden Age are baroque fancies. Take the first murder in *The Hollow Man.* The victim drops dead in a snowy street – watched by witnesses – as a gunshot rings out. Forensics show the gun was pressed to his skin when the bullet was fired. But only his own footsteps lead to the corpse, and the witnesses saw nobody else, and there is no gun. Impossible, surely? Solution: simple. He was already fatally wounded when first seen standing in the street. The killer took a second shot. The victim collapsed at the sound and died, but not from the shot the witnesses heard. That bullet whistled past. Another good example is *The Nine Tailors* by Dorothy L. Sayers – but I won't ruin that one for you, although it too is beautifully simple.

The bad news for crime writers is that it is far more difficult to come up with simple, graceful, solutions than complex ones. In art as in life, less is more. You have to search out those fundamental mistakes of perception which we all make – and which policemen often make – when trying to interpret what look like the facts. One of Colin Dexter's finest Morse mysteries is based on a simple, everyday, mathematical false assumption. Put one of these plot-twisting moments at the heart of a gritty modern crime novel and I think you've got a winner. If – by the way – you want to solve the mystery in *Death Wore White* for yourself I can suggest three things you might need: half a dozen Dinky toys, the map of the crime scene provided, and a clock without glass so that you can manipulate the hands. Good luck.

Laura Lippman: Getting ideas

Laura Lippman, a 'literary figure who's chosen to write mysteries' (Booklist), was born in Baltimore and began writing her best-selling novels while working as a reporter. She has won most of the major US crime awards.

Have you ever met a kid without imagination? Actually, I've met a few, but it's rare. Sometimes, adults tell me they have no imagination and I always counter with: 'What would you do if you won the lottery?' They always have an answer. Always.

I mention this because it seems to me that a lot of writers have lost faith in their imaginations. They talk about their research. They confess which moving passages have been lifted, virtually intact, from their own lives. Both are fine, good, even. But whatever happened to making stuff up? That's what I heard Donald Westlake say early in my writing life. 'I became a writer so I could make things up.' Bingo!

The problem, I think, is that we believe imagination is magical and therefore not something we can control. You can't will yourself to have an idea, can you? Well ... actually, you can. And it doesn't have to involve wandering the moors or brooding darkly for days. Just gather up the tools of your trade – a pencil and pad, a laptop, a sketchbook – and tell yourself: *Time to have an idea. What interests me now? What would I like to read? What's going on in my life, in my head?* I think about crimes from my childhood, figuring if they've stayed with me for forty-plus years, there must be something to them, a subtext to be explored.

I know, I know: it's not supposed to work that way. We should begin our novels and stories only when we feel passionately about a character or a plot or an idea. A person might as well will herself to fall in love and use the Internet to do it. Like that could ever happen!

Still, we cling to the idea that the systematic search for an idea makes one a hack. OK, then call me a hack. I'm a novelist. It's my job to have ideas. Sometimes, they come unbidden, out of nowhere. (That's what people in my second home town, New Orleans, call lagniappe, an unexpected gift.) Sometimes, someone says, 'Can you write a short story about ...?' and I do, and I love it. And, sometimes, I simply sit and stare into space for a few days, thinking about life and what I have to say about it.

If we make writing mystical, we place it out of our control, we give ourselves another reason not to do it. If we hold our ideas to the standard of blinding love at first sight, then they will be few and far between. Find the idea, start to write. Trust me, the emotional highs and lows will follow. You might even have days where you feel inspired. But you'll have plenty of days where you don't and you have to get through those, too. Writing a novel is like a very long, happy marriage. Sure, there are hard days, but ultimately one is rewarded just for showing up every day.

Gayle Lynds: Fascinate me

Gayle Lynds, the award-winning author of nine spy novels, has been called the Queen of International Espionage. *The Book of Spies* introduces museum curator Eva Blake and intelligence operative Judd Ryder.

Today we're gifted with an abundance of mysteries and thrillers that are technically fine, even superior. The characters are finely drawn, the background is interesting, and the villain is strong and intelligent, a worthy foil against whom the hero/heroine (classically put: protagonist vs antagonist) can believably find unknown inner strength and bravery.

Still, many lack something. I call it fascination – the author's.

Fascination can't be taught, and it doesn't have to be. It's a natural human characteristic too often underrated. So fascinated was Mario Puzo by the workings of the mafia, how it affected individuals, the cost to them, the wars, courage and treachery, that like millions, I was completely captured in the universe he created in *The Godfather*. I felt the same about *The Spy Who Came in from the Cold* by John le Carré. How compelling it was to enter le Carré's grey world of intelligence, and how I missed it when it ended.

Information, even knowledge, about the mafia or espionage was not enough to have made those novels great. No, it was that Puzo and le Carré were themselves fascinated, swept up by and in their subject material.

In 1989 I discovered an article in the *Los Angeles Times* about Ivan the Terrible's long-vanished Library of Gold – a collection of illuminated manuscripts covered in gold and precious gems, dating all the way back to the Greeks and Romans. Many of the books are lost to the world today, a literary and historical tragedy. I was instantly fascinated, but I write spy thrillers that are contemporary. So I carried the clipping around, losing it, refinding it, researching the library, muttering about it, until I finally had an idea that I hoped would work. Twenty years is a long time to be fascinated, but that's what can happen to a writer. The result was *The Book of Spies*, both a spy novel and an homage to libraries, published in 2010. It was recently nominated for the Nero Award for Literary Excellence in the Mystery Field.

Some authors seem to know that if they're fascinated, they have a better chance of fascinating readers. They find what enthrals their imagination, then they figure out how to use it in a story. I suspect they feel inspired when they do. I know I, as a reader and a writer, feel inspired – and grateful.

Alex McBride: Using real evidence

Alex McBride is a criminal barrister, and author of *Defending the Guilty: Truth and Lies in the Criminal Courtroom*, from which this edited extract has been taken.

Evidence is the most important thing in a trial. 'Real evidence' – defined as any tangible object, from a document to a baseball bat – is a prosecutor's friend: it's straightforward, easy to understand and interactive. Juries can touch it, admire its qualities, feel its weight – evaluate how much it would hurt to be smacked in the goolies with that baseball bat.

The two pieces of real evidence that are often assumed to be the most 'probative' (the legal word for a persuasive piece of evidence) are DNA and CCTV.

We have, thanks to shows such as *Crime Scene Investigation* and *Waking the Dead*, bought heavily into DNA evidence. DNA is an amazing evidential tool that has transformed criminal investigations and enabled the police to solve crimes that had baffled them for years. This has given people the impression that it's infallible. It isn't. DNA is fragile and easily damaged. It is susceptible to contamination. Ten per cent of crime scenes are inadvertently contaminated by the police's own DNA. The danger is that because DNA is sexy and cutting-edge, we accept the findings without thinking critically about them.

Statements from expert witnesses, combining forensic science and probability statistics, and typically using bafflingly large numbers, are difficult to interpret. Let's say that a witness statement reports that the defendant's DNA is a good match for that found under the fingernails of a murdered girl; if the DNA had come from someone unrelated to the defendant, then the chance of obtaining a match with the defendant would have been one in one million. Aha! you think: if the DNA has only a one-in-one-million chance of being from someone else, then this is decisive evidence against the defendant. But you'd be wrong. In fact, assuming that the male population is twenty million, then the statement would indicate that around twenty people in the population have the same profile. On this evidence alone, the chance that the DNA came from the defendant is only one in twenty.

Juries love CCTV. For them it's the best real evidence there is. It's their chance to play detective. For barristers, on the other hand, CCTV is a pain in the arse. If you're defending, you have to ask the prosecution for it, and if you're prosecuting, you have to hassle the police to go and get it. Officers then go down to the shop that's been turned over, or the train station where some kid's been robbed, to find that the CCTV:

- Wasn't switched on;
- Was broken;
- Was pointing the wrong way;
- Was unplayable;
- Wasn't loaded with film;

- Was already erased;
- Was lost;
- Was on a two-second stop-go frame speed which missed the crime;
- Or, as is mostly the case, was of such poor quality that it showed nothing of evidential value.

Even though Britain has more CCTV cameras than any other Western nation (there is no official estimate for the number of cameras in Britain but it's certainly many millions) it is estimated that only 3 per cent of crimes are solved by 'real evidence' from CCTV.

Val McDermid: Series or standalone?

Val McDermid, born in Fife and educated at St Hilda's, Oxford, was a journalist before beginning her crime-writing career in 1987. She has won awards around the world and is a fixture on best-seller lists.

Series fiction is attractive and satisfying for writers and readers alike. When it's done well, it's like a friendship – as the years go by, our understanding of the central characters and their world grows and we watch their lives affected and altered by the events they experience. We all want to know what comes next – and that generally applies to writers as much as to readers.

Standalone novels offer a different sort of satisfaction – the contained pleasure of a single play or a film, as opposed to an ongoing developing drama. That singularity gives a writer complete freedom to do what they will without having to imagine the consequences.

For the last dozen years, I've been alternating series novels and standalones. That's partly because I have a low boredom threshold and can't actually bring myself to write two novels back-to-back with the same characters. But it's mostly because that cycle allows me the freedom to write whatever story is clamouring most loudly to be heard.

Writing a single series has major limitations for a writer. Whatever the professional role of your central investigator, there are only certain kinds of story in which they can hold centre stage. In my standalones, I've had the burden of the story carried by a journalist, a greetings card manufacturer and an academic studying Wordsworth, among others. These are not sleuths who have a second novel in them, by and large.

Me, I hate limitations of any kind. So I embrace the standalones as a way of telling the stories that burn in my heart and my head but can't be homed with any of my series characters.

I'm often asked if there's any difference in the writing of these two types of novel. There is, but it only really has any significance in the early stages of the process.

Every novel starts with an idea. Sometimes it's a quirky nugget of information that suggests possibilities. Sometimes it's an anecdote told over a dinner table. Sometimes it's a throwaway line on the radio. But always, it's something that sets me thinking, 'What if ...?' It can take years to learn all the possible answers to that question, but quite early on in the process, it will be clear to me whether the shape and the subject of the story that's emerging fits existing series characters.

Finally, the story will have reached a stage where I know enough about what it is and where it's going and how it gets there. What happens next depends on whether it's a series novel or a standalone.

If it's a series novel, my starting point is the nexus of characters who move from book to book. Tony Hill and Carol Jordan are the key characters in their series, but there are family members and colleagues who have accompanied them through several stages of their journey. First I need to remind myself where I left them at the end of the previous book. So I have to do a bit of background reading, to be sure I've got all the details at my fingertips.

Then I have to consider the effect of the events of the previous books on the characters. How will they respond to what they've seen/heard/experienced? What damage has been done to them? What lessons have they learned?

Once I've got that straight in my head, I have to figure out how the story shapes itself around them. Series characters have individual clusters of limitations and abilities and the writer is stuck with those. The story has to accommodate that and it's not always easy to make that happen. But you have to labour through it because consistency is crucial, not just out of respect for yourself as a writer but also out of respect for the readers who have made a commitment to following your books.

When I wrote the first Hill and Jordan novel, *The Mermaids Singing*, I intended it to be a standalone. Looking back at it now, and the consequences of some of the decisions I made for plot reasons, I do wish I'd taken into consideration the fact that I might still be writing those characters fifteen years later. It left me with some interesting hoops to jump through over the years. I might not have made Tony Hill permanently impotent, for example, which would make his relationship with Carol all the more complex and tantalising. And I might have chosen to set the books in a real city rather than bind them to a fictitious one, to root them more firmly in terms of authenticity.

With a standalone, however, the story is the starting point. I have the luxury of working out how to make the different plot elements cohere so that the whole thing hangs together without the reader having to go, 'But wait a minute, that doesn't make sense ...' Only then do I turn to the characters and, rather like a psychological profiler, start asking myself 'What sort of person would behave like this? What personal history would provoke this attitude, these responses, those dreams? Why would someone react in one particular way rather than another?'

But once I'm past this initial stage, both forms converge into the same sort of biofeedback system, where the more I learn about the characters, the more the story possibilities cohere. And the further the story gets, the better I understand my characters, and so on in an endless progression. Sometimes the moments of illumination come suddenly. I can still remember struggling for a long time in *The Last Temptation* with why a Dutch cop and a German cop would be sharing confidential information about their cases. I was literally in the shower one morning when I slapped myself on the forehead and shouted, 'Because they're trying to impress each other into bed! Because they're lesbians, you numskull.' You'd think if anyone was going to work that one out it would be me ...

Which do I prefer, series or standalone? Well, the truth is, neither. I love them both. Because whatever I'm writing, my method means I'm passionate about that particular book. What's not to love about that?

Dreda Say Mitchell: The city as a setting

Dreda Say Mitchell is an East Ender whose parents came from the island of Grenada. She has been a journalist and broadcaster, and won the Creasey Award in 2004 for *Running Hot*.

I am, and always will be, in love with the city of London. It's the place of my birth and the place that I've chosen to set all of my current crime novels in. Crime fiction can be set anywhere. From the high society murder to the street drug deal gone wrong, crime writers find material at every level of society and in every background. It's worth giving the social backdrop at least as much thought as you do to your characters, because in the best writer's work, that backdrop will become a character.

Cities have always been a popular setting for crime fiction, from the days when Fagin's gang were out on the streets of Victorian London, through to Chandler's *femmes fatales* in LA, and into our own time with Rankin's Rebus getting to grips with a murder in Edinburgh. A city may well be the setting for your book. If it is, what are some things you need to consider when you're putting it together?

One of the first questions to ask yourself is, why choose to write about this particular city and not another? What is it about this location that is going to help you link the story, the characters and the theme at the centre of your book? In my case London reflected some of the key themes that I wrote about, such as people living on the margins, criminals, isolation, social misfits, justice. London is recognised throughout the world as a place that welcomes all types of people, but what if two very different people with differing lifestyles and views meet? What if a crisis develops between them? You have the recipe for a disaster, a crime writer's dream.

What makes your portrayal of the city distinctive? One way of doing this is to observe the unseen and unnoticed, the people and places that have passed others by. Consider the introductory line of my first novel, *Running Hot*: 'Mehmet Ali lay in East London's number one outdoor spot to die.' Here I wanted to convey to the reader not only that the victim was dying, but something about the place where he was dying. This part of East

London was not where anyone would want to find themselves at dead of night.

When I first started writing I began to realise that it wasn't so much London I wanted to write about but East London. So is there a certain part of the city that you've chosen that draws you? And why does it? East London has got a rich, but also explosive history, and I found myself particularly wanting to write about the experiences of people who grew up on housing estates. I didn't want to portray the usual 'Aren't housing estates awful places' image, but to give a much more rounded and realistic perspective. For example, in my first three novels, I created a housing estate where my characters live in two blocks called Aneurin Bevan Tower and Ernest Bevin House, nicknamed by the locals, Eric and Ernie. This setting acted as locations for my characters, but by using past politicians' names for the buildings I also point to the political and social history of the area.

The vocabulary and rhythms of city speech are another issue that writers need to think about. Nothing catches a moment more than a popular phrase or expression, but of course by the time your book hits the shelves, the slang that was hot when you wrote it will be deader than a Christmas card in January. Anthony Burgess famously got around this problem by inventing an entire Russian-based argot for his characters in *Clockwork Orange*. There's no need to go that far, but you can consider doing what a nephew of mine suggested for my novels and that is coming up with your own slang. This is what city people do; they invent their own and the good ones go into common usage while the others die away. You might even achieve the ultimate accolade for any writer of having one of your phrases pass into common speech.

Writers want to develop their own distinctive voice. We all use different voices every day – the formal voice you use at meetings; the voice you use with your family; the voice you use with your closest friends. But which one do you choose to write your book in? In my case the rhythm and the patter of the housing estate voices I grew up with – Cockney and Caribbean – hugely influenced the style of writing for my books. I hadn't consciously realised that the city I was breathing life into on the page was also giving life to the very words I chose to use.

I'll finish in the words of the protagonist from *Running Hot*, who, even though he knows that getting out of London is the only way to start a new life, still finds it hard to leave the city of London behind:

> *Schoolboy stood with his faithful hood, bandana and last bit of smoke in East London's favourite open-air spot for lyrical disobedience ...The fear of leaving stalked him. How could he up and leave a place where people were so frank and fresh in their openness with the world?*

Sara Paretsky: Why are we writing?

Sara Paretsky revolutionised the mystery world in 1982 when she introduced V. I. Warshawski, challenging a genre in which women typically were either vamps or victims. She is a founder of Sisters in Crime.

I began living in a world of stories when I was a child. As is true for many children, the books I read sparked a desire to become part of the narrative, to jump from a fire hydrant and land in Narnia, or hide in a window embrasure and become Jane Eyre. The desire to be part of the narrative led to writing my own stories, and ultimately, to creating my own narratives.

As a reader, I look for four things in a novel: a care for language, at least one character I can like, genuine emotion and believable dialogue. I don't look for brands or slickness. I'm turned off by high polish that doesn't have true feeling underneath it.

Too much of contemporary crime fiction is written for effect. People who have no street experience glory in a cop ride-along and imagine that they understand cop worlds, or 'perp' or gang worlds, that a sprinkling of rap or jargon will make us believe that they have street cred.

We are not just encouraged, but urged by publishers to create brands. I have at this writing (2012) published fifteen novels about my series character, V. I. Warshawski, and two standalone novels. My publishers tell me that the standalone novels, which helped stretch me as a writer, by challenging me to use language and to think of narrative in new ways, are outside my brand. When I leave my brand, I lose readers and the publisher loses income; I have been told not to do that any more.

I am better off than Melville. When Melville published *Moby-Dick* in 1851, the reception by both public and critics was hostile: he had left his brand, which was the travelogue novel. During Melville's life, this astonishing masterpiece sold 500 copies. In a bitter weariness, Melville wrote Hawthorne: 'The silent grass-growing mood in which a [person] ought to compose – that can seldom be mine. Dollars damn me.'

In a previous life, I sold computers to insurance agents. I would get on a plane, go to a small suburb which, whether it was in New York, New Jersey or Michigan, looked the same. I would go to the same office, where women did the clerical work and a few men owned the agency, try to persuade them of the value of automating their offices, have a mediocre lunch, be shown the accoutrements of their success – cars, sometimes yachts, once even a yacht outfitted with Uzis – and the next day I would do it all over again.

Writing 'brand' fiction feels the same as selling computers to insurance agents. Brand writing takes the joy out of losing myself in story. It deadens the soul.

Creating brands is not just unfair to readers, but it is dangerous for the future of the human spirit. We readers have become accustomed to getting the same hysterical recycled news wherever we turn; now we are being trained to accept slickness instead of the examined soul.

We writers owe a duty to our gifts. We've been given the gift of language, and we need to dig deep into words. We need to relish wordplay, not rely on clichés as we stumble towards the marketplace, or settle for the slick, repackaged street-talk we pick up from rap and TV.

And we owe a duty to our other gift, our stories. In the cacophony of sound that fills our broadband waves, amid the lies and shrill self-promotions, it is essential that we writers return to Melville's silent grass-growing place and find the truths that fiction can lay bare.

Jill Paton Walsh: The author's voices

Jill Paton Walsh was born in London, educated at St Anne's, Oxford, and writes for children and adults. She received the CBE for services to literature, and was elected a Fellow of the Royal Society of Literature.

Any working writer will have received blame they did not deserve and, if they are honest, praise they did not deserve. In my case the undeserved praise has been for being able to write in the voice of another writer – Dorothy L. Sayers. People suppose this must be a terribly difficult thing to do. There are two reasons why it is not so hard, one trivial, and one profound.

The trivial one first – she wrote the King's English, in a straightforwardly fluent and unmannered style. I am now so ancient that the King's English is the dialect I was brought up to read, speak and write. It comes naturally to me.

The more profound reason is that I, like any other reasonably competent fiction writer, can write in many voices – it is an essential part of the job to be able to write the dialogue for many and various characters, who must sound as unlike each other and as like themselves as reality requires. Writing in the voices of Dorothy Sayers' characters – bringing off Lord Peter in his mercurial moods, catching the light-hearted chatter of his mother, and the essentially serious timbre of the voice and thought-patterns of his wife, Harriet, is difficult; I am conscious when doing it of an exercise of skill acquired over years of writing, and of the possibility of failing to get it right. But it isn't perceptibly more difficult to catch the narrative voice – that voice is one of the characters in the novel, like any other.

This point is quite obvious if the story is told in the first person by one of the participants as, for example, in *Jane Eyre*. But it is just as true of the often colourless voice of the 'author' in third-person narration.

Very unsophisticated readers, and inexperienced writers, can easily forget that the narrative voice is one of the characters. The reader thinks of the story-telling as direct speech in the mouth of the author, and more or less autobiographical. Thinly disguised memoir. And it is perilously easy for a writer to drop the mask, and start putting in opinions and observations which are personal to the living author, and not necessary or appropriate to the voice telling the tale, as though they were writing down personal speech. But the narrative voice in a work of fiction is a *persona* – that is, not a real person, but an imaginary person. Just as imaginary as one of the characters in the tale being told.

A good deal of very high-level fun has been had with the concept of 'the unreliable narrator' in literary fiction, including great masterpieces like *The Turn of the Screw* by Henry James, and *Huckleberry Finn* by Mark Twain. In twentieth-century fiction it became so common a device that it is almost a surprise to find a narrative voice that can be trusted. Perhaps its widespread use was a spin-off from the theory of relativity.

Unreliable narration is widespread in that now flourishing area of detective fiction which overlaps with traditional literary fiction, and is powerfully more realistic than the Golden Age detective story. But even in that Golden Age the game was played – think of Christie's *The Murder of Roger Ackroyd,* for instance.

Dorothy Sayers, however, saw that such a device was problematic in a detective story, and had strong rules about it. A detective story writer had to play fair by the reader, so that the reader could make an intelligent guess at the answer to the mystery, and that ruled out lying to the reader. To make her point with my example, it would be all right to say 'The Butler thought he saw the figure of Moriarty moving in the shadows,' but not all right at all to say 'The Butler saw Moriarty moving in the shadows,' if the person seen was actually someone else. For Sayers, what the reader is told in the narrative voice must be 'true', even if what the reader is told by the entire cast of characters is biased and deceitful.

Writing as Dorothy Sayers I keep this rule rigorously. I can't say that I would like to keep the rule always in all my writing; but the essential point is that the narrator in a work of fiction is not someone you can invite to tea, or take a creative writing class from. It is a mask, contrived to the particular needs generated by the telling of this particular story.

Mask wearing is a form of personal set-aside – about as far as it could possibly be from that weasel idea 'self-expression'. Self-sublimation would be more like it. And it has a moral quality. Whatever you are writing, tuning the narrative voice to be the best possible medium for the telling of *this* story, to give satisfaction not to yourself, but to the hoped-for reader, will give your work an extra dimension.

And extra dimensions are always empowering.

George Pelecanos: One book, one teacher

George Pelecanos has been called 'the poet laureate of the DC crime world' for his fifteen award-winning novels, as well as his work in film and television.

At the age of sixteen, Washington, DC native R. Dwayne Betts pleaded guilty to a felony, carjacking, and was charged and sentenced as an adult to a nine-year term in a Virginia prison. He did much of his time in solitary confinement, in a place known as 'the hole'. Inmates housed in the hole lose many privileges, among them the ability to use the library or to receive books. But Betts and others in solitary found a way to share books using a system of weighted water bottles, ropes and pulleys, a process which they called 'fishing'. Basically, they tossed out their lines to the general population in the hopes of reeling in a precious tome.

One day, a book, *The Black Poets*, was slipped into Betts's cell from an anonymous benefactor. For the next two months Betts copied poems by Langston Hughes, Robert Hayden, Etheridge Knight and others on to paper, which he eventually bound into a notebook. It is not an exaggeration to say that this book changed him profoundly and probably saved his life.

Many professional writers will confess to a similar transformative experience at some point in their lives. Often it is one book that flips the switch. For me it was a teacher at the University of Maryland, who turned me on to crime fiction, which I recognised immediately as 'the people's literature', egalitarian art. To Charles Mish, and to every teacher who has impacted a student in such an important way, I give thanks.

I first read about Mr Betts in an editorial he wrote for the *Washington Post*. This was around the time that Virginia correctional officials had blocked Quest Institute, a non-profit group, from providing books to the state's prisoners through their Books Behind Bars programme. The reason given was that items such as CDs and paperclips had been found inside the books, but really the ban was about punishment and a show of power. The prison industrial complex is big business in America, where we lock up more of our citizens, primarily minorities, than any civilised nation in the world.

For years I have been conducting reading programmes in adult prisons and juvenile facilities around the area where I live. My focus has been on New Beginnings, formerly the infamous Oak Hill complex, which houses juvenile offenders convicted in Washington, DC. The experience is not always a pleasant one, nor is it meant to be. First there is the matter of visiting a prison, which can be intimidating and downright depressing. There are days when the young men are inattentive, rowdy and sometimes hostile. Often I walk out of there thinking, 'Why did I bother?' Knowing, with some degree of guilt, that I *am* walking out of there, to my nice car, which I then drive to my nice, safe house where I live comfortably with my family. Knowing, too, that the boys I visited will soon re-enter their 6-by-9-foot cells, the doors closed and locked behind them.

I have no illusions that I am doing something 'good' that will positively alter the course of these young men's lives. But, the thing of it is, I don't know for certain that I haven't reached someone on some level at the end of one of those sessions. I do know this: if one boy takes a book into his cell at night, and goes somewhere else – if, in effect, he escapes his cell through the power of imagination via the written word – then the visit has been worth it. Any teacher will tell you, the practical objective is to reach one kid.

A couple of years ago I got on the board of Pen Faulkner, our local organisation that promotes reading on a national level. One of Pen Faulkner's most notable achievements is the Writers-in-Schools programme, which brings in noted authors to meet with students in the DC public system. We have recently expanded the programme to include students who are housed in prisons and juvenile facilities.

Recently I did a session at the DC Jail, organised by the excellent Free Minds Book Club. The inmates housed in this block of the jail are juveniles charged as adults; eventually they will 'transition' into the adult population of this nation's prisons. In other words, they are considered to be dangerous individuals who need to be incarcerated for relatively long periods of time. To my surprise, this was the most attentive, focused and respectful group of inmates I have ever visited. Sitting among these young men in their orange jumpsuits, I was struck by their determination, their engagement with the subject matter we were discussing, and their connection to the books that had been placed in their hands. At one point they left the room for ten minutes and returned with poems they had written on the spot. As they read these poems, I was convinced that many of them were talented and creative individuals who had the potential to move well beyond their current circumstances. One or two of them might actually be writers. They had been impacted by what they read and inspired to create something personal and, yes, artful.

And what of Dwayne Betts today? He is the author of *Shahid Reads His Own Poems*, and the memoir *A Question of Freedom*, which won the 2010 NAACP Image Award for Literary Excellence. He is a devoted husband and father, a mentor to students and inmates, and an advocate for juvenile justice reform. All because of a poetry collection that landed, like a miracle, in his cell.

Such is the power of books.

Ian Rankin: The accidental crime writer

Ian Rankin, born in Fife, spent three years writing novels when he was supposed to be working towards his PhD in Scottish Literature. His Rebus novels have brought him awards including the Gold Dagger, the OBE, and several honorary degrees.

I never set out to write crime fiction.

I'd always been a writer though. As a kid, I would fold pieces of paper in half to make little four-page booklets, filling each side with strip cartoons, emulating the comics I was devouring at the time. Around the age of eleven I began buying pop records and decided to start a group of my own – in my head and on paper. They were called Kaput (and, later, The Amoebas). The singer was Ian Kaput. I wrote all his lyrics. In our English class at secondary school, we were made to write short stories and poems – no hardship for me. I wrote a story called 'Paradox' about a man who thinks he is the US President but is actually an inmate of an institution. The teacher wanted to know why I'd chosen that title. I told him it was the name of a song by Hawkwind. He sent me home after school to look up the word in a dictionary. At seventeen, I entered a poem called 'Euthanasia' in a competition. It won second prize. So I thought of myself as a poet when I arrived at Edinburgh University. I kept writing – poems, song lyrics, short stories. I was 'gallus' (Scots for *daring*) and would read my work aloud at gatherings, while garnering a fair collection of rejection letters from magazines and the BBC.

I was a postgraduate, working towards a PhD on the novels of Muriel Spark, when I wrote my first novel. It was a black comedy set in a Scottish hotel. A few more rejection letters went into the drawer. My next attempt, *The Flood*, found favour with a small publishing house in Edinburgh. An agent contacted me and asked if I was working on anything new.

My PhD research had taken me in interesting directions: from Spark to Miss Jean Brodie and from there to Brodie's supposed ancestor, a real-life Edinburgh character who had been gentleman by day and housebreaker by night. William Brodie had inspired the writing of *Doctor Jekyll and Mr Hyde*. I was intrigued by the theme of the doppel-gänger and the nature of evil. I'd also been reading contemporary Scottish Literature and had relished William McIlvanney's novel *Laidlaw*, featuring a dour, philosophical Glasgow-based detective. I had read only a very few crime novels in my life, but I could see that the figure of the detective allowed the author access to many layers of society, from the highest echelons to the marginalised and disenfranchised. I invented a cop called Rebus (the word means a type of puzzle), and gave him a doppel-gänger who is out to destroy him. The crime would be solved with the help of a literary theorist at Edinburgh University. The whole book would be playful as well as visceral.

That book was meant to be a one-off, but Rebus himself had other ideas. He refused to vacate the premises. Gradually I learned the crime novel's manifest strengths: sense of place; the potential to tackle big moral questions; pacing and plot. Every theme I wanted to explore could best be contained within the crime novel, with the figure of John Rebus as my guide.

I'm thankful he found me, and decided to stick around.

Peter Robinson: How to deal with exposition

Peter Robinson was born in Yorkshire, and moved to Canada in 1974. His books have won major awards in Canada, the United States, Sweden and France. In 2006 he was invited to join the Detection Club.

When she got home, the frightened woman locked all the doors, turned on the lights and headed straight for the telephone, which she picked up with a trembling hand. She was certain that the hooded man she had seen in Sainsbury's that afternoon had followed her all the way from the Red Lion. Her name was Charlotte James. She was five feet six inches tall, with blonde hair cut in the page boy style. She wore little make-up except around her eyes, which were deep violet, and her most striking feature. Slim and athletic, she had the sort of body women envy and men desire. Charlotte came originally from Cheadle Hulme, where she had attended the local infants' school, then the comprehensive, where she had excelled in history and English literature. After that, she got a place at Leeds Metropolitan University, where she studied fashion design. She was now living in Neasden because of her work. Her mother had disapproved of her choice of career right from the start, and they had had many arguments about it during the various holidays she had spent back home in the little suburban semi where they lived with her stepfather, Len,

her two half brothers, Tim and Tony, and their dog, Spot. Charlotte was now thirty-three years old and doing very well for herself. There had even been talk of promotion to head of the creative division. Work had taken its toll on her love life, however, and her relationship with Andy ...

One of the problems of teaching crime writing courses is that, more often than not, the most I see is the first chapter or so of a work in progress, and if I had a pound for the number of times I've read an opening similar to this one, I'd be a rich man. The impulse to give a physical description and a complete biography of a character you have just introduced often seems too strong to be resisted. But resisted it can be, and should be.

This is what is called exposition, and while it seems to be one of the trickiest things to handle in narrative fiction, it is actually one of the easiest, once you remember a few basic rules. There are many elements of writing that can't be taught, but this one can. It's a practical matter.

The first step of course, is to learn to recognise it when you see it. According to Ansen Dibell, 'Exposition is the thing in fiction most like thought, least like action.' When you also remember that Graham Greene once said when you're writing action there's no room for thought, you can see how exposition might become a problem. Books need strong openings, and exposition, being static, is weak.

It is also, however, necessary. Of course, we all want the depth and colour that background, description and research bring to a novel, to its characters and places. Without those things the story will seem flat and lifeless. The problem is how to get them in without boring the reader because, important as it may be to the story eventually, all that stuff about Charlotte's background slows down the book.

Research is often the biggest problem. Many writers assume that because they have done a lot of background research into the milieu of a story – the arms trade, investment banking or people-trafficking, for example – they have to make sure they get every last scrap of this research into the book, no matter how. The same applies to background. A science fiction writer might get so caught up in explaining the social development of the Betazoids (which she has spent many pleasurable hours creating) that she forgets her hero's journey for two chapters. In the same way, a crime writer can get bogged down in police procedure or knowledge of how the Russian mafia operates, and in doing so lose track of the story's momentum. Don't assume that, just because you have enjoyed doing your research and making up a whole new universe, your readers will necessarily be interested in reading all about it. In the same way, you don't have to put in everything you know about a character the first time he or she appears. After all, who knows everything about anyone, and how long does it take to get to know someone well?

Once you have recognised exposition for what it is – background information, description, research – and realised that it needs handling, how do you deal with it?

First of all, you can always leave it for later. One useful rule of thumb is to have no exposition at all in the first scene, and, if you can manage it, none in the whole first chapter. That way you give yourself a chance to get the story moving, get the readers so interested in your characters, their story and the world they inhabit, that by the time you get around to giving them that background, they will actually be crying out for it. First drop the people out of the helicopter, then show us how they got there.

Secondly, cut it up into bite-sized chunks. There's nothing worse than slogging through page after page of character background, the history of a building, or the mechanism of an AK47, no matter how well it's written or how relevant you may think it is to the plot. Give it to us in small pieces, and do your best to make it fit smoothly with scene it is in.

Thirdly, you should strive to make sure that the exposition comes naturally out of a situation. It shouldn't intrude. The way to do this is to make it part of a scene, part of the action or the dialogue. If it is important that a character is getting divorced, it would be far more dramatic to have him receive an annoying demand from his wife's solicitor, or even his soon-to-be-ex wife herself, when he is expecting a phone call that is important to the plot, than to write simply: 'Charlotte and Sam had been married for sixteen years and had now decided to get a divorce because of irreconcilable differences.' The exposition you get across is the same, but the first method has drama and emotional power, and can enhance characterisation, whereas the second is dull and flat, simply conveying information.

Be very careful when you use dialogue for exposition, though, and avoid exchanges such as the following:

> 'Good evening, darling,' said Charlotte. 'Did you have a good day at your office in the city, where you are now a successful merchant banker?'
>
> 'Yes, my love,' replied Sam. 'And did you have time to look at the dream house we are hoping to purchase now that our relationship is working out and we plan to have children?'

If I need to tell you what is wrong with that, even this book won't help you! (One of the reasons why seasoned writers are sceptical about *The Da Vinci Code*, in spite of its status as a best-seller, is because of the way the author uses dialogue almost entirely for the purpose of exposition.)

If the passage of exposition is lengthy, such as the history of a village or a house, and it can't be easily broken down or made dramatic, then try to use it as a pacing device between scenes of action or suspense (what used to be called the 'comic relief' in Shakespearean tragedies). If you have just written a tense dramatic scene and have set the reader up for more mysterious and exciting things to come, either through action or revelation, then you can afford to slacken the pace for a while. Use the exposition here to give the reader a short breather – but don't do this until you are well into the story.

Exposition can also be transformed by the voice in which it is presented. Many writers tend to use the omniscient, objective voice to tell the reader things about a character or a place. In other words, they simply set down the necessary information. You could, however, present this same exposition from the character's point of view. This would not only make the information more lively, it would also add to the characterisation and show us, for example, that a character is afraid of spiders or uneasy about her childhood and her relationship with her parents. She can speculate on these worries and problems, and through this gain the reader's sympathy in addition to giving important information about her background.

Instead of telling the reader, for example, 'The mature valley, where the river meandered, had lush green sides rising up to steep cliffs far in the distance,' why not say, 'Charlotte loved the old valley. It was a wonderful escape after so long in the city. She loved the lazy way the river meandered through its lush meadows, and the towering cliffs in the distance took her breath away.' There is nothing wrong with a well-written piece of descriptive prose, but sometimes it helps to give us the character behind it, the point of view. Put some human feeling into it.

What you are essentially doing when you learn to handle exposition properly is turning a problem into an advantage. By following the advice given above and adding colour and dramatic impact to information that lacks it, you are not only adding depth and resonance to your story and characters, but moving the plot forward at the same time.

S. J. Rozan: Categorisation and its discontents

S. J. Rozan, a native New Yorker, was an architect focusing on police stations, firehouses and zoos before she turned to writing her award-winning series featuring Lydia Chin and Bill Smith.

A lot has been written about crime novel subgenres, detailing which narrative elements each focuses on and listing various practitioners. But there's one aspect of the subgenres – and the genre itself – that remains to be discussed: why they exist.

Does a writer sit down to write a cosy, a thriller, a hard-boiled novel? Do we look to sets of rules and check our work against them? No. We write the story that presents itself. While some books fit clearly in the centre of a subgenre, others – many, many others – occupy grey areas, the no-book's-land where two, three or more subgenres meet. These books are hard to categorise. Then why try? Because the days are long gone when books were hand-sold in independent specialty – that is, book – shops by people whose avocation was reading. Wholesale book buyers today, at the chains, the online retailers and the distributors, are inundated with titles. If 'noir' does well in one market, 'cosy' in another, they want to stock more of them in those places; if 'procedurals' sit untouched on particular shelves, they want them identified so they can avoid them. It's a matter of retailing ease.

This is true of the larger genre groupings, too: mystery, romance, science fiction, western, horror. If I had a nickel for every time I've heard, 'Why do you write mysteries? Didn't you ever want to write a novel?' I'd have double my first advance. I do write novels. I write fictional narratives, full of invented incident and made-up characters; those are novels. In mine, crimes – causes, solutions and effects – figure prominently. That makes them crime novels. That's a more encompassing term than 'mystery', but it's still a category.

Am I complaining? No and yes.

No, because the crime world's a great place to be. The readers are voracious and loyal, actively seeking out new writers. And the writers are generous and kind to each other. It's rare, here, to see the sort of sniping you find on the 'literary' side of the fence.

But yes, because there's a problem, too.

I'm a genre writer. That makes me, in the eyes of some, *ipso facto* not serious. Real writers write in the literary mainstream. Genre books are written by hacks.

What is this book-world version of cultural elitism really saying? That discernment and refined understanding are the province of the few. If a book appeals to the many, that very fact proves it cannot possibly be of high quality.

What happens, then, when a genre novel comes along of such undeniable quality that that argument doesn't stand up? Take Alexander McCall Smith's *Number One Ladies' Detective Agency*. In this best-seller (one strike against it), a woman sets herself up as a private eye and goes around solving cases (two); but it's so beautifully written, no one could call the writer a hack.

The solution? Books like this 'transcend the genre'.

As we say in the Bronx, Gimme a break. If you take off all the cream, you can't blame the cow when the milk is skimmed. OK, we don't make cow metaphors in the Bronx. But you get my meaning.

But it *is* skimmed, you say. Even granting my premise that when Joyce Carol Oates and John le Carré write books with crimes in them, they're crime novels and fit squarely in the genre, it's unarguable that the genre also contains a lot of trash. All those serial killers! All those chases! All that plot-driven drivel!

Yes, it's true. Many bad books are published in the crime genre, and in the other genres, too.

Why?

Because unlike most mainstream fiction, genre novels tell ur-stories.

The purpose of art, after all, is to tell us about ourselves. To show us our dreams, our fears, our hopes.

The crime genre's ur-story is *explanation*. Real life is arbitrary; bad things happen for no reason. Not so in the crime novel. There, justice may not be found but an answer is. Evil may not be controllable but there's the solace of understanding.

The other genres have ur-stories, too – romance deals with human connection; westerns with the border of the known and unknown – as do the subgenres. The PI novel, for example, is about moral ambiguity and the meaning of honour.

And readers are so hungry for ur-stories, they'll put up with mediocre books that tell them. Crime readers want to hear, over and over, that there's a reason. If they've read all the good books that say that, they're willing to read the bad ones. This isn't true in mainstream fiction. Mainstream fiction does have genres – the coming-of-age novel – and subgenres – the coming-of-age-in-the-south-in-the-sixties novel – with ur-stories. But by and large mainstream books have to stand on their own, with less cultural resonance. If a book's not good, people have no reason to read it. It won't sell, so it won't be published. In the genres, a bad writer can get away with more.

But a good genre writer soars. The best genre books carry their full measure of literary value – character, setting, theme, elegant prose – and, in addition, reverberate with the ur-story behind them. These books are, in fact, transcendent. They transcend not their genres, but the quotidian world.

Guy Saville: Thrillers that sell

Guy Saville has lived in South America and North Africa. *The Afrika Reich* is a thriller set in an alternate history where the Nazis have conquered Africa.

It took me twelve years and six rejected manuscripts to get a publishing contract. I like to think that other unpublished writers can draw inspiration from that. Beyond inspiration, I suppose the most interesting thing is why did book number seven succeed where the others failed.

That's a tricky question and one I've reflected on at length (if I'd been able to work it out sooner I might have saved myself years of heartache!) I think there were two elements in particular that made the difference, both of them vital to a commercial thriller. Concept and pace.

Concept. You need something original, something to intrigue an agent or editor. You must also be able to sum up your concept quickly. I'm always reluctant to reduce fiction to the level of soundbite, but this is the reality of mainstream publishing today. My book, *The Afrika Reich*, is a 'thriller set in an alternative history where the Nazis have conquered Africa'. Twelve words to summarise 120,000. The concept doesn't necessarily need to be a milieu. The originality of something such as Stieg Larsson's *Millennium Trilogy*, for example, comes from the character of Lisbeth Salander.

A word of warning. Be careful of choosing something too original. It can scare off publishers, as they won't know how to market your book. Ideally you're looking for a fresh and unusual take on something that's already been successful. With *Afrika Reich* I was able to point to other thrillers such as Len Deighton's *SS-GB* or Robert Harris's *Fatherland*. You need to push boundaries rather than break them.

Once you have a concept, don't waste it. The error some writers make is to leave their idea as little more than a backdrop. Instead make it integral to the story; make it so that your concept and plot cannot be separated. This reinforces both, giving your novel a stronger and more satisfying structure. In my book, although the swastika flies from the Sahara to the Indian Ocean, the true focus of the narrative is an SS conspiracy to dominate the rest of the continent. The specifics of the story can only work within the world I've created.

The second thing I'd encourage you to do is write a page-turner. Just before I started *Afrika Reich* I accosted an editor at a big UK publisher and asked what she thought the most important element of a thriller was. She replied without hesitation: 'Pace. It's everything. Your book must rocket!'

It was a simple but very important piece of advice. Readers, especially readers of thrillers, are looking to be entertained. You must move the narrative forward with a relentless momentum. And do so effortlessly; the reader shouldn't even be aware of the pages turning. That doesn't mean you can't develop your characters or explore themes that are important to you, just that these more 'literary' concerns must serve the pace of the narrative rather than the other way round.

The mechanics of doing this are complex and best learnt through studying writers you admire. One of the techniques I always use, however, is to imagine my reader late at night. He is exhausted, has an important meeting the next day, wants to sleep. So how do I get him to read just one more chapter before lights-out?

The key is deferment. In a culture that's preoccupied with instant gratification, a novelist's duty is to buck the trend mercilessly. Your reader wants to know what happens next. Don't tell them. Withhold information for as long as possible to keep them turning the pages.

Which brings me on to an important qualification about pace. There's nothing less exciting than non-stop excitement. So avoid the monotony of constant action; instead texture the pace. It's the quiet moments of *Afrika Reich* – characters reminiscing over beer and mango juice, the villain enjoying the afternoon sun – that makes the mayhem elsewhere so frenetic.

Ultimately there's no magic formula to writing a publishable book. If there was we'd all get published with our first novels and live happily ever after (at least until the follow-up). An original concept and fast pace aren't enough on their own. You need a good plot, credible characters, atmospheric setting. A dash of luck is essential, as is the ability to persevere. But if you can muster all of these, then you've every chance of succeeding.

Yrsa Sigurðardóttir: Location, location, location

Yrsa Sigurðardóttir is an Icelandic writer of crime novels and children's fiction, who has a second career as a civil engineer.

If the major elements of a crime novel – the characters, the plot, and the time period, say – are effectively in place, that novel can transport the reader to a world born wholly or in part within the author's imagination. What can make or break a story set in a foreign place is the way the author uses the location itself.

To begin with, it is best to imagine a novel as a play or a movie that is enacted in the reader's mind. Hints as to what the characters look like suffice, as most people fill in the gaps in textual descriptions of flesh and blood, and prefer not to be spoon-fed when it comes to character. The plot must be carefully woven in so as not to jump out and yell for attention. The time period must be handled with care, as on it depend the tools available to the characters and the way they interact. But apart from these, the location is crucial if the 'movie' is to play against something other than a blank background.

Landscapes and location are of increased importance when a novel takes place in a part of the world not familiar to its readers. To be able to follow the characters through the paths they take, to see what they see and to feel the elements that confront them, the reader must be acutely aware of the setting. At times, the setting will play a role in the plot itself; it may have an influence on the decisions the characters make or it may limit their choices dramatically. In such instances, it is obviously vital that the setting is accurately conveyed.

If done in the right way, location can be used to fix a mood ranging from gloomy to cheerful and everything in between. Cold, snowy climates bring to mind emotional chill and at times cruelty, whereas extreme heat is more likely to evoke fierceness. The landscape in any area can be used to the same effect. The characters can be made to feel (and seem) vulnerable alongside creepy natural formations; they can appear insignificant alongside majestic ones. When this is done in an accomplished way, the result can be very effective. The reader can be transported with the characters into the situation and can empathise powerfully with their plight.

For those living in big cities, at a distance from nature, landscape may not play a large role. But when one comes from a country that is not densely populated, landscape is ever-present. I need only drive for some minutes from my home in Iceland and I've left the tarmac behind; I'm surrounded then by the land as it was before settlement. Driving further takes me into even more remote areas, ruled by strong forces, utterly lacking in human compassion. In such places mankind and all its endeavours seem very small. Finding the words to describe dramatic surroundings such as these is not always easy.

The best location and landscape descriptions do not always use a large number of words. More often than not, it is the succinct sentences that capture the essence of a place, the sounds, smells and sights that make it what it is. To find these words it is clearly best to visit the location and take in for yourself the major effects it has on the senses. When travel is not an option, authors have to call on all their reserves of imagination. In such cases, photos, books and video clips provide a second-best way into the experience of being on the spot. The rest must be fantasised; oddly enough, authors have received praise for such descriptions, while, in the same novel, being criticised for other descriptions based on actual experience. Perhaps descriptions that arise from imagination are more readily translated into words than are the sensory images that arise from true involvement.

Lastly, when using landscape and location in writing it is very important to keep in mind that the effort made in laying these two out well can make or break the impact the novel will have on the reader. Poor description, tedious; accurate description, thrilling. Perhaps the phrase 'location, location, location' applies to writing as much as to real estate.

Dana Stabenow: Those 'Eureka!' moments

Dana Stabenow was born in Anchorage and raised on a seventy-five-foot fish tender in the Gulf of Alaska, before deciding that writing offered her a better chance to stay warm.

Writing successfully is sweat equity. Butt in the chair, hour after hour, grinding out sentences and paragraphs and pages, none of which, one is grimly aware, may make the final cut when it comes time to edit.

That is especially true of crime fiction, because, really, how many different ways are there to kill someone? And how many different motives can there be? In the end it all comes down to money and sex. At most a writer can create an original variation on a tried-and-true theme.

Crime fiction series are, pardon me, deadliest of all. Here we have the same character on yet another case, investigating the same kind of mayhem (Knife? Gun? Blunt instrument?) following the same kinds of clues (Entry wound? Calibre of ammunition? Blood splatter?) to the same kind of perpetrator (Murderous).

Something that helps me down the narrative road is that one small, seemingly insignificant detail, written in simply to set the scene. Sort of like the spoon in the place setting when the menu doesn't include soup. Sometimes it's pretty, sometimes amusing, but it was not as originally written in any way associated with My Master Plan.

Right now, *mirabile dictu*, I am writing the nineteenth Kate Shugak novel. Kate's undercover, looking for somebody ept enough to back the screw off an oil filter on a Piper Super Cub just enough for it to come off in flight, thus causing the plane to crash and killing the pilot. This kind of ept is pretty thick on the ground in Alaska, however, and matters are not helped by the lack of esteem in which the deceased was held by pretty much everyone who ever had anything to do with him. So Kate's really going to earn her fee this time.

She has wangled her way into the mother-in-law apartment over the victim's garage with an eye towards getting into the house and tossing his office. Yesterday I described the apartment, adding in details of what I've seen in real apartments created over real Alaskan garages. This fictional apartment was recently built, and it has some leftover construction materials stored in it, as well as some fishing and camping gear and a chest freezer. Nobody in Bush Alaska ever throws construction materials away, and a chest freezer is a staple of Alaskan life, necessary especially in small Bush towns and villages where a lot of people hunt subsistence. This chest freezer is empty and unplugged, stored because it's too old to sell but too good to throw away.

Today Kate headed for her undercover job as a waitress at the local watering hole. She's late coming home, as I shut that bar down at about two a.m., by which time all but the most sincere drinkers should be in bed. She slipped into her landlady's house and headed for the office, where she found some interesting records that may or may not have something to do with the landlady's husband's murder.

She got away clean, which may have led to a certain amount of, shall we say, overconfidence, and headed back to her apartment, accompanied by her sidekick, a half-wolf half-husky dog named Mutt. The staircase up to the door of the apartment over the garage is narrow and Kate had to get to the door first to open it, so she went in first. Whereupon someone who had the same idea she did, only to find out more about her, drops a gear bag over her head and throws her in the freezer and slams the lid down.

A second later the freezer opens again and Mutt is dropped in on top of her, and the lid slams down on both of them.

I had absolutely no idea why that freezer was in that apartment until that moment.

It is often these small 'Eureka!' moments that make the writing life worth living.

Andrew Taylor: Creating a good plot

Andrew Taylor worked as a boatbuilder, teacher, librarian, labourer and editor before becoming a full-time writer of crime and historical novels. *The Times* (of London) listed *The American Boy* as one of the top ten novels of the decade.

Ask any writer of fiction – not just a crime writer: in terms of the writing process, plotting is what we hate most. It's a common source of writer's block. Characterisation, theme, setting and dialogue seem to flow naturally and often enjoyably. But plot is where the process gets painful.

I've learned from bitter experience that there are no simple remedies – it's one thing to write a wonderful opening to a story but, to continue it and bring it to a satisfying ending, we writers need to be able to plot. Our stories need plots as our bodies need skeletons.

E. M. Forster famously wrote that '... a story [is] a narrative of events arranged in their time-sequence. A plot is also a narrative of events, the emphasis falling on causality.' It's more complicated than that, but Forster does suggest a useful distinction between narrative – i.e., how a story reaches its audience, how its events are ordered – and the story itself. I think of the plot as a combination of the two: it's the underlying sequence of events together with how you filter those to the reader.

When I was writing *The American Boy*, for example, I had often little idea where the story was going – but I did have a vivid sense of what my characters would do next because I knew what fitted their personalities and situations, and also what the rhythm of the narrative needed. If something feels right in terms of both the characters and the narrative, it probably is right.

On the other hand, sometimes I find it helps to stand back from my characters and the narrative and look at what I know of the overall plot. That can suggest the best way to move forward, especially when I'm hesitating between various options.

I know that some writers plan their plots in detail before they start writing. Sometimes I envy them. But too much preliminary planning can suck the juice out of an idea and result in a bland and flavourless book. I start writing with only the first few chapters mapped out in my mind and a vague idea of where the story will be going after that. E. L. Doctorow memorably summed up this approach: 'Writing a novel is like driving a car at night. You can only see as far as your headlights, but you can make the whole trip that way.' I wrote the whole of the *Roth Trilogy* on the basis of that advice.

Personally I find it easier to do the plotting as I write the first draft, allowing characters, setting and theme to develop a joint momentum with that of the story. In a sense, plotting is as much about discovering the story as about creating it. Then I tidy up the result as I produce the second draft. Reginald Hill, author of the intricately plotted Dalziel and Pascoe novels, once said that the plot is something he puts in afterwards. I regularly change my mind about the identity of the murderer as I near the end of the book. Why not? I'm telling myself a story as well as the reader.

Many first novels have over-complicated plots because their authors are desperate to keep their readers interested. But a good plot doesn't have to be complicated. It doesn't even have to be fully resolved. Perhaps the best plots give you the sense that their stories continue beyond the covers of the book. Plots are about what doesn't happen as well as what does. Chekhov said that when you've written your story you should cross out the beginning and the end because 'It is there that we authors do most of our lying.'

Good crime writing, like good comic writing, needs particularly tight, careful plotting. Timing and misdirection are both crucial, just as they are for stand-up comedy and conjuring. A plot needn't be plausible, but it does need to aim for internal consistency – especially if you're writing for a print medium, because a reader has more opportunity for analysing what's going on than the average viewer does.

I try to remember that readers like books whose stories come at them from unexpected angles. The danger of creating formulaic plots is the great occupational hazard of crime fiction. But it needn't be. As John le Carré once put it, 'The cat sat on the mat is not a story. The cat sat on the other cat's mat is a story.' A predictable plot is dull, however well constructed.

There are no hard-and-fast rules in writing fiction, only guidelines, opinions and suggestions. We read Chandler for his language, not his convoluted and improbable plots. But genius can get away with anything, even technical incompetence. The rest of us need to remember the importance of plotting, where the art of a story becomes a craft.

Charles Todd: A look at settings

'Charles Todd' is a mother-and-son writing team who live on the east coast of the United States. Caroline and Charles turned their love of England into an award-winning series set in post-First World War Britain.

Every mystery – or any novel for that matter – has a setting. It is necessary in order to ground characters and actions in a specific place. There are several approaches to this.

Make up your own – the sci-fi writers do this as a given. If you take this route for a mystery, you must give your created town all the attributes of a real town, for the simple reason that it gives you flexibility in describing action to know where Maple Street turns left, or if there's a shallow doorway at the bakery on the High Street, or where the hospital is located. It's also useful to know where characters live in relation to each other, if your mystery revolves around where suspects were at the time of the murder.

Another choice is to use a real place. And there are several approaches to doing so. David Liss mentioned on a panel that he visits the setting after he writes the mystery, and grounds it then. Another author uses the Internet to give him all he needs to describe and move about in his setting. All well and good. Their books demonstrate the fact that it works for them.

We do our research for the setting before starting the writing. The advantages here – for us – are several. While walking through a town on the north coast of Norfolk, we could see that the centre looked exactly like photographs we'd seen of it. What they failed to show – because that centre was of greater interest to the traveller and thus got great coverage –

was a fascinating church just behind where the photographer was standing. And this church provided several important scenes involving suspects. Such surprises on site give the setting greater reality. Another town we had hoped to use in a mystery turned out to have no ambience whatsoever. Time had changed it to the point that even our imaginations couldn't resurrect it. Several miles farther along that same road we found a village we hadn't even considered initially, and it spoke volumes to us.

Going there for us expands our options for characters, action and suspense. A mystery always has a mood, and sometimes this feeling, this sense of place, becomes another character. Think the easy streets of LA and Philip Marlowe, or Scarlett O'Hara's wartime Atlanta. The very popular Scandinavian mysteries are a part of their Northern culture and therefore strongly influenced by it.

There's another angle, too. People are usually of their place and time. If your character was born in Northumberland, he or she will be marked by that. If he or she comes from London, that too will determine much of what he or she is, innately. Therefore, the setting of a murder mystery can contribute to the types and personalities of the characters put there. Agatha Christie used this in two different ways – Poirot, the Belgian policeman, can stand aside and regard the English almost as objects under his microscope. He has no personal involvement with them, their way of life, their viewpoints, their needs. And so he can judge them in a very different way from Miss Marple, whose own small village is a reflection of human nature. She can solve a mystery by drawing on her personal experience and knowledge of the inhabitants of St Mary Mead, no matter where she may presently be involved with a murder.

Finally, settings often offer reasons for a murder to happen. Again, Agatha Christie sometimes used the newcomer to a village, who wittingly or unwittingly knows something he or she shouldn't about someone there. It can also work in reverse – in the opening scenes of our *A Long Shadow*, the fact that a constable went into a wood near the village aroused suspicion. And someone, always on the alert for just such a trespass, was forced to act. In doing so, a nearly perfect murder was brought to light. Was the wood really there in the setting we had chosen? Not as close to the village as it is in the book. Sometimes we must make allowances for the passage of time from 1920 to the present day. However, a wood could – in fact, should – have stood there, because the way the land sloped meant it wasn't good pasturage or grazing, and therefore it was ignored, damp and overgrown.

It's important to think of setting as an asset to a story and an integral part of that story: the people, the crime, the action, the dialogue and the ambience can evolve from it, and your mystery can be richer in texture because of it. How you go about it must spring from your own way of handling setting. But handle it you must.

Laura Wilson: Crime fiction set in the recent past

Laura Wilson's crime novels have been awarded the CWA's Ellis Peters Historical Award and the Prix du Polar Européen. As well as being the author of ten psychological crime novels, she is also the crime fiction reviewer for the *Guardian*.

According to both the Historical Writers' Association and the CWA Ellis Peters Award for Best Historical Mystery, a historical novel is one that is set 'beyond thirty-five years from [the present]'. That takes us back to the region of 1975, and one good thing about writing a crime novel set before 1975 is that you are immediately freed from the shackles of such developments as DNA profiling and mobile phones, both of which can really mess up a decent plot. In the UK, you will also have the benefit (as it were) of capital punishment (until it was finally abolished as a punishment for murder in 1969), the existence of which ups the ante considerably, as your murderer, guilty or otherwise, will have a lot more to lose than liberty. You will benefit also from the grey area of legalised police brutality at a time before the Police and Criminal Evidence Act of 1984 and the placement of CCTV in police stations. You will be able to use to the advantage of your plot various bits of now-defunct legislation such as the draconian divorce laws and the acts that made suicide attempts, homosexual acts and abortion (decriminalised in 1961, 1967 and 1967 respectively) illegal.

All of these are great fodder for writers, but the flip side is that you must employ constant and paranoid vigilance in order to ensure that your characters aren't doing, saying or thinking anything anachronistic. I once, in an absent-minded moment, had a character zipping up his fly in 1940. The mistake was only spotted – quite by chance – just before the book was printed, and fly buttons substituted. While this isn't quite on a par with, say, a medieval herbalist heating up his potion in a microwave, it is still very definitely a 'schoolboy error' and not the sort of thing you want ending up in print. There's also the matter of ensuring that all the historical detail you've painstakingly researched does not overwhelm the plot. Remember: if it's not germane to the story, then it shouldn't be there at all.

The recent past may be closest to us chronologically, but in many ways it is more remote than the Dark Ages. Even if it happened during your lifetime, it can still be hard to believe that British people thought that some races were inherently superior to others, or that masturbation would make you go blind or insane, and so on – but they did. Lots and lots and lots of them. So, in order to make your novel ring true, you need to adjust your own mental 'default settings' while writing, and attempt, as far as possible, to jettison your assumptions and beliefs (especially those which have to do with political correctness).

The single most important thing to remember is this: the past is *not* the present in fancy dress. Remember, too, that history is littered with 'facts' that, on closer inspection, turn out not to be facts at all, but popular misconceptions, and the twentieth century is no exception to this. This is true of your brain, as well, so never trust your memory, no matter how good you think it is. Always, always check. Reading a novel requires suspension of disbelief, and historical gaffes, once detected, will bring that suspension crashing to earth, and with it, your credibility as a writer.

You also need to remember that your characters – however enlightened and perceptive they may be – are not soothsayers. Yes, the carnage of Flanders was terrible, but no one in the 1920s could have predicted the Holocaust or the atomic bomb. Similarly, fashions and gadgets took longer to filter down through society than they do now, so that the time-lag between 'early adoption' of anything from cars and fridges to mini-skirts and slang expressions, to general usage and acceptance, might be years rather than days, weeks or months.

You are on a much stickier wicket writing about the recent past than about, say, 100 BC. You can't just make stuff up: not only are there people around who will remember the time, but the twentieth century is the most documented century in history. This, of course, can work in your favour, because you can get an excellent idea of the mindset of a decade from period newspapers, magazines, novels, diaries, films and (if applicable) television programmes. Memoirs, too, can be helpful. The History Channel's not bad, either, but nothing beats getting it straight from the horse's mouth by talking to an older person. This can be especially useful because, for a lot of the twentieth century, there was an enormous gap between what was publicly acceptable and what actually happened in private (as shown up, to general horror, in the Kinsey reports of 1948 and 1953). Just be sure you verify any facts before setting them down on paper.

Part 3:

Write on:

Getting your story across

The tools of writing

Now is the time to take those early Part One thoughts on the genre spectrum, idea-gathering, decision-making and research, and turn them into tools to build your novel. By now you should have some sense of how you want to go ahead. Are you thinking of a thriller, or a historical detective story? Set in your home town, or an exotic foreign land? First-person, or multiple third-? And most important, are you Orderly or Organic?

We talked about our different methods of writing in 'Reflections', and followed that with suggestions of how to use the Orderly and Organic systems. Two things to remember, as you sharpen your pencils or charge up your laptop:

TOP TIP FOR PLOTTING

Your outline is there to guide you, not to be a straitjacket. If a better way of moving your story from a to b occurs to you as you write, then go for it. If a character wants desperately to take a step in a different direction, give it a try. (You can always retreat to the original outline if the new idea doesn't work.)

As Patricia Highsmith says, in *Plotting and Writing Suspense Fiction*:

> *... a flexible plot line lets the characters move and make decisions, like real people, gives them a chance to debate with themselves, make choices, take them back, make others, as people do in real life. Rigid plots, even if perfect, may result in a cast of automatons.*

The 'Organic' writer flirts with disaster, every day, every book. Remember the main character in Michael Chabon's *Wonder Boys?* If you find that you are piling up the typescript with an increasing sense of desperation, as the story flails and goes nowhere, that may be a sign that Organic isn't for you.

Now: to write!

Plot or character: chicken or egg? by Michelle

Plot and character together are the vital organs of crime fiction. Your plot can be water-tight, every scene taut as a drum, every chapter linking seamlessly to the next, but if it isn't peopled by credible and engaging characters, it will be – as some say of history – just one damned thing after another. Without both well-developed character *and* well-crafted plot, there's no heartbeat. The story is dead.

Those who look down on 'genre' novels say that 'literature' is character-driven while mysteries and thrillers roll along entirely on plot, with card-board characters too flat and single-dimensional to propel the story. This prejudice is based on a narrow (and probably outdated) range of reading; certainly, a crime novel is more likely to have a tight plot than is a 'literary' novel – that is part of the popular appeal of crime writing. But that doesn't mean that character is neglected. Crime and thriller writers from Graham Greene to John le Carré to Patricia Highsmith to John Harvey and – dare I say it – my co-author Laurie R. King have demonstrated over and over their capacity to write crime novels in which both plot and character are lifted to the level of art.

FOR MEG GARDINER on ...

the thriller as an exploration of character, see 'Tips and tales – guest contributors', p. 121.

TOP TIP: PLOT OR CHARACTER?

Plot and characters must necessarily be developed hand in hand. The plot developments must be consistent with who the characters are and what they're searching for. The characters must initiate, and respond to, the events of the plot. Not one – but both.

But how does a writer create plots and characters that mesh? Stephen King, in his candid book *On Writing*, argues that the best stories are character-driven, but they don't necessarily start out that way. He explains, 'The situation comes first. The characters – always flat and unfeatured to begin with – come next. Once these things are fixed in my mind, I begin to narrate.'

Say, for example, you were drawn to the idea (in Part One) of the wife Joanne who finds the phone number of a murdered neighbour in the jacket pocket of her husband, Declan. Your developed scenario might go like this: Joanne tells the police about the scrap of paper, establishing Declan as a murder suspect. But in fact, Joanne and Harry (the murdered woman's husband) are lovers, who planned and carried out the murder of Harry's wife, intending to frame Declan for the killing.

This sounds like the basis for a twisty thriller full of tension and suspense: is Declan really the murderer? What will Declan do when he finds that Joanne betrayed him to the cops? Can Joanne trust Declan, or is her life in danger, too? Why does Harry (appear to) dislike Joanne? And so on.

But before beginning to turn this scenario into an outline, it would be useful to put some serious thought into your characters and how they interact. Joanne is especially tricky: what kind of woman would be capable of conspiring to murder another woman, and to frame her own husband for it? Where does the motivation come from? How is she able to combine her nasty acts with a convincing performance as the concerned wife? As for Harry, the apparently grieving widower: how could be so callous as to take part in his wife's murder, and frame another man? Why didn't he simply get a divorce? (And surely you can do better than the old stand-bys of a Catholic upbringing or a reluctance to share the estate?)

EXAMPLE: SYNCHRONISING CHARACTER AND PLOT

It is only once you have fleshed out your characters – including the victim – that you will make headway with the detailed plotting we talked about in Part One. Some of the outline will emerge out of your brief character portraits. Let's say that Joanne dreamed in her youth of being a famous actress: she takes pride in acting out the concerned wife while actually framing Declan. Once you decide this, you will need an item in your plot table – maybe a flashback to childhood – where her dream of acting is revealed (see **Scenario to outline** in Part One p. 87). Place this quite early on, so the significance of Joanne's fantasy about acting is not immediately apparent. (Aha, I hear you say: but wouldn't this give the game away? Not if you do it properly – see the section 'The clue', below.)

And on you go. There is really little point in elaborating the twists and turns of the plot in your story, unless you can synchronise these with the nature of your characters. It won't do to have Harry overhearing a crucial conversation between Joanne and Declan through the bedroom wall if it later turns out that Harry is deaf as a doorpost. So your characters and your outline must develop hand in hand. That way, you can be confident that the things that happen in the course of your novel will make perfect sense in terms of the characters who people it.

Plot vs story, by Laurie

If any one thing distinguishes crime fiction from its mainstream cousins – other than the obvious element of a crime at its core – it is the genre's dependence on a strong plot. And yet, even a teacher of literary fiction such as John Gardner (in *The Art of Fiction*) declares that plotting must be the primary concern of *any* writer:

> *The writer's first idea for the story – what Henry James calls the 'germ' – may not be an event but an interesting character, setting, or theme. But whatever the origin of the story idea, the writer has no story until he has figured out a plot that will efficiently and elegantly express it.*

Much has been written (and shouted) concerning the difference between 'plot' and 'story', but for our purposes, let us call the story the end product, and the plot the machinery at its core.

The plot is the sequence of events, given chronologically or causally, in which the story's characters are involved. Plot is to story as skeleton to mammal, the thing that keeps the organism from collapsing into a fleshy puddle.

The story is the entirety, the wider meaning that is woven out of plot and character, mood and setting, language and intent. Or as Aristotle would put it: plot, character, theme, dialogue, music and spectacle.

At some point – during the outlining process or as the first move in a rewrite, or both – you must make certain that your plot works, that all those bones connect and move together.

There are basically three ways of constructing a plot. One is to start at the beginning, and feel your way towards the end. Then there's the opposite: to have the end clearly in mind, and construct the story that leads to it. Alternatively, a plot may be borrowed in its entirety, a duplication of an existing storyline from, say, Shakespeare, or yesterday's headlines.

Often, the final plot will be reached by a combination of two or all three methods, as a catchy beginning links together in the writer's mind with a pleasing ending, and the plot develops as a way of bringing the two together.

The tricky bit with plotting is to make the machinery work so smoothly, to make it so natural an extension of the characters and their setting, that the mechanism becomes imperceptible. And this is where the criticism of crime fiction as nothing but plot has some justification: when the story limps along on a poorly set bone; when the reader is aware of a grinding noise from the mechanism at the story's core.

> **TOP TIP**
>
> *The best plot is a simple one, clean and elegant. You should be able to state the core of your story in one sentence (also known as the one-line, or elevator, pitch): young Mary Russell meets Sherlock Holmes in 1915 and becomes his apprentice, then his partner (Laurie's* The Beekeeper's Apprentice*). A rich executive hires a hooker as a convenient date, and falls in love (the film* Pretty Woman*). A middle-aged crime novelist looking for stability returns to her university, only to find turmoil and murder (Sayers,* Gaudy Night*).*

Language, by Laurie

Language is the tool for building a story. The kind of language used depends on the story.

For the most part, language, like plot or typeface, should be invisible. It should blend so seamlessly with the other elements that the reader is no more aware of it than the viewer is of the brush strokes in a Constable. A thriller tends to have stripped-down prose, particularly as the action accelerates, with short sentences and paragraphs, sharp verbs, crisp dialogue. A country-house mystery, on the other hand, may be permitted a more leisurely approach, with long descriptions and meandering conversations that, upon reflection, conceal some deft sleight-of-hand on the part of the writer, hiding some vital clue or revelation of character.

Nonetheless, there may be times when you don't want your language to be invisible. If in your story, the language is part of the point, and especially if the story is told in the first person by a narrator with a distinctive voice, the vocabulary, grammar and rhythm used will stand out more sharply. My character Mary Russell, for example, speaks in a voice dripping with Latinate words and archaic structures. I use a thesaurus to write Miss Russell, producing language that would jar in one of my police procedurals or standalones, but which is necessary for the memoirs of a proud, eighty-plus academic.

> **TOP TIP ON USING DISTINCTIVE LANGUAGE**
>
> *Unless, as in the case of Mary Russell, an idiosyncratic vocabulary and syntax is key to your story, it is best to keep language in the background, making it a strong, vivid means of conveying the actions and personalities of your characters.*

Below are some points to consider regarding language; none of them replaces a book of basic English grammar for language structure and a copy of William Strunk Jr and E. B. White's *The Elements of Style* for, well, style. If you are uncertain as to the use of the semi-colon or have to think about the use of *among* and *between*, you need Strunk and White's little book. If you suspect that you misuse the words *comprise* or *hopefully*, you need the book. If you want a survey of style that states, 'To achieve style, begin by affecting none,' you need this book. Any writer serious about craft should keep Strunk and White close to hand, if not committed to memory.

> **TOP TIP**
>
> *Short and Anglo-Saxon is generally stronger than long and Latin-based. Would you rather a reader know that your character is* pissed off *or* irritated? shocked *or* unnerved? *that she will* scold *or* admonish *a child? This is not to say that short is* better *than long – the word you need may be five syllables and Latinate – but when it comes to forward motion, short is sweet, dictionaries are bad.*

- Prose is built of nouns and verbs. Adjectives and adverbs are modifiers, and can often be made redundant if the basic verb or noun is strengthened.
- Adverbs can be a warning sign of cheap writing, by a writer who can't be bothered to hunt down the correct verb. Respect your reader, and

watch every *–ly* (the majority of adverbs, and a few adjectives, end in that suffix) to make sure it's the right word for the job.

EXERCISE 1 ON LANGUAGE

Make the following passage more effective by eliminating unnecessary adjectives and adverbs and substituting stronger words for weaker ones.

The court reporter had to abandon her typing at this point, because there was such a huge noise in the courtroom. Two loutish fellows in the public gallery had their hands cupped to their mouths, and were shouting furiously at the prosecutor. The witness was crying copiously and desperately looking around as if to be rescued. The judge was gesturing angrily at the ushers to put a stop to this. Members of the jury pulled back in alarm, as the defendant lifted his arm high in the direction of the gallery in a kind of salute.

- Good fiction is active. This is why writers are told to avoid the passive voice, although as with most rules, there are times when this one may be bent a bit. ('The best-seller was written by me' is in the passive voice, since the subject of the sentence – the best-seller – didn't perform the action. 'I wrote the best-seller' is active voice, and active in its impact.) There are odd cases where the passive structure is simpler: *I was paid in dollars* is generally better than the vague third-person, *They paid me in dollars.* And used with care, the passive can provide contrast: *While Jerry was being investigated, he secretly jumped into action* is better than using an indefinite 'they' in, *While they were investigating him, Jerry secretly jumped into action.* Better would be the specific: *While the FCC were investigating him, Jerry secretly jumped into action.*

  For the most part, the passive voice should be avoided by ... a writer should avoid the passive voice. The active voice makes for active writing, concise and direct.

EXERCISE 2 ON LANGUAGE

Wherever possible, in the following passage, change the passive voice to active, and evaluate the effect of the change.

After being dropped by Tom in his rush to escape, the innocent-looking capsule lay unnoticed at the side of the road for several hours. At 11.10 a.m., just fifty minutes before the charge was due to be detonated, the container was picked up by a little girl on her way to the shop. It was stuffed alongside a gum wrapper and a fifty cent piece in the pocket of her duffle coat. While she was being served with a packet of liquorice, the child had no idea that the minutes of her life span were ticking away.

- Flabby words leach away the vitality of prose. If dinner is *nice*, you're just too polite to say it's lousy; if something is *almost* certain, then it isn't. And why use *very cold*, *very small*, and *very hungry* when *icy*, or *minute*, or *ravenous* would do a better job?
- Fiction needn't be literal: if you say, 'John was a rock, when Sarah needed him,' the reader won't rise up and accuse you of deception when John reaches out his non-sandstone arm for a cup of coffee.
- Beware of cliché and cardboard. If you can't come up with an analogy that feels fresh and appropriate, it's best to leave it off and just go with a simple statement: 'She ran like the wind' might be better simply, 'She ran.'
- Beware of clutter (or as Strunk and White say: 'Omit needless words!') 'Clearly' is more often an admission that something isn't; 'the fact that' gets in the way of the fact; 'he is a man who' is permissible only if you are being paid by the word.

EXERCISE 3 ON CLICHED AND CLUTTERED WRITING

Rewrite the following passage in simple, straightforward English, eliminating clutter and replacing cliché with phrases that are fresh.

The rain was pelting down when Joe emerged from South Kensington underground station. He wasn't the kind of chap to hang around when there was work to be done, so, quick as a flash, he headed for the Natural History Museum. The opening of the new Palaeontology Archive was an auspicious occasion, and a golden opportunity for Joe to demonstrate to the fullest possible extent his new technique for reconstructing pterodactyl skeletons. Notwithstanding the fact that the question as to whether or not he would succeed in winning the committee's support was still unsettled, Joe was determined to rise to the challenge, and to use draconian measures, if necessary, to secure the contract.

- Keep your prose intimate, narrowing the distance between action and reader. 'Detective Lisa Carson knew that La Cienega took a jog just south of the I-10' is less immediate than 'La Cienega would jog as soon as she passed the I-10.' 'He turned and saw that the two dogs had begun to snarl' is less involving than, 'He turned. The dogs were snarling.'
- Conjunctions accumulate. If you can get rid of some *ands, howevers* and *althoughs,* do so.
- Choreography is valuable, but dangerously addictive. If every scene has someone tapping a pencil, rubbing their eye, squinting out the window or lighting a cigarette, it's time for the editorial pencil. (See also 'Dialogue and body language' below.)
- Every writer is plagued by his own quirks of repetition. One of the blessings of word processing is that it's easy to check how often you've used a distinctive word, and rid yourself of a few. Repetitions are one

of the things to watch for in the final draft. (See 'When you're "finished": the rewrite'.)

- Concrete words are more vivid than abstract ones. Something that's bloody should not be considered sanguineous, unless the character is writing a coroner's report.
- Fashionable words – *groovy! awesome!* – are like fashionable proper names: they date your writing. (Two females, Iris and Brittany: which one has wrinkles?)

EXERCISE 4 ON LANGUAGE

Write a conversation between two British or North American fifteen-year-olds in 2012. Let readers know these two are teens, without saying so, and without using particular slang words that might date.

- The rhythm of language matters, and not only because an increasing number of 'readers' are now 'listeners'. Rhythm comes through subtly even on the printed page. The opening of Daphne Du Maurier's *Rebecca* grabs the reader by the ears – 'Last night I dreamt I went to Manderley again' – in part because it's an iambic hexameter. Chandler's description of the crime hero – 'But down these means streets a man must go who is not himself mean, who is neither tarnished nor afraid' – begs to be read aloud. John Gardner (*The Art of Fiction*) spends many pages analysing rhythm, although, as with much of his work, he goes a bit farther than most people need. Suffice it to say, you should be aware of the rhythm of your prose, on the page and on the tongue. One of the best ways to become aware of rhythm is to read your writing aloud. (See 'When you're "finished": the rewrite'.)
- When describing a scene, consider all the available tools of a writer. For the most part, description needs to be prosaic, in both senses of the word, giving details without the distraction of fancy speech. But at times, particularly when setting a scene of some importance to the story, the poet's toolbox can be of value.

EXAMPLES OF POETIC CRIME WRITING

In Raymond Chandler's 'Red Wind', a lot more is moving around than hot air:

> There was a desert wind blowing that night. It was one of those hot dry Santa Anas that come down through the mountain passes and curl your hair and make your nerves jump and your skin itch. On nights like that every booze party ends in a fight. Meek little wives feel the edge of the carving knife and study their husbands' necks. Anything can happen. You can even get a full glass of beer at a cocktail lounge.

James Lee Burke, who might be called a poet of crime, uses the Southwest's landscape in a similar fashion, in *Feast Day of Fools*:

> The night air was dense with an undefined feral odor, like cougar scat and a sun-bleached carcass and burnt animal hair and water that had gone stagnant in a sandy drainage traced with the crawl lines of reptiles. The wind blew between the hills in the south, and he felt its coolness and the dampness of the rain mist on his face ...

- Poetic imagery can be useful in less extended forms, in places where you would like the reader to pause briefly to reflect on the sensory meaning of the story. However, take care that your poetic metaphor doesn't distract the reader right out of the fictional dream you've been working so hard to construct. When in doubt, leave out the metaphor.

TOP TIP

Beautiful language is functional to the task, elegant in its simplicity – in other words, invisible. If the reader pauses to reflect on the beauty of a particular piece of prose, it could be because the reader is extraordinarily aware of words – or because the writer is extraordinarily full of himself. In either case, that reader has fallen out of the author's dream world.

- Punctuation. This is one of those places where, like the abstract artist, it is better to immerse yourself completely in the traditional rules before you decide to ignore them. If your manuscript is too creative with its punctuation, or overlooks the rules entirely, it provides a hard-worked editor with an instant excuse to pass on it. Blood is shed at conferences over semi-colons; the serial comma has threatened marriages; there are people devoted to the exclamation point as well as real exclamaphobes (like Laurie, who doubts she has used a dozen exclamation marks in twenty-two books); and your publisher's copyeditor is sure to have a policy on the serial comma that disagrees with yours. However, when it comes to punctuation, remember: the semi-colon is quite formal for fiction; the exclamation mark is at the other end of the spectrum! Neologisms and foreign phrases can be used to add a *soupçon* of flavour, although too many can overwhelm the palate and are best reserved for the verbal tics of a character. And as for beginning a sentence with a conjunction, the rules, once understood and acknowledged, are made to be broken. But *avec* care!

Description

As John Gardner points out (in *The Art of Fiction*), 'Vivid detail is the life blood of fiction.' This is particularly true for a genre such as crime, which rests on detail-based clues.

However, while detail may be the lifeblood of fiction, when it haemorrhages all over the page it's a distraction. All detail should be *telling* detail: if it isn't a plot point, doesn't give us something about the character, and isn't necessary to set the stage, do we need it?

FOR PETER ROBINSON on ...

the craft of exposition, see 'Tips and tales – guest contributors', p. 146.

- A gambler's 'tell' is an unconscious gesture that gives him away – a 'tell-tale'. Whether you are writing about character or place, you need that telling detail that gives away something about the personality of the person or the setting: the tattooed biker who stops to rescue a weeping child's toy; a piece of brutal pornography on the shelf of an apparently pious man; a warm, leafy street with the steep roof-lines of snow country.

EXERCISE 1 ON DESCRIPTION: THE GAMBLER'S TELL

In 150 words or fewer, show us an apparently poised, genial and confident man who, under closer examination, gives away that he is neurotic and deeply anxious.

- A large reason why readers return to mystery stories is the challenge, to see if they can outwit the protagonist – and the writer – by assembling the answer out of the clues given. Fair play demands that the necessary information be given. Respect for your reader demands that you make him work for it. Detail is where the clues lie.

TOP TIP

All description needs to be specific, concrete, and vivid, and essential to the story. If it doesn't move some element of your story forward, it doesn't belong there.

- Description, like Dialogue (see 'Dialogue and body language'), needs to do more than one job. If you describe the moose head on the wall of your protagonist's study, what are you telling us about the man? If you pause to note the state of a woman's fingernails, are you talking about her concern for grooming, or letting us know that she's done something with those hands that left the polish chipped and one nail torn? Or both? If some detail does not contribute to the story, look to see if it can be taken out. As Chekhov said, if you show a gun early on, you'd better use it before the play ends.

EXERCISE 2 ON DESCRIPTION

Write a single paragraph of description of each of the following:

- The bedroom of a woman who was recently widowed
- A man in a newish suit (a gift from a charity) but who is himself penniless and homeless
- A ten-year-old girl who seems sweet as pie but who is, in fact, a persistent bully

- Often, a leisurely description evokes the apology attributed to Pascal (among others) for sending a long letter because he lacked the time to make it short. Description that is general or long-winded is often a sign that the writer wasn't certain, or wasn't concentrating. Long passages of exposition can be distracting – Umberto Eco is more interested in semiotics than story-telling, when he spends an entire page describing the carving of an arch – and should cause you to consider the dictum of best-selling writer Elmore Leonard: leave out the parts that people skip.
- It may help to write those lengthy passages in your character studies or background notes. Then, when you are sure of your way, return to the story feeling as if you have explained all that to the reader once already. You can always add material in the rewrite.
- Beware the use of brand names as a short-cut to description: if I spend my life in sneakers, will I know who Jimmy Choo is? Unless I read fashion magazines, will I hear what you're telling me by having your character put on his True Religion jeans? Clothes and possessions are the outward manifestation of personality, but they should be the result of close scrutiny, not stereotype. Brand names also carry the certainty of dating your story, a generation from now.

EXERCISE 3 ON DESCRIPTION

Show a woman of fifty years of age in an action that reveals she is extremely wealthy, without using brand names or any explicit reference to material riches to make the point.

Setting – place and time

We spoke of your book's period in Part One, under 'Early decisions', and followed it with suggestions concerning research of place and time. But now that you're immersed in the actual writing process, how do you implement those early choices?

Make sure you have a solid feeling for the time and place (see 'Research', in Part One). It is a good idea to have a collection of photographs before you as you write, and listening to music of the period, if you can, helps get you in the mood.

Don't limit yourself to the customary detail. As H. R. F. Keating pointed out, if the writer is trying to 'place' a scene firmly in Victoria's reign, it is less effective to talk about the expected bustles and antimacassars than to mention the boiled mutton on the breakfast sideboard.

EXERCISE 1 ON SETTING: TIME AND PLACE

Write 250 words about a policeman walking the beat in New York, using unexpected detail to place the scene firmly in the 1930s.

And speaking of the smell of mutton, details include all the senses. Does the air smell of mildew, or roasting coffee, or rotting oranges? Is the sound from the nearby freeway so omnipresent one ceases to notice it? In Victoria's reign, the sounds of iron wheels grinding against cobblestones made for a constant din, to such an extent that hay was often spread on the street outside a sickroom. Crossing-sweepers were employed to keep streets from becoming mucky swamps – imagine the odour on a warm day. A Londoner's eyes would burn from the haze of coal fires. And even to those whose noses were accustomed to crowds of people dressed in wool who had a bath once a year (whether they needed it or not), wintertime journeys on the Underground must have been ripe.

- The devil is in the details: if your character is standing with others in a row, what he's doing depends on where he is. If he's a New Yorker, he's on line; if a Californian he's in line; if British, he's in a queue.

Laurie says: I find that often I overwrite detail when I'm uncertain, as if I had to feel my way into its meaning. If there's a passage you've had trouble with, go back later and see how much of it you can simply leave out. You'll probably find quite a bit.

EXERCISE 2 ON SETTING: TIME AND PLACE

Your protagonist is in a public waiting room, hoping to see a police investigator, in: rural Vermont; central London; Morocco. Without saying where he is, use telling detail to build that waiting room.

Atmosphere, or, In defence of weather, by Michelle

It's obvious that historical period helps to determine the setting; the sixteenth-century London of C. J. Sansom is definitely not the gangland London of Jake Arnott, nor is the 1909 New York in Jeb Rubenfeld's *The Interpretation of Murder* much like the city of Ed McBain's 87th Precinct series.

But weather (or climate) also defines a setting. Elmore Leonard, in his celebrated rules for crime writers, insists that you should never write about the weather. It works for him; but for the rest of us, it may not be the best advice.

The setting of a story helps to ground it in sensory reality, and weather is a crucial aspect of this. You want your readers to capture the taste of your region, to experience its smell, to soak up the atmosphere – whether dry dust, or brisk breezes, or rain, rain, everywhere.

EXERCISE ON WEATHER

Select a place – a pine forest on the edge of a lake, the Tokyo metro, the walled city of Dubrovnik, or wherever – and write two different accounts of your central character walking there. Ground each description in a different type of weather – one on a mild summer's evening, the other in the build-up to a major storm. What details would the character notice, experience, sense, on these two outings?

Weather enables readers not just to 'look at' the setting, but to feel it in their bones, as in the opening paragraph of Chapter 1 in Robert Crais's *L.A. Requiem*:

> *That Sunday, the sun floated bright and hot over the Los Angeles basin, pushing people to the beaches and the parks and into backyard pools to escape the heat. The air buzzed with the nervous palsy it gets when the wind freight-trains in from the deserts ...*

EXAMPLE OF THE IMPACT OF WEATHER ON THE TONE OF A STORY

Attending to weather can give a different tone to a story, even where, within a series, the physical setting remains the same. Michelle's series books are set in Cambridge, England. *Nights in White Satin* opens with a May Ball at St John's College, and taps into the glamour of May Week:

> The ball had taken place, as May Balls should always do, on a warm night in the middle of June – a champagne and oysters kind of night, following a strawberries and cream kind of day.

But the opening section of *In the Midnight Hour* takes place towards the end of January, when:

> The city of Cambridge huddles against the damp and chill. Long gone are the May balls, the leafy walks, the picnics by the river. Rows of punts lay chained up together by Magdalene Bridge, with water puddling in the bottoms; the river is dark and deserted except for the odd indifferent duck.

See? Cambridge still. And a Cambridge instantly recognisable to anyone who knows the city well. But distinctly cooler and laced with melancholy.

TOP TIP

Aim to convey the impact of the place on the senses, using weather as one of your tools. Aim for an atmosphere – chilly and damp, icy and slippery and treacherous, cool and mysterious, or hot and humid and overgrown. Think in terms of light or dark, serenity or excitement, silence or clatter, old or new. The weather should underscore the theme of your novel.

Remember that fiction is about forward motion, and all description – weather, setting or the character's footwear – must contribute.

Divisions – sentence, scene, chapter, book

The sentence, or sentence fragment, is the basic building block of prose, spoken or written. On the page, however, lacking gestures or the rhythms of speech, one needs to pause from time to time for the psyche to take a breath.

A stretch of unrelieved prose can be daunting for a reader. Page after page of it, even for the expert reader, may create an anticipation of heavy going, whereas pages of dialogue, with lots of white showing, look like a fast read. Now, unless you're e. e. cummings, it's silly to write for how your words will look on the page, but the appearance of too-heavy blocks of print can be a sign that your story has become bogged down in description – or worse – a dumpload of everything the reader might need to know. At the other extreme, many serial pages of white dialogue space may signal the risk of confusing the reader as to who is speaking and what is going on.

Vary your sentences, too, as you vary your paragraphs, to give a natural and interesting rhythm to the story.

EXERCISE ON VARIATION IN SENTENCE STRUCTURE

Find a paragraph (one that you, or somebody else, has written) that strikes you as stodgy. Rewrite this passage, varying the sentence structure, and evaluate the result.

A short, punchy sentence works especially well at the end of a paragraph, to bring home the central point.

TOP TIP

Short is catchy. Make use of it.

How many chapters, scenes, books?

Michelle says: When I was partway through my first novel, I began to think about this thorny issue of divisions. What was a chapter, anyway? How many should there be in a novel? How did a chapter differ from a scene? I analysed existing crime novels in search of an answer, and found them nothing if not varied. The truth is, there is no formula.

TOP TIP

***A chapter** is the right length when it is complete. It is too short when it feels to the reader (initially, yourself) insubstantial, as if the story hasn't moved on. It is too long when it makes readers feel as if they have been stuck for ages in one place.*

Each scene has a point. When the reader enters the scene, s/he needs to know what the character is after, what her goal is. The scene works through that goal, watching the character push aside the obstacles to getting what she wants, and then we see her move on to the next scene, the next challenge.

EXERCISE ON SCENE WRITING

1) Your character, Maggie, enters a rather squalid flat in Glasgow, where an impromptu and raucous party is taking place. Write the scene.
2) Now write the scene again, but this time Maggie has a goal: she is trying to track down the pusher who sold her younger brother a fatal drug.

A scene is a segment of the story with clear boundaries. The intervals between scenes may represent times when nothing significant happens – the hero sleeping, driving to a job, brushing his teeth – or they may be filled with narrative passages when the protagonist is reflecting on what he has seen or considering what to do next. When two scenes need a greater division than a paragraph break but don't require a new chapter, use a pair of asterisks on a line, so that when a scene break comes at the end of a page, it will still be clear.

A chapter may be made of one long scene or a number of shorter ones, but generally the scenes within a chapter are related, if only chronologically – chapter twelve may show what several characters are doing in an afternoon, while chapter eight is what happened the week before we left for Costa Rica.

Chapter lengths are also related to the kind of book you intend to write. Shorter chapters, or chapters broken up by scenes, increase the pace of a novel – which is good for thriller writers, but may feel choppy in a novel that deals in suspense and atmosphere rather than in wham-bam incidents.

EXERCISE: HOW DO WRITERS USE CHAPTERS AND SCENES?

Take a book that you've enjoyed. Divide a sheet of lined paper into six columns. The columns, left to right, will be: 1) the number of pages in the book; 2) the average word count on a page (the easiest way is to count the words on five random lines and divide by five, then multiply by what seems the book's average number of lines on a page); 3) a list of chapters, giving one line to each; 4) the number of pages for each chapter; 5) the scenes in each chapter – you can as easily pick six or nine random chapters, equally spaced through the book, for this, rather than working from beginning to end; 6) a column for notes. Then repeat the exercise with another book with a very different writing style – e.g., if your first book was a thriller, the second might be a classic mystery. Compare the two sets of results.

Are the chapters similar in length throughout, or is there a more complex pattern?

Use the final column to make a note of ways in which you feel the length of a chapter affects the flow of the story.

Do the same with other story elements, such as the number of words in a typical sentence, or the kind of language (when does this author use shorter words, when longer?)

As you read other thrillers or crime novels, repeat this analysis, and compare the results, thinking back to the experience of reading each book. Did the length of chapters and number of scenes affect the reading experience, and if so, in what way?

In a large novel, or one with two or three vastly separated times or places, you may also consider dividing the whole into two or three 'Books'. If paragraphs represent breaths taken and a new chapter a turn of the page, a Book is the psychic equivalent of getting into a car to drive around the corner. However, if every other chapter involves a major jump in time or place, it hardly justifies the attention-getting device of a page declaring Book Two.

Preface and prologue

A preface is an introduction, such as when 'editor' Laurie R. King explains how she comes to be publishing the memoirs of one Mary Russell (*The Beekeeper's Apprentice*). (See below, for a discussion of beginnings under 'The story's arc, or acts'.)

A prologue has a greater degree of independence from the book that follows. It may take some time for the reader to grasp how it ties to the story itself.

TOP TIP

Many readers (and editors!) loathe prologues, because they are so often misused as a substitute for Chapter One. The prologue should be at a remove from the action of what follows, not only in time or place, but in characters. It should be succinct and tantalising, and it should not take away from the opening words of Chapter One. If you can possibly envision replacing the word 'Prologue' with the words 'Chapter One' at the beginning of your novel, do so.

(Laurie says: My editor once permitted me to get away with not one, but *three* prologues to a novel [*Touchstone*]. I was in a fragile state at the time, and she didn't want to trouble me.

She should have troubled me.)

A prologue draws up the curtain, with drama. If there is no other way to set a mood, introduce an apparently unrelated but ultimately revealing event, or suggest a character trait – if you feel that the book would be starting on the wrong foot without it – you may need a prologue, but only as a last resort.

EXERCISE ON PROLOGUES

You have completed a novel about the search for a missing child in the aftermath of the Bosnian war. You decide that the opening chapters are not engrossing enough on their own, and that readers need to be aware of an event that took place ten years earlier. Write a Prologue (*500 words maximum*) that alludes to, or arises from, a massacre in which members of the child's family were murdered.

Dialogue and body language

In dialogue on the page, aim for verisimilitude, not authenticity. The *ums* and *ers*, repetitions and cross-speaking that take place in any normal conversation can be baffling on the page, since readers don't have the non-verbal elements essential to any real conversation. Dialogue should *seem* natural, not *be* natural.

Similarly, dialect – speech that indicates strong regional connection – should aim at the flavour without the confusion. Too scrupulous a rendition of how the character sounds risks making him into a caricature. Unconventional grammar and a colourful vocabulary are much better indicators of region than a literal transcription of the sounds.

Show, don't tell. If the speaker is angry, don't *tell* me that she said something angrily, *show* me in the sharp words, the brief sentences, some giveaway gesture. The reader needs to feel that he is the surrogate hero, actively participating in the investigation or adventure, and that won't happen if the author keeps inserting distance between reader and protagonist.

EXERCISE 1 ON DIALOGUE

Draft an exchange between a secondary school (high school) teacher and the parent of a pupil. Show through their speech and gestures that the parent is anxious and the teacher is impatient (*300 words maximum*).

On the other hand, body language, as mentioned earlier, can accumulate and clutter the scene. Gestures, facial expressions, noises and the like are valuable adjuncts to dialogue, but take care not to over-choreograph your scenes, crowding them with giveaway gestures and nervous tics. The telling gesture should tell, by itself.

- Attributions should be limited to the signposts of 'he said' and 'she said'. *Asked, answered* or *replied* may be used sparingly, and even more occasionally *whispered, murmured, snapped* and the like. The stronger the speech verb – *sneered, retorted* – the more sparingly it should be used, but unless you are writing period farce, there is little cause for oddities like *demurred, rejoined* or *reproached. Hissed* may be used only when the words spoken have the 's' sound in them. And as for verbs that have nothing to do with words coming out of mouths, do not use them for speech, ever: *'No,' she laughed. 'Please,' he sobbed. 'God!' she vomited.*

If the smile, the laugh or the stomach's distress need to be there, give them a sentence of their own, however brief.

- Dialogue is action, not exposition. If there is information that you feel is absolutely essential, some of it can be inserted – briefly – in dialogue.

EXERCISE: 2 ON DIALOGUE

Scenario: Jim and his wife, Fiona, bump into a woman colleague of Jim's at a fundraising event.

Write a brief three-way conversation in which readers – and Fiona – gradually realise/come to suspect that Jim and his colleague have been lovers in the past.

- Dialogue must feel natural, not forced. When two old friends reminisce about a past event as a way of providing backstory (see below), it mustn't feel like the writer filling in the characters' history. They might argue about the details, but they can't tell each other about them.
- Every bit of dialogue must reflect its character. If a teenager is talking to her grandmother, the reader should be able to tell them apart without the attributions. The more similar the people, the harder this is, but even then, the reader ought to be able to tell them apart in her own mind.
- Lengthy dialogue can be as flat to read as lengthy narrative, and needs a rhythm. Back-and-forth talk can be woven through with actions such as assembling a meal or an explosive device; a witness's lengthy monologue can be broken up by the waiter coming to take an order or the dog diving into the bushes.

EXERCISE 3 ON DIALOGUE

Write an exchange (*maximum 300 words*) between a Filipina hotel maid and a hotel guest who is an international banker. He accuses her of stealing his mobile phone; she denies it. Use as few speech attributions as you can, but throughout, make it absolutely clear who is speaking.

Humour

Laurie says: Humour is tricky when it permeates the entire book. For every Carl Hiaasen, there are dozens of comic novels (or, would-be comic novels) that die unseen. Even successful ones are not universally so – *Pirate King* was written as farce, embracing the ridiculous from beginning to end, but even then, people objected that such things wouldn't happen and furiously demanded that I go back to the adventure format. Still, it made a number of best-seller lists, so I'd guess some people got the jokes.

Humour within an otherwise non-comic novel, on the other hand, can be a valuable means of pausing the forward action while the reader catches his breath.

A humorous subplot can be a convenient way to conceal a clue in plain sight, since the reader is not expecting straight information to be nestled in the ravings of a green-haired manicurist or trotted in by the protagonist's chronically misbehaving basset hound (see 'Red herrings' below).

Titles

A title needs to evoke the book, not give it away.

- The best-seller list tends towards brief titles. Thrillers tend towards two- or three-word titles. Very occasionally, a long title works well, particularly to indicate an idiosyncratic novel at the cosy end of the spectrum – Alan Bradley and Alexander McCall Smith come to mind. As for Stieg Larsson's six- and seven-word best-selling thriller titles, those only go to prove that there are no unbreakable rules in the publishing world.
- Wordplays or titles with the words *death* or *murder* in them are often signs to the reader that this is a traditional mystery, where the body is a plot device and not a family ripped apart.

EXERCISE ON TITLES

What kind of book would you expect from each of the following titles:

- *Midnight by the Oasis*
- *Death Where Is Thy Sting?*
- *Blood River*
- *Hit and Run*
- *The Man Who Wouldn't Give Up*

Characters

Characters in crime fiction, by Laurie

If plot provides the bones of the story, then character is its beating heart. The complaint is sometimes made (not entirely without justification) that Golden Age fiction is all plot and no character. Thus John D. MacDonald, in *The Mystery Writer's Handbook*:

Too often in mystery fiction, the attempt to devise a real and believable detective has degenerated into a complication of props rather than expanded into a complication of character, a subtlety and complexity of the spirit. The original fault is perhaps due to that misinterpretation of Sherlock Holmes which places too much weight on the needle, the violin, the pipe. We remember Holmes as a man who, primarily, was troubled in spirit, was obsessed with the sense of evil, whose arrogance was defensive. Yet we see around us today a score of fictional detectives who have been given merely the props without the spirit ... with the childlike faith that through eccentricities [one] could define character.

In Golden Age fiction, the focus on cleverness – a preternatural level of cleverness, not only in the detective, but in the villain, the method of killing, the means of escape, in all aspects of the tale – sometimes made it hard to see around the plot to the individuals wrapped up in the actions. It may be no coincidence that this kind of fiction seized the publishing industry just as the craze for crossword puzzles erupted in the 1920s, since what the 'tec reader wanted was essentially a crossword without the grid: arcane and misleading clues, the goal of figuring it out without a cheating glimpse of the answer, and if a person was lucky, a pleasing design overall.

Many readers still read with the goal of figuring it out before the final scene – there is no doubt some vital portion of the brain that lights up and goes *Aha!* when two facts in a story link together and lead to a third. But even puzzle-readers are more demanding today, and find that if there isn't something interesting going on with the people on the page, reading is a lesser experience.

Bookshop customers may pick up a book because of the cover, they may even buy it because their friends liked it or they were hooked by a compelling first page, but they return to that writer because of the characters. And in those all-important conversations about books, over the phone or in chat groups online, the intellectual stimulation of a clever plot or the author's deep research comes second to the reader's involvement with the fictional people.

We buy books for the characters: we become interested in them, get caught up in their lives, fall in love with them. And then we happily watch them put through hell.

TOP TIP

What bring characters to life and make readers want to follow them on their adventures are thoughts and feelings, perspective and passion, not mere quirks. To create characters who are believable, distinctive and interesting you have to get to know them yourself. Know their past, and their present. Know how they walk, how they speak, and what pushes their buttons. Know far more than you'll ever use.

- Characters need to walk the line between stereotype at the one extreme and grotesque at the other.
- As John MacDonald said, aspiring writers try often to develop unique characters by giving them unusual interests, pastimes or physical

characteristics. But constructing a detective who is seven feet tall, a dedicated nudist, and carries a traditional Korean violin with him everywhere is not going to win you any readers. What's unique about your character is internal not on the surface.

- Some writers use real-life people for their fiction, and find that only the good guys recognise themselves on the page. Still, it is probably better to adopt only *portions* of actual friends and relations, especially in a series, since you may be forced to have that character do something that would outrage the original.
- A physical description of the character matters less than what the character does with that body. Appearance can tell us what others see there, and it can hide more important characteristics – a burly Marine whose passion is for the flute, a dithery blonde who runs a powerful lobby firm. Many of the most vivid characters in fiction are in fact vivid only to the reader's inner eye – indeed, if you look at the fiction of both current authors, you will find very little precise physical description for the principal players.

EXERCISE 1 ON CHARACTER

Scenario: Three men are driving along the motorway in the middle of the night when they have a blow-out and have to change a tyre.

Write this scene, in 300 words or fewer, showing us by their actions and their dialogue that one man is powerfully built and gung-ho, another is shy and awkward, and the third is large and lazy.

- Many writers find it helpful to produce detailed biographies of their characters before beginning to write, with background, tastes, education, appearance, family etc. Little of this will go into the final book, but it helps the writer to know the people before they walk on to the stage.
- Build a library of characters, complete with backstories. It's fun to do, and it exercises your writerly imagination.

EXERCISES ON CHARACTER

1. Choose one character from the following list: the chef with high blood pressure; the champion ice dancer; the elderly Pakistani woman who came to England as a young bride; the party-seeking tourist; the best-selling science fiction writer. Write a sketch of his or her life, in 250–500 words.
2. Notebook in hand, take a seat in a cafe, on a train, or in a busy park – anywhere you can observe other people. Choose one person who interests you, and jot down the details of their appearance. Then imagine what their background might be, and what their current life is like. Turn this into a biography of 250–500 words.
3. Write one or two pages describing a middle-aged woman teacher: her appearance, her taste in clothing, what she likes to do in her time off, her primary relationships etc. Do the same for a young man who designs computer games.
4. Then, write a page with dialogue showing a person who can only be that middle-aged teacher confronting a noisy neighbour, without giving any of her biographical information. Have the computer game designer do the same thing.

TOP TIP

Most of us have a limited understanding of the lives of people whose ages, circumstances and upbringing differ from our own. You can extend your knowledge, and therefore the range of characters you can create, by reading biographies, or even better collected letters and journals, and by scouring the obituary pages of major newspapers: letters and diaries are immediate and personal, while obituaries can be condensed biographies, giving insight into the backgrounds of people from a wide range of generations and cultural milieux.

What do the characters *want*? by Michelle

On their journey through a novel, readers follow a character. Or two characters, or three.

To be interesting enough to follow, the character must *want* something. What is wanted might be trivial – to get a phone call from his daughter, to find an open petrol station, to catch a bit of shut-eye – but the longing must be potent. If you can make clear to readers what is wanted, and why, and what will be the consequences for your character of running out of petrol, then readers will stick with your character all the way.

EXAMPLE

Graham Greene's most stunning achievement in his novel *Brighton Rock* is the vivid way he reveals what his characters most want. Pinkie yearns to leave behind for ever the shabby estate where he was born, and to be rich and admired like Mr Colleoni. At one point in the story, Pinkie is summoned to visit Mr Colleoni at the grand Cosmopolitan Hotel. Pinkie is wildly impressed, and takes to heart Mr Colleoni's assertion that he *likes things good.* From then on, the Cosmopolitan looms in Pinkie's mind. Again and again, 'the memory of the luxury of Colleoni's circumstances, the crowned chairs at the Cosmopolitan, came back to taunt him':

> 'Pinkie was conscious for a moment of his enormous ambitions ... the suite at the Cosmopolitan, the gold cigar-lighter, cigars stamped with crowns ... he was at the beginning of a long polished parquet walk, there were busts of great men and the sound of cheering, Mr Colleoni bowed like a shopwalker, stepping backwards ...

Then something happens to trigger Pinkie's insecurity again, and... 'The parquet floor rolled up like a carpet.'

Desire is the key to drive in the novel. When you turn your idea into a scenario, and your scenario into a story – when you shape the characters that make your story happen – inject into your characters that powerful 'wanting'. It will become your story engine and push the story forward.

But it doesn't stop there. In every scene you write, make sure at least one character wants something out of the encounter – whether it's money that's owing, or a name, or the satisfaction of planting a fist in the other's person's face. A scene written like that will not be merely a list of things that happened; it will have energy, and verve.

Elizabeth Benedict's *Joy of Writing Sex* is more than the title suggests. It contains excellent advice on how to give vitality, individuality and drive to your writing, and how to move beyond cliché. She emphasises the importance of adding desire, with this piquant bit of advice:

> *But whatever your character wants, remember that in fiction it is always more interesting if he does not get what he wants, or gets what he wants and finds that it is not what he wanted after all, or has to pay a heavy price for what he has gotten.*

Knowing your characters means worming your way inside their heads. It means knowing what they relish, what they would most hate to lose, and what they try to disguise.

EXERCISE

What would your character say about himself/herself when first getting to know a business colleague/co-worker? In other words, how would he or she want to be seen? Write up your idea in a maximum of 250 words.

continued →

EXERCISE *continued*

Now, repeat the exercise – but imagine that your character has had a few too many drinks, and is becoming a little indiscreet. What might he or she say now? What might be let slip? How would he or she come across when the guard is down?

Narrators and protagonists

From the opening words, the reader needs to know who is telling this story – not only the point of view, but the personality.

EXERCISE

Scenario: the novel is about a fatal traffic accident which turns out to be a murder. The protagonist is a newly qualified police officer, not yet confident in her role. Write an opening paragraph (*maximum 300 words*) in which she arrives at the scene of the accident.

The protagonist needs to be sympathetic, but not simplistic. Nobody wants to spend 300 pages with a two-dimensional person. On the other hand, no one wants to hear *everything* about that protagonist's life, what they ate for breakfast and how they get to work and the first boyfriend in high school and the arm they broke when they were six and —. What is most interesting, most immediately *telling*, about your character? That should be first in your mind as you write the character – although that characteristic may not make its open appearance for many pages.

Use every opportunity to build your character on the page: every action, reflection, or observation should bear the stamp of that character's personality.

EXAMPLE

Mary Russell, the narrator of Laurie's Russell–Holmes series, describes Sherlock Holmes at their first encounter:

> [I] glared down through my spectacles at this figure hunched up at my feet: a gaunt, greying man in his fifties wearing a cloth cap, ancient tweed greatcoat, and decent shoes, with a threadbare Army rucksack on the ground beside him. A tramp, perhaps, who had left the rest of his possessions stashed beneath a bush. Or an Eccentric. Certainly no shepherd.
>
> He said nothing. Very sarcastically. I snatched up my book and brushed it off.

This passage would read far differently if the person coming across this seated figure was a more traditional fifteen-year-old girl:

> I gave an alarmed squeak and backed rapidly away, laying my hand above my pounding heart as I looked down at the sitting figure. He was a tall, thin old man in raggedy clothing, one of those tramps one was warned about. But he made no move towards me, and he said nothing, so I tentatively snatched up the book I had dropped.

The description says as much about Russell as it does about Holmes.

Introductions matter. Let readers become interested in your character (and, preferably, the story, too) before they're buried under a load of detail. A succinct opening monologue by a first-person narrator is one way of firmly establishing that character in the reader's mind. Sue Grafton makes expert use of this technique in the opening page of *A is for Alibi*; her style (echoed later in the 'Death is my beat' opening of Michael Connelly's *The Poet*) sets the tone for the long and successful series to come.

My name is Kinsey Millhone. I'm a private investigator, licensed by the state of California. I'm thirty-two years old, twice-divorced, no kids. The day before yesterday I killed someone and the fact weighs heavily on my mind.

TOP TIP

Let readers see a character in action, and make their own judgement about that character, before you ply them with character description. In the early pages of Nikki French's creepy thriller, Beneath the Skin, *we first meet Zoe, a young schoolteacher, when she fells a mugger with a watermelon. The scene is vivid, entertaining and telling; readers are immediately drawn to this resourceful young woman.*

- When it comes to fictional sleuths, the professional and the amateur come with different advantages, and problems. A professional detective, whether she's a licensed private investigator or a police officer, has very definite rules and regulations to limit her actions, but at the same time, has experience, resources and authority to back her up. An amateur, on the other hand, has a world of freedom in how he approaches his investigation, but is severely limited by his amateur status.

A series with an amateur sleuth will forever be saddled with an air of the impossible. This is known as the Miss Marple syndrome: how many people can die in a tiny English village, anyway, before the Home Office looks into it? If you want a series with a greater degree of reality, your amateur needs to be someone whose job, or life, might plausibly come into contact with a series of murders: parole agent, criminal lawyer, pathologist. Crime writer.

- Review also the section above, 'Description'. In the city where your story takes place, will your hero speak with a coroner, or a medical examiner? Does your Victorian lady speak in anachronisms, with *teenagers* and *weekends*? Does your 1930s detective zip his flies? It is terribly easy to knock a reader out of the dream by anachronisms or research failures, and while some mistakes may be forgiven, make too many and you've lost a reader.

Heroes and villains

The protagonist of the book is the *primary actor* (*proto* + *agonistes*). The subtle difference between *protagonist* and *hero* acknowledges that the main character may not always be particularly heroic. But no matter: she or he will do as *hero* until the real thing comes along.

Crime fiction is a moral genre; that is, it addresses moral questions, though it may do so, as Patricia Highsmith does, from an amoral point of view. But crime and thriller writing is more compelling when it resists the tendency to produce heroes who are perfectly good and villains who are perfectly bad.

TOP TIP

Imperfections in a hero or heroine – a streak of selfishness, a nasty habit, a tendency to mouth off – enables readers to identify. Vulnerabilities heighten readers' concern: Superman's adventures would be far less exciting if he were not in danger from Kryptonite; V. I. Warshawski, Sara Paretsky's private eye, is brave enough to take on thugs and clever enough to outwit them, but her empty fridge prevents her seeming intolerably smug. Could we bear it if she returned from a day of sleuthing to whip up a gourmet dinner for the neighbours?

And a streak of something decent in a bad guy – a demonstration of tenderness, an act of charity, an innocent pastime – can make us care what happens to them and increase the tension. Even Hannibal Lector, perhaps the best-known and most admired fictional killer of our age, had his finer points. Intelligence and erudition, gourmet sensibilities (even if rather macabre ones), a feel for fashion – all of these raised him above the level of your average serial-killing cannibal, and made him a character who, once met, is never forgotten.

TOP TIP

The villain needs to be worthy of the hero, and vice versa. They should be so equally matched that the outcome is no sure thing.

Never forget that the villain is the hero in his own story. Even an extreme psychopath shouldn't justify his actions by saying that he just feels like being evil. Inside his own mind, his actions are justified.

- If crime fiction is a quest, then your hero must be worthy of that calling. Chandler's description – 'down these mean streets a man must go who is not himself mean, who is neither tarnished nor afraid' – is misleading. Our hero may be tarnished, and he may be afraid, but his essential being is pure, his fear of failure is greater than his fear for himself.
- The villain in a detective story, where the goal is to discover Who Done It, needs to be introduced early, and he must blend in with the rest of the characters. The impulse to commit murder, or at least felony, is tucked away behind a façade of normality, and any clues pointing towards the villain's identity are ambiguous until the moment of revelation at the end, when all falls into place. If you fail to introduce the villain early on, readers will feel you've cheated them of a fair chance to solve the mystery.
- The identity of the villain in non-whodunit varieties of crime fiction, from suspense to thriller, is likely to be clear earlier, even from the very beginning. Here, the tension of Will He Succeed? is paramount.

Sidekicks, suspects, supporting actors

Do you need a Watson? All of us deserve a Watson, of course – an ever-willing and ever-admiring sidekick would be terribly useful in daily life, and do wonders for the ego. However, if we can look past the bumbling Nigel Bruce interpretation of the good doctor, we see a Watson who is much more than a not-so-bright chronicler of the Great Detective. In the

Conan Doyle stories, Watson is Holmes's partner, with strengths that help compensate for the detective's weak spots. The two men are in many respects complete opposites, but both are strong and competent, and Watson's presence opens doors for Holmes. Keep this in mind as you seek out the outlines of your protagonist's partner.

TOP TIP

Secondary characters are the supporting actors on the stage, whose interaction with the hero gives him depth. Make them worthy of him, neither clichéd nor extreme – exaggerating every character makes none of them memorable. Supporting actors should give the reader the impression that they might be interesting people, if the reader had the time to get to know them. That they might also be villainous people only moves the plot along.

Supporting characters are there to drive the plot, but they are also there to add dimension to the story, and to the protagonist. When we see the hero through other eyes, we see the hero.

Minor characters don't need the full treatment. Spending a lot of time developing a character who plays a minor part in the story annoys readers, who have been led to think that this is someone who matters.

On the other hand, even minor characters deserve sharp pen portraits.

EXAMPLE: SUCCINCT PORTRAITS OF MINOR CHARACTERS

'The guard didn't laugh. He looked out the window at the huge, flat expanse of the prison farm, his eyes narrowing whenever we passed a trusty convict walking along the dirt.'

(James Lee Burke, *The Neon Rain*).

'Charlie came in a few minutes later and closed the office door behind him. He was a man in his early thirties, with a good-humoured and ugly face, considerable energy and ambition, and a calculatedly indolent manner.'

(John D. MacDonald, *The Executioners*).

- Don't tell me *about* the character, *show* him to me. If I know that his hair is like electrified snakes and his teeth are mottled brown, I have more of a feel for the man than if you say that his hair is unkempt and his teeth bad. Is he very angry? (Yawn.) Or does he upend the table in a fury?

TOP TIP

A strong crime novel has no mere onlookers. Each character is there for a reason, and preferably more than one: a child whose presence in the story appears to be just a way of showing the hero's soft side (or the villain's nasty one) may also deliver some key piece of information, a fact only noticed in retrospect. The nerviness of the suspect's young secretary may tell the protagonist that the boss is a short-tempered tyrant, but it may also conceal that the secretary is involved in a behind-the-scenes power play.

Suspects, so necessary to the mystery story, are the character equivalent of the clue/red herring element (see below). Most of them are innocent, but their presence hides a villain, or more than one. And all suspects have secrets, all lie about something, all appear to have both reason and opportunity to do away with the victim.

EXERCISE

Many writers have taken a sidekick and turned him into a protagonist – or vice versa (Laurie hasn't been the only one to put Sherlock Holmes into a supporting role; Bob Crais's Elvis Cole stories have branched into a new series with Cole's sidekick, Joe Pike.) Look at a story with a sidekick, and try to envision it from his or her point of view.

The victim

In a traditional mystery, the victim often appears early, and we get to know him for the most part by seeing the effect his death has on those around him. Spend some time thinking about your victim: what called an untimely death to him? How is he related to the protagonist, and the villain? You might want to develop a biography for the character – even if you never use any of it in the final book, the impression of that person as a personality will come through when you write about him.

TOP TIP

The victim, like the villain and the suspects, has secrets. Some of those contribute to the solution of the mystery, some are red herrings, but even a dead person lies.

Distinctive elements of crime fiction

We talked in Part One about the spectrum of crime fiction, with a description of some of the major divisions of the genre. Here, we go into the question of how the craft builds each type, whether you are writing a mystery story or a thriller.

Coincidence and fair play

Father Knox's *Decalogue of Crime Writing* was mentioned in the Part One discussion of detective stories. In the same vein, the Oath of the Detection Club, as writ by founding member Miss Dorothy L. Sayers, includes the following:

> *Do you promise that your detectives shall well and truly detect the crimes presented to them, using those wits which it may please you to bestow upon them and not placing reliance on nor making use of Divine Revelation, Feminine Intuition, Mumbo-Jumbo, Jiggery-Pokery, Coincidence or the Act of God?*

This applies primarily to the mystery or detective story, but even thrillers require that the writer keep to the rules of fairness, and not bring in impossibilities.

Remember, just because something happens in real life, doesn't mean it's OK in a crime novel. Coincidences frequently happen in the real world; they are rarely acceptable in crime novels.

Some degree of coincidence is acceptable at the very beginning of a book: after all, the story has to start somewhere – why not with an overheard conversation or the chance meeting of an old friend? It doesn't even have to be entirely plausible – the daily news is filled with impossible stories that any self-respecting editor of fiction would instantly slash to pieces with a blue pencil. So although an unlikely event is a shaky beginning, most readers are willing to suspend disbelief if everything that follows is firm. You could even have your character reflect on the improbability of the matter, then move on.

TOP TIP

Coincidence is unwelcome in crime novels, but it is unforgiveable when the solution depends on it. The vicar cannot be arrested, the world cannot be saved from annihilation, because of a pamphlet the investigator happens to spot on the dashboard of a parked car or a random conversation overheard on the subway. It is a different matter, naturally, if the investigator was hunting for that pamphlet or the hero had laboriously positioned himself to overhear that very conversation. Anything else is a deus ex machina, *a god of solutions who hops out of the plot's machinery to save the day, thus causing any rational reader to flip the book over the railing into the sea.*

The clue

Detective stories are built out of clues, but even suspense and thriller novels depend on them. In Greek mythology, Ariadne gives Theseus a ball of string – a clew – with which to find his way through the Labyrinth. In crime fiction, the investigator (and through her the reader) is given a series of clues which, when followed, lead to the solution of the problem. The trick comes when the writer has concealed the clew in a landscape that is strewn with bits of string.

We spent considerable time earlier talking about description and detail, not only because detail breathes life into your prose, but because in a crime story, it is in the details of the situation – objects, gestures, slips of the tongue, unexpected relationships, a scuff of the shoe – that the investigator discovers the correct bit of string to lead her out of confusion.

Details can be clues, and they can be red herrings (more on those below). Dorothy Sayers planted a clue – a missing clue – literally out in the open, in a list of paint tubes (Sayers, *Five Red Herrings*). Peter Dickinson uses a newspaper clipping in *Perfect Gallows* to send the hunt off in one direction, only (spoiler!) to have the reverse of that clipping prove to be the more important bit. Position is everything with this technique: you want your reader's eye to skip over that essential, to notice it but to zero in on something right next door that seems far more suspicious.

Clues may consist of physical details such as cigarette ash, or bits of information like the time of the 4.10 to Paddington. But clues may equally be details of character – the fact that the gentle social worker in Michelle's *Standing in the Shadows* becomes angry when inquiries are made about his wife reveals that he has something to hide.

Your reader is probably brighter than your investigator, when it comes to recognising a clue. He has been trained by ten thousand pages to suspect the obvious and snatch at the obscure. Keep this in mind when you go to hide your clues, since you can then turn the tables on your reader, tempting him into cleverness when the actual string leads elsewhere.

When crime novels have a detection or mystery element, readers generally expect that they should have a chance, however slim, of solving the mystery before the protagonist does. They expect fair play – that all information the detective uses to solve the crime should be available to them, too. But how to lay out the clues without giving the game away?

TOP TIP: PLANTING CLUES

The key is to provide the information clearly and openly, but in such a way that the reader overlooks it. As Edgar Allan Poe's story 'The Purloined Letter' demonstrated, it is entirely possible to 'hide' clues by putting them in full view. You can:

1. *Slip the clue into a series or group of similar points. A character drones on and on about all the places he went to on his world*

cruise: that he was in Goa on New Year's Eve may be an important clue, but if it is lodged in the middle of a long list, readers will probably not take it in.

2. *Let the information come from a character who is not taken seriously. The character who drops the clue may be presented as a clown, or an idiot, or someone trying to grab attention. The character's vested interests or prejudices may make readers doubt their information: who would believe a Klansman when he said that he saw a sinister-looking black man running away from the scene? Other characters may pooh-pooh the information, or be dismissive or scornful of the person delivering the clue. A phrase such as,* Oh, is she on about that again? *can come in very handy.*
3. *Offer another, plausible, explanation for the presence of the clue in place of the correct one – the face at the window may have been kids mucking about; those scribbles in blood may have been left by the local graffiti artist.*

EXERCISE

Raise your eyes and look at what lies before you. Choose one element – a book, a chair, the cup belonging to the reader at the next table – and write a scenario in which that element is a clue with a good chance of going unnoticed by the reader. Then write another scenario in which that element only appears to be a clue, and distracts the investigator – and reader.

That distraction is the red herring, used to distract the reader – and the detective.

Red herrings

A red herring in crime writing is a nice, fat, tasty clue that the investigator – and the reader – cannot resist following: an overheard argument between victim and suspect that turns out to have been about something else; suspicious behaviour that turns out to have a good explanation; an object that appears to point in one direction, but ends up going elsewhere.

INTERESTING FACT

A red herring is, literally, a kipper, a salted fish with a strong smell to it. Tradition has it that the red herring was used to lay a trail for scent hounds, which would follow its scent instead of pursuing that of the quarry. The figurative meaning was laid across history's tracks by a political journalist, and crime readers have joyously pursued it ever since.

The red herring is a large part of playing fair with the reader, particularly in the detective story – don't forget Father Knox's Eighth Commandment: 'The detective must not light on any clues which are not instantly produced for the inspection of the reader.' The writer's job is to make clues available, but at the same time to distract the reader by dragging an enticing alternate scent across the story.

The closer your novel follows the tradition of the detective novel, the more essential the role of red herrings: your detective may pounce upon a clue and run it to earth, while the experienced reader of mysteries knows full well to keep her eyes on a discarded clue. Ideally, the true trail will follow a third possibility, discounted by both detective and reader.

The more hard-boiled end of the genre, the police procedurals and thrillers, make use of red herrings too, simply with less whimsy. Overlooked clues and undetected lies steal valuable time and attention from the investigator or hero, until it is *almost* too late.

Conflict and violence

It may be out of place to mention conflict as an element of crime fiction, since conflict is the major element of all fiction, period. However, it is worth remembering here that without conflict, your hero has no purpose, your villain no heft. You are writing about a battle – of wits, of moral strength, of resources – and the ground being fought over is the value of human life.

Even when the 'murder mystery' turns out not to be a murder, the pressure of feeling that there is an untimely death must remain. (For sly and intricate plotting along this line – although this acts as a spoiler – take a look at Josephine Tey's *To Love and be Wise*.)

Violence is an inherent part of crime fiction. Even a classic detective story has at its core a piece of brutality, one person taking the life of another. How much of that violence you show will determine where the book stands on the crime spectrum, but even in a cosy, it is there.

Extreme rage is required to beat a person to death; poison, on the other hand, is a tool of cold deliberation. Unless your murderer is trying to get clever and mislead the investigators, the violence shown to the victim needs to reflect the relationship between victim and villain.

Pace and progression

The thriller is all about pace – a thriller writer is composing a symphony of tension that ratchets up, slacks a little to permit a breather, then tightens again, and again. The writer of a detective mystery may be working on a more cerebral plane, but there too, pace is essential to plot. We will speak more of the story's forward drive in the section on 'The story's arc, or acts'.

Once readers are into the story, page-turning depends on the story's forward pace. When a story has progression, it moves forward; readers won't know exactly what's coming next, but they should feel confident that you the writer are driving the story in a definite direction, and that they can safely hitch a ride.

To ensure a good sense of progression, first be sure of your story. (The Part One exercises on p. 87 should help you with this, as well as the upcoming sections under 'When you're "finished": the rewrite'.) Unless you know your eventual destination, you're likely to wander into culs-de-sac, take wrong turnings, and dawdle by the roadside while you wait for inspiration. And unless you have removed those meanderings in your final draft, your readers are going to suspect that you're taking them into a dead end.

TOP TIP

Demand of every scene, every chapter, that it push the story forward. That it move closer to answering the question that was suggested early on in the book, to solving the problem or escaping from the trap. If readers feel that they're getting somewhere with the issues that brought them on board in the first place, then you have achieved progression.

If you prefer a more Organic approach to plotting, you may leave some of the decisions about the book's pace until after the basic storyline is worked out. During your rigorous editing process, you'll tighten the pace and trim any sections that go nowhere. Either way, if your writing self is entranced by a scene you've written, step back and ask: does it further the story or seriously contribute to understanding the characters? If not, then – no matter how seductive your image or how delicious your prose – out it goes.

Stay true to your niche?

Crime fiction readers tend to have their favourite niches. One loves mysteries that include recipes, another thrills to woman-in-jeopardy suspense stories, a third searches the shelves for paranormal thrillers. (Laurie says: I was once in a lift with a reader who asked if I wrote serial killer stories. When I said no, not really, this cheery blue-rinsed lady shook her head and declared, 'I just *love* serial killers!' The lift emptied soon after.) This means that publishers like writers who fit a neat niche. If you do so, your chances of finding a publisher edge up a fraction.

If your book doesn't fit a niche, its chances of publication may go down; however, if it *does* get picked up for publication, chances are it will be considered a bigger book than a button-collecting or cat-grooming mystery.

TOP TIP

Once you understand the genre spectrum of crime (in Part One) and have read widely in the various categories, you may find that what you are writing doesn't seem to fit any of them – or rather, it crosses lines between them. If you are writing for selling, you may wish to reconsider. If you are writing because you are on fire with the story, then by all means continue. You may be defining a new genre.

When the going gets tough

Writer's block, by Laurie

The crime writer Lawrence Block (interesting name, for our purpose) has been known to write horror stories – at least, for the would-be writers among his readership – in which he describes writing several hundred pages in a book before it went dead, and he abandoned it. More than once. As writers go, Block must be one of the bravest out there: rather than obsessing on the book, he would stick it away and start another that he *could* finish.

Everyone has days when the sunshine tempts and the life of the bonbon-eating reader takes over. The occasional submission to holidays is a necessary part of one's mental health – after all, there are enough drawbacks to self-employment without working for an oppressive boss. A more serious state, when days drag on with an unfinished manuscript groaning at your shoulder, needs more serious treatment than someone else's new hardback.

Writer's block can be your friend. Honestly. I find that when a first draft begins to bog down – when I discover that I have nothing to say and the ironing simply must be done and the closet cleared out, when scrubbing the oven with a toothbrush seems a more appealing task than continuing to eke out one ... word ... at ... a ... time ... – it's often because the story is developing some problem that I'm not seeing.

I was once having some work done at the house, putting a walkway from one building to another, which involved changes in both height and angle, with a tree and a tank in the path. My contractor has one guy who always gets these tricky jobs, and it was a revelation to watch him at work. He made a highly detailed sketch of the ground, measured to the quarter inch. He figured out how many steps he'd need and their exact rise. He stood looking at it for a while. And then he went off and did other things for a couple of days. When he came back, you'd have thought he was working to a prefabricated design, the whole thing went so easily. I've watched him do the same with three different complex projects, and never seen him rip something apart, once he had it in his head.

And that is what I do. After a day or two, when the ironing is put away and the closet floor vacuumed clean (but before tackling the oven with the toothbrush), I trudge back upstairs and take a look at my printed-out manuscript, beginning at page one. And nine times out of ten, I'll find some tiny problem, festering in the corner unnoticed, waiting to grow in the dark and turn into something systemic and fatal. Early detection saves lives.

And the tenth time? The time when writer's block persists yet there appears nothing amiss in the story? It may be time to trudge upstairs and take a look at my life. Am I happy with what I am doing? Is my life more or less balanced, or have I been working all day, every day, for weeks on end? Am I getting fresh air and exercise? Am I eating reasonably well? Do I get out and see friends?

And still, if the idea of putting yet more words on a page, idiotic and meaningless words, fills me with deep loathing?

That's when I go upstairs and I sit down and I write. Because ...

TOP TIP

... sometimes, writing is just about putting words on a page. Bad words, awful words, meaningless and grey words, but words. Because unless I'm going to accept that this writing gig is a delusion and not for me, I'm going to have to put words on a page. One ... word ... at ... a ... time ...

At least they'll be there, on the page. And sooner or later, a few of them will be good.

Lawrence Block, faced with a partial manuscript he can't figure out how to finish, sticks it away: after all, it's just a bunch of paper with ink on it. Many other writers don't dare move off a page until it's right, and would rather cut off a hand than leave a book unfinished. Who is right? They both are – for them.

- Is it writer's block, or frustration? In some ways they are opposite ends of the spectrum, but they tend to have the same solution: step back, rethink, re-attack.
- If you get to a point where every potential act of your characters feels either pointless or just confusing, try skipping ahead to a scene that excites you. It may be that you need to see where they're going before you know how to get there.
- Change how you write. If you compose on a laptop, try a fountain pen, or dictation software. If writing in the mornings isn't working, try setting to in the evenings.

> **TOP TIP**
>
> *There will be days when every scene you produce feels dull, every character worthy only of being a candidate for the next murder. Those days, remind yourself that a novel is a marathon, and even long-distance runners are not swept up in the joy of exertion every step along the way. Even dull writing is better than no writing: once it's there, you can improve it. And believe it or not, when the book is finished, even you won't know which parts were written with fire, and which slogging through cold mud.*

Writer's block often creeps up in mid-book, when the plot seems to sag and interest wanes. Take a look at our next chapter here, 'The story's arc, or acts', where we include suggestions about what to do to keep your middle taut and fit.

- If writer's block takes over, take a look not at the plot, but the motivations behind it. Perhaps you're trying to get your cop to do something – say, manipulate the district attorney into freeing a suspect so he can get his hands on the man – and every idea you come up with seems just pointless. Stand back and look at what the cop *really* wants. Is it simply to shake information out of the man? Or is there something deeply rooted in his past that's driving him to take short-cuts to justice? Your writer's block could be the door to a better story.

- It often helps to take a look at the foundering manuscript and decide what it is you *do* like about it. When you read it, where do you find your interest piqued? Can you take the entire book in that direction?
- Physical exercise can be an antidote to depression; moving your body can get your story moving again as well.

Working with others

Educated criticism is hard to find for a new writer. Your mother will clap her hands in surprise and exclaim how lovely it is that you've written a book, your best friend will say that it's better than anything she's read all year, but when it comes to knotty questions about plot problems and whether or not that character's motivation makes sense, family can be less than forthcoming, while book doctors or freelance editors can be expensive. Many writers find writing groups enormously helpful, a second family whose veins run with words instead of blood. These creative communities can be found both in person and online (though with an online group, it's harder to share coffee or a glass of wine). Writing groups can also be destructive to a writer's prose and to his sense of worth, if egos flare and the community goes toxic. If you begin to feel that a group is pummelling *you* harder than your bad writing habits, look elsewhere.

The best writing groups – the real gems – are those where the feedback on your work engages with what you're really trying to do. If, on the other hand, feedback tends to consist of lectures about literary technique, and (unfavourable) comparisons between your work and George Eliot's, it may be time to pull out.

Other writers are rarely ideal editors, but they can be mentors. If there is a local mystery group – Sisters in Crime, Mystery Writers of America, Crime Writers' Association – join it, and stay on for a drink after the meeting. If you're too far away for meetings, you might contact other writers in your area and get together informally, at the bookshop's coffee bar or in the local library. Writing is a solitary business; we all need a community.

If you are hard at work on a novel, but confronting problems you cannot seem to solve, a professional mentor may help to move your work on to another level. In the UK, agencies such as Gold Dust will (for a fee) link a talented amateur writer with a more established colleague, who will work with them one-to-one on issues such as plotting and pace.

Laurie says: When it comes to feedback, I never show any portion of an incomplete manuscript to anyone. Period. I don't even talk about it much. Once I have a first draft, I send it to my editor, who knows my Organic system well enough not to be shocked by an unreadable novel with vestigial characters and ragged plotlines. She and I hammer out what it needs, and I go back to work. Later, when the book is more or less finished, I give it to a handful of family members and friends who have shown that they can help make it better.

Michelle says: Ditto. When it comes to writing, I'm a bit of a loner. Most of my novels have stayed with me until I regarded them as finished. My editors in London and New York seem to agree, because they never ask for anything other than the most minimal of changes. (Perhaps more pressure from other people would have made for better books: who knows?)

TOP TIP

Writing classes can be life-changing. In England, the Arvon courses provide inspiration, feedback and masterclasses in technique for new writers, while in Canada, the US and the UK, many conferences and literary festivals have panels and workshops that focus on craft. An afternoon workshop may be just what you need to pep you up when your motivation is flagging. An intensive week-long course, or an evening class spread over several weeks, may allow time to test out some of your ideas and to brush up your technique. We talk about some of those at the end, in 'Resources and reading'.

The story's arc, or acts

If you are an Orderly writer, your early stages in a novel will find you wrestling with the mechanics of plot, the arc of your story. If you're a more Organic writer, you'll just be diving in and piling up the pages. But whether you're of the Orderly or the Organic school of writing, at some point you need to step away and look at the overall arc of your story. (We'll talk about the series arc below, too.)

How does the plot of a crime novel look? Well, as the King of Hearts said to the white rabbit, 'Begin at the beginning, and go on till you come to the end: then stop.' Like any novel, a crime story has a beginning, a middle and an end, plus the occasional preface or afterword. Unlike other novels, the point is in the tension being built. It may help to visualise the story as a shape. Take an actual arc:

Here, your reader starts with a certain level of tension, which keeps building, then begins to slacken, until the book ends. More common in crime fiction is building to a sharp climax, followed by a dénouement that gives the reader a sense that life will go on with the characters he has come to care about:

Both of these patterns leave a somewhat mechanical feel in the mind, since there is little variation. Thus, a good crime novel aims to crank the tension in degrees, with two or more climaxes, or sharp twists in the plot, or threats met – more roller-coaster than cliff-jumping:

Let's look at how the beginning, middle and end combine to produce this effect on the reader. For sake of simplicity, we have divided the story into three acts, a format that fits some novels but not all. If your story seems to fall more comfortably into four, or two – and if you are satisfied with its overall pacing – then feel free to adapt our suggestions to fit your work.

And now: cue the curtain!

The curtain rises

> **TOP TIP**
>
> *Page one is your empty stage. The audience waits to see if you begin with faint birdsong, a narrator's voice from the wings, or an explosion. The tone of that first moment will remain with the audience to the end.*

The opening, by Michelle

Strong openings in crime fiction may be forged in a single sentence, or may run to an entire chapter. They can draw their power from a number of different sources:

From a reference to death or violence:

> Wednesday, 11 December 1963. 7.53 p.m.
>
> 'Help me. You've got to help me.' The woman's voice quavered on the edge of tears. The duty constable who had picked up the phone heard

a hiccuping gulp, as if the caller was struggling to speak.

(Val McDermid, *A Place of Execution*)

"The corpse without hands lay in the bottom of a small sailing dinghy drifting just within sight of the Suffolk coast.

(P. D. James, *Unnatural Causes*)

"We were about to give up and call it a night when somebody dropped the girl off the bridge.

(John D. MacDonald, *Darker than Amber*)

"The moment Bryan Judd's sister died – that very instant – he was sitting on an abandoned sofa on the waste ground behind Erebus Street.

(Jim Kelly, *Death Watch*)

"The kid in the alley had been dead for 48 hours.

(Chaz Benchley, challenged at a crime convention to produce a compelling first line for a thriller)

From a sense that a character has arrived at a turning point, so that there is a feeling of urgency about what happens next:

"I don't know who sent it. There wasn't a letter, just the cutting, with the date, Sat 14 Aug '76, scrawled across the top.

(Laura Wilson, *Hello Bunny Alice*)

"I am outside. Not far from the front door, not yet, but I am out and I am alone.

(Sophie Hannah, *Little Face*)

"I was down in Surrey, on business for Lord Cromwell's office, when the summons came.

(C. J. Sansom, *Dissolution*)

From sheer surprise, without even a hint of the sinister – from a mention of something bizarre or unexpected, that tugs readers into the world of the novel:

> Lacey Dowell clutched her crucifix, milky breasts thrust forward, as she backed away from her unseen assailant. Tendrils of red hair escaped from her cap; with her eyes shut and her forehead furrowed she seemed to have crossed the line from agony to ecstasy. It was too much emotion for me at close quarters.
>
> (Sara Paretsky, *Hard Time*)

> 'Balls!' said the Bursar and continued skipping vigorously. As her skirt rode higher, vast quantities of satin eau-de-Nil directoire knicker were exposed to Amiss's enchanted gaze.
>
> (Ruth Dudley Edwards, *Matricide at St Martha's)*

From statements that propel the reader into a character's mind. This is especially effective when the character is – like David in the example below – moved by powerful emotions:

> It was jealousy that kept David from sleeping, drove him from a tousled bed out of the dark and silent boarding house to walk the streets.
>
> (Patricia Highsmith, *This Sweet Sickness*)

> We owe respect to the living, Voltaire tells us in his Premiere *Lettre sur Oedipe*, but to the dead we owe only truth.
>
> (Andrew Taylor, *The American Boy*)

> The crime scene was in the low 30s around E, on the edge of Fort Dupont Park, in a neighborhood known as Greenway, in the 6th District section of Southeast DC. A girl of fourteen lay in the grass on the side of a community vegetable garden that was blind to the residents whose yards backed up to the nearby woods. There were colorful beads in her braided hair. She appeared to have died from a single gunshot wound

to the head. A middle-aged homicide police was down on one knee beside her, staring at her as if he were waiting for her to awake. His name was T. C. Cook. He was a sergeant with twenty-four years on the force, and he was thinking.

(George Pelecanos, *The Night Gardener*)

The smart, slick opening sentence can, as we have seen, be incredibly effective; but enthralling openings often extend to a paragraph or more.

EXERCISE

Consider the opening paragraphs below, and identify the source of their power to ensnare the reader. Select the one you like best, and write a similar opening paragraph for a crime novel set among a group of actors on tour.

It wasn't the first time she'd been locked in the cage, but this time was different from the others. Before, it had always been because she'd done something wrong or hadn't done what they wanted her to do. This time it was different. It was because of what she had become, and she was really scared.

(Peter Robinson, *Aftermath*)

A sudden swell threw Giles sideways. His elbow cracked against the wheel, and pain spiked up his arm like an electric shock. The momentary agony made him sicker than anything since the markets had crashed around him in 2008 and he'd had to sink three bottles of fizz in twenty minutes to dull the horror ... Waiting for the pain to recede, he silently added his niece to the list of people he'd be happy to see dead at his feet.

(N. J. Cooper, *Face of the Devil*)

It was about eleven o'clock in the morning, mid October, with the sun not shining and a look of hard wet rain in the clearness of the foothills. I was wearing

continued →

EXERCISE *continued*

my powder-blue suit, with dark blue shirt, tie and display handkerchief, black brogues, black wool socks with dark blue clocks on them. I was neat, clean, shaved and sober, and I didn't care who knew it. I was everything the well-dressed private detective should be. I was calling on four million dollars.

(Raymond Chandler, *The Big Sleep*)

My name is Mary Katharine Blackwood. I am eighteen years old and I live with my sister Constance. I have often thought that with any luck at all I could have been born a werewolf, because the two middle fingers on both my hands are the same length, but I have had to be content with what I had. I dislike washing myself, and dogs, and noise. I like my sister Constance, and Richard Plantagenet, and Amanita phalloide, the death-cap mushroom. Everyone else in my family is dead.

(Shirley Jackson, *We Have Always Lived in the Castle*)

Exceptional opening sentences are likely to linger in the reader's mind. But always bear in mind that an effective opening sentence (or two, or three) only works if it links seamlessly with the rest of your opening scene, and blends in with the book as a whole. If you are writing an eerie suspense novel about a scholarly antiques dealer freaked by the thought that the cabinet he's just acquired had once belonged to Hitler, a noir-ish opening along the lines of *The kid in the alley had been dead for 48 hours* would set the wrong tone and trigger the wrong expectations. As Noah Lukeman (*The First Five Pages*) says, 'Don't write an opening for the sake of an opening, but for the sake of the story that follows.'

EXERCISE

Write an intriguing opening (from one sentence to one paragraph) that sets the mood for:

1. a classic mystery

continued →

EXERCISE *continued*

2. a noir PI novel
3. a suspense novel
4. a thriller

The opening, by Laurie

It's called 'the hook' for a reason: once it snags the reader (in a shop or across an editorial desk) the book is sold.

A reader, particularly a first reader (the editor) wants nothing better than to be caught by a good, strong hook. Any reader longs to be taken in hand and led into the dream, lulled into submission by a sure authorial voice.

As Michelle says above, there are any number of ways to open a book. One of the more effective is, don't begin at the beginning. The temptation is to start a novel with the background you think the reader needs to know, and then move into the action. Go ahead and do that – but then exchange that first chapter with the second. That gets things moving with Chapter One, then uses Chapter Two to let the reader look around and see where she's standing.

This carries the danger of being formulaic – every other crime novel begins with an exclamation or argument or a sudden corpse, in the belief that therein lies the interest. In fact, if you go through the examples above, you'll see that the more intriguing ones – those that make you wish we'd included the next paragraph – all have a twist: the macabre image of a handless gent in a drifting boat. Two guys peaceably night fishing when a body splashes from the bridge overhead. The in-your-face humour of Chandler's, *I was neat, clean, shaved and sober, and I didn't care who knew it.* Shirley Jackson's self-introduction where, beneath the haughty assertion of mature idiosyncrasy, one hears the voice of a girl who is young for her age.

The opening contains the book. A strong opening steps straight in and sets the stage for everything that follows, whether it be furious action, dark humour, or the vivid voice of the narrator. From the first sentence, a reader needs to know the direction of this particular story.

EXERCISE

Look at half a dozen novels that have lingered strongly in your mind. In what way is the personality of the book contained in its opening lines?

The opening needs to be specific: we need to be greeted at the novel's entrance by a person, or by a place if it is going to play the part of a character in the novel.

FOR JILL PATON WALSH on ...

finding the author's voice – for this particular story, see 'Tips and tales – guest contributors', p. 140.

The opening is rarely the place for a flashback or exposition. Let things move along for a chapter or two before asking your reader to dawdle.

- Don't write fancy. *It was the best of times, it was the worst of times* worked for Dickens, but even that is only fancy in its philosophising: note the monosyllables. Begin with straightforward prose, and your reader will trust you.
- Write with energy. The opening is no place for excess words or hesitation: keep it clean and simple, and let your reader engage with the character.
- If, as you write, you're not satisfied with your opening, make some notes as to why, but keep writing. Write down different opening paragraphs – make a file of them, and later, consider how each affects the flavour of the story. But don't interrupt the story to go back and polish, then polish again – you'll never finish the book.

TOP TIP

The story's end needs a touch of the beginning. Once you finish your novel, take a look back: is there some echo at the end of the opening scenes, some faint reminder and an acknowledgement of expectations met?

Act one: the beginning

The opening is the doorway to the beginning, which merges into the middle, then builds towards the end: three separate entities, each with different demands, each essential to the whole.

The beginning sets up the story. It introduces the majority of characters, sets the subplots in motion, lays the foundation for everything that comes after. In a quest, the hero's journey begins with a call, which he promptly refuses. A mentor then intervenes, and off the hero sets, into the unknown.

Not all crime fiction follows the structure of the quest, but in each there is a set-up that drives the protagonist into the investigation, or out of comfort into suspense. Act One lays out the goal and raises the spectre of complications.

The beginning sets the machinery moving: we meet the characters and find out what they want. The goal of the story should become clear early on – even if, later, events crop up to change that goal.

- At some point, take a look at your novel's opening pages. If your story gets underway with long sentences and one or more hefty blocks of type, you may want to break the prose up somewhat. Time enough for lengthier discourse, once you've hooked the reader.
- Follow the playwright's dictum: begin your story as close to the end as you can. Not chronologically, but experientially: you want your reader to feel the pull of the ending from page one. Dithering kills suspense.

The set-up

The traditional mystery novel begins with the corpse, since the story is about the investigation of that death. In some, the death is in the first line, while others take a couple of chapters to work up to it, but this variety of story requires the victim to appear within the first third of the book, or the reader will fidget.

Generally speaking, the more suspense in the novel, the later the body may be introduced, since the whole point is, clearly, the suspense. However, the reader must have the clear sense that death is coming: that the threat is imminent and will be fatal. In a thriller, looming catastrophe, whether it's personal and individual or something that affects a whole swathe of humanity, presses on the reader with increasing urgency.

TOP TIP

During the Golden Age of crime fiction, readers were satisfied with a victim who was an ON switch rather than a person. Now, the world is full of fictional corpses: make your reader care about this particular victim, this specific investigation.

Action, by Michelle

Action and suspense are both page-turning qualities that can keep readers up late into the night. But each operates in its own way, and calls for different skills on the part of the writer.

By action scenes, I'm referring to chases, fights, attempts to escape from danger or to block a catastrophe – all those sustained series of movements that generate excitement and get readers' hearts pumping. Action scenes are not as easy to write as they sometimes seem. Moreover, such scenes usually work best when they are 'set up' at an earlier stage in the story. A few simple techniques can help.

EXERCISE

Take the following paragraph and make it tight and vivid. An example follows:

Troy used his own key to enter Lucinda's apartment. They'd been lovers for a while, back in the days before he'd come out as gay, and he'd never got around to returning her key. As he stepped into the darkened entrance hall, he heard a sound. A sharp, clicking sound. He stood stock still, listening. The entrance hall was large for this type of apartment – maybe eight feet by ten – with a substantial run of IKEA cupboards where Lucinda stored the necessaries for training.

continued →

EXERCISE ***continued***

As a triathlete, Lucinda's schedule called for stacks of equipment of different kinds, but she insisted that it shouldn't be allowed to clutter her apartment. In the dark, through the opaque glass doors of the cupboards, Troy could make out a stationary bicycle. He peered at the next set of doors, but just as he was trying to focus, the louvred blinds that screened the living room clattered open, and something – or rather someone – stood there. It was the man who'd followed Troy into the dry cleaners earlier today. He certainly didn't look like a weakling. On the contrary, he had shoulders as wide as a refrigerator, hands like hams, and there was the same suspicious bulge in the right pocket of his ex-military overcoat that Troy had noticed earlier in the day. For a moment, they stared at each other. Then Troy, anxious not to let the intruder get the upper hand, threw himself at the fellow's lower legs. His many years of amateur rugby served him in good stead and he managed a terrific tackle. The big guy came crashing to the ground ...

Here's an example of how it might be done if some of the information had been given earlier:

Troy used his key to enter Lucinda's apartment. As he stepped into the darkened entrance hall, he heard a sharp click. He froze, scanning the glass-fronted cupboards; nothing. Then the blinds that screened the living room clattered and a shape loomed there – the wide-shouldered man Troy had spotted earlier, his overcoat pocket still showing that suspicious bulge. Troy and the big man stared at each other for an instant before Troy dived for the fellow's legs. The big guy came crashing to the ground ...

The revised example is not merely shorter, it is faster-paced and more exciting. The actions – stepping into the apartment, hearing the sound, seeing the man, registering how scary he looks, the stare and the tackle

– are exactly the same, but the impact on the reader is much more intense. Why? Because extraneous description – of character, of background, of setting, of earlier events – has been removed. Anything needed to make the scene work in its pared-down form has been introduced earlier in the story, so that readers already know what Lucinda's apartment looks like, and that: Troy was once Lucinda's lover; he has a key; the entrance hall contains a row of glass-fronted cupboards, in which Lucinda, a triathlete, stores her equipment. They know that 'the big guy' is powerful, that Troy used to play rugby, and that daring tackles were his speciality. Introducing this descriptive information earlier keeps the action crisp.

It is especially important to introduce earlier any special features of the settings (such as trap doors, fire escapes, or dangerous protrusions) or any items (antique swords, a pair of scissors, a wind tunnel) which might affect the action. Otherwise, when you come to describe them, you will slow down the action. More to the point, they may seem like gimmicks dreamt up at the last moment to put the heroine in danger – or allow her to escape. With a brief mention beforehand, readers will take the special feature for granted.

EXAMPLE

Nights in White Satin contains a tense action scene in which two men attempt to use a big four-wheeler to crash the car driven by protagonist Laura Principal and her passenger Katie. I established the setting earlier – Laura visits the road and notes its narrowness, its isolation and the fact that there is no escape – so in the action scene, all I had to do was to remind readers of what they already knew:

> Even in the gloom, Fleam Dyke Road ... still resembled a Roman road – ruthless, puritanical almost, in its refusal to go anywhere but straight. It was still bordered on either side by tall, impenetrable hedges, walls of prickly hawthorn that formed a tunnel. But this time round, night had tossed its black tarpaulin between us and the flat blue sky.

> As the story goes on, with Laura injured and the men closing in, Katie reaches for a heavy club – but it isn't just a lucky find, since that earlier visit included a comic episode with a dog and a stout stick. Katie needs only to make a passing mention of the dog, and the presence of the cudgel is no longer a 'convenient' device, but perfectly credible.

Suspense, by Michelle

Action scenes stir readers up and grab their attention. But an equally powerful way of gathering in your readers, and keeping them entranced, is through suspense. Whereas action is about something happening – often something frightening or heart-stopping or dangerous – suspense comes entirely from anticipation of something that might happen. Think of those long sequences in horror films where the girl treads slowly, painfully, step by step, through the darkened corridor, bracing herself at every turning; the impact on the audience comes not from action, but from holding our breaths in dread.

> **FOR MARK BILLINGHAM on ...**
>
> the creation of true suspense, see 'Tips and tales – guest contributors', p. 109.

In novels, suspense arises because you the writer lead your readers to anticipate something, whether it is the lover sinking to his knees to propose or the murderer leaping out of the closet. Suspense is achieved by giving readers a vivid idea of what might be at stake before the suspenseful moment arrives, and building towards it. The consequences have to be firmly fixed in readers' minds before the suspense can kick in. A scene where the consequences were mooted at the same time as the 'suspense' is a caricature:

Elaine stepped out of the sunny terrace and into the darkened hallway. She stopped, suddenly aware that the door had been unlocked and that this meant that Butch might already be inside. Elaine moved slowly, step by step, overwhelmed by what she knew of Butch. Butch! Butch was ruthless; look at the way he'd killed his own granny so he could inherit her cottage. Butch was determined to get the jewels, and, because of Drew's letter, Butch knew that Elaine had them. Butch was the sort of man who would stop at nothing to get what he wanted. Elaine reached in her bag and drew out a small torch. She switched it on and ...

What a wasted opportunity! The scene would be far more compelling if readers knew already of Butch's dastardly ways, if Elaine hadn't had to tell us at this crucial moment about the jewels. It would be even better if Elaine doesn't realise the significance of the fact that the door is unlocked, but readers do. (Perhaps readers had been shown Elaine elaborately locking the door on the way out, but when she'd returned, she'd been gossiping on her mobile, and opened the door again without really thinking.) Suspense is heightened when readers are aware of an imminent danger that the potential victim seems to have overlooked; those are the scenes have us screaming: *Stop, Elaine, don't go in there!!!*

Backstory and the series novel

We now illustrate the need for maintaining suspense by pausing to consider backstory.

If a story's arc rises on the impulse of action and suspense, it stumbles beneath the weight of exposition, when the author breaks into the story to give the reader information about the characters or their world. We talked about this under 'Description', but here we consider backstory or, what went on before the story opened. Sometimes this is an explanation of the characters and their relationships in a series novel, but even a standalone novel may require the writer to feed the reader a certain amount of information. You just don't want to bog down the machinery of the story while you're doing it.

- A list of characters at the start of a novel is an admission of failure, the writer acknowledging that there are so many people, with such impossible connections, that the reader is going to need a list to keep them straight. A nice touch for a comic novel, perhaps.

> **TOP TIP**
>
> *Simply depositing a load of information – called an 'info-dump' – can be a sign of too much research or too little respect for the reader. Make a list of everything you're tempted to insert about what happened before this novel begins. When you're finished, go through and decide which information is absolutely necessary if the reader is going to understand the story, or the character.*
>
> *Then, cut half of it.*

Some backstory can be slipped in through dialogue – remembering always to maintain the voice of the person speaking. A conversation between two old friends will not lay out information, but it may refer to events, as well as giving insight into the long-term effects those events had on the pair. (Also see 'Dialogue and body language', above.)

- If there is a vivid and defining event that can be encapsulated in a short narration, it is tempting to tell it as a flashback or a dream, permitting the reader to experience it along with the narrator. Because even a lively flashback puts brakes on the plot, consider its position with care: breaking into the story at a point of great excitement does guarantee that the reader will be eager to return to the story, but it also means the reader will not have as much patience for the interruption. See if you can do without it, or compress it somehow.
- For a series novel, the goal should be, how *little* backstory can I give? If your novel depends too heavily on an earlier volume in order to make any

sense, maybe you need to change the novel. Even a series story needs to stand alone, since (with luck!) even the reader who knows you and has been waiting a year to snatch up the new book may have forgotten some of the details. Reminders can be scattered gently, in snippets of conversation and moments of reflection.

- In writing a series novel, it's best simply to proceed with the first draft as if the reader is sure to know the progress of the series as well as the writer does (if not better). Then, in the rewrite, read the early chapters with the cold eye of a complete stranger, watching for places where just a touch of explanation would help clarify matters.
- The arc of a series – the overall story from meeting to last fade-out – is not found in every series, many of which can be read in any order at all. Even in those where the protagonist develops as she goes along, where the characters are not at all the same in book seven as they were in book one, they need to hold true to themselves within each book. Treat each story as a standalone, with any plot elements that run through more than one book – a developing romance, a dying parent – limited to a discrete segment of its span.

The thematic arc of a series may be visible only when the series is complete. The Martin Beck series by Maj Sjöwall and Per Wahlöö, for example, can be viewed as a ten-volume meta-novel of social criticism. Each volume is complete unto itself, but when one reads them all, in order, a higher intent can be seen.

Act two: the middle

If the beginning sets the plot running, and the end brings everything together, the middle is that dangerous suspension bridge connecting the two.

In the classic quest, once the hero sets off on his journey, he encounters tasks and tests; he meets his enemies; he goes ever farther from his safe haven. At first, things seem to go well. Then problems crop up, and compound, to pummel him from all sides. The second act of a quest is all about trials and tasks – trials that include temptation, tasks that may encompass facing up to his past.

The middle of the book is all about character: the protagonist, his friends, the enemy (who may be a shadow, or a clear personality). It is about plot, yes, with information gathered, clues followed and suspects identified; but primarily it is about the protagonist feeling his way into this foreign country of his investigation, becoming ever more hedged about with complications – many of which stem from his own actions. Everywhere he turns, problems loom; everything he does, only makes matters worse.

TOP TIP

The middle is the part where you, the author, hit your protagonist while he's down. Then you kick him.

Subplots strengthen throughout the middle, becoming more complex, distracting the protagonist from his goal. Towards the end of the middle section the subplots begin to coalesce, allowing your readers to see how the story they thought they understood is actually quite a bit simpler, and larger.

In addition to the internal momentum that propels the hero out of the beginning, external forces emerge to give him a shove. Tension builds, with one or more smaller peaks along the way – peaks that end up being merely steps to the climax.

In the middle, the protagonist is largely reactive, responding to one threat after another, cornered by his inabilities and misunderstandings.

- Tension is the driving force in the middle: ever greater threat, a continual narrowing down of options, a closing in of walls all around him, bigger and harsher complications that the protagonist finds increasingly difficult to keep up with.

FOR TESS GERRITSEN on ...

tension – 'what happens *before* the action explodes' – see 'Tips and tales – guest contributors', p. 122.

The middle is the place for a shock, a twist that turns your story inside-out: a revelation that a friend is an enemy, or that what appeared to be a cold case from the past has abruptly gone hot, or for your detective to return home to find his wife missing and signs of a struggle. Just when the reader was settling down for the book's second half, s/he is struck by the tingling awareness that the story is taking on a whole new dimension.

Descriptive passages begin to drop away as the middle section progresses, fewer characters are introduced, as the story narrows down to the character and his task.

Pace – peaks and valleys

Remember the third illustration of the story's arc, that builds and drops off a bit, builds higher and drops again? That rhythm is your goal for the middle section of your novel.

Crime novels and thrillers should have a good pace. But that doesn't mean they all have to gallop along; nor does it mean that car chases and shoot-outs are *de rigueur*. Some stories are contemplative, pursuing a problem or an issue (or a case) with stately dignity, letting readers revel in the richness of the language or savour the intricacy of the plot. Others rip along, from one scene of intense action to another.

Whether the story you're writing calls for Formula 1 speed or a steady trot, pace is important. A novel is too slow if readers feel their attention flagging, or get the notion that nothing (that really matters) is happening. There are two simple ways to improve pace.

First, introduce variation. If your story is a stately one, with your Detective Whicher musing over every scrap of evidence, slip in the occasional scene of action or high emotion. A sudden accusation, vigorous denouncement or pitched argument will raise the reader's pulse and kick the story along.

Second, keep up the pace by cutting anything that doesn't move the story forward. Pare. Trim. Edit. Prune. *When in doubt, cut it out* – also known as *Kill your darlings*. Remember the exercise under 'Action'? It is amazing how a page that drags can be rehabilitated simply by cutting excess words.

On the other hand, if your story is the kind that publishers describe as 'an action-packed thrill ride', then allow for a quieter scene from time to time. As Guy Saville points out in his guest essay in this volume, 'There's nothing less exciting than non-stop excitement.'

FOR GUY SAVILLE on ...

the relentless pace of the thriller, see 'Tips and tales – guest contributors', p. 153.

The middle is often the trickiest part to write, mostly because it is so dependent on momentum. In terms of physics, momentum is the product of mass and velocity. In terms of a novel's momentum, mass is required here as well. If the protagonist lacks a kind of moral weight or if the problem he is battling is too thin or frivolous, the middle of the novel can lose momentum. Keep in mind what your protagonist wants – and that goes for his deeper needs as well. He may think that he wants to deal with his fiancé's troublesome ex-boss, when what he really wants is to build a future.

- If you find your story sagging in the middle, look at ways to reinvigorate it. Raymond Chandler famously said, 'When in doubt, have a man come through a door with a gun in his hand' – although he was not recommending the technique, merely commenting on the mechanical aspects of some detective stories. Still, a vivid reminder of threat is a great way to up the ante for your poor besieged hero.

Making things worse for your hero isn't simply about bringing on more of the same. This is one of the drawbacks of the serial killer genre, when the Gothic horrors of the first part have no place to go but more lurid, more explicitly gruesome. A single gun, sitting unused upon a desk for several chapters, can generate more excitement than a dozen gun battles; in the same way, a dozen mangled bodies, dragged in whenever the plot threatens to sag, can be less suspenseful than the foreknowledge of a single death.

Act three: the endgame

In chess, the endgame is the final battle, when both players are reduced to a bare minimum of pieces and the movements become a flurry of attack and counterattack.

In a quest, the third quarter sees the hero's brush with death, the loss of an ally through death or treason, and his increasing isolation just as the enemy is growing stronger. In the classic quest journey, however, the hero may be saved by outside help: not in your novel. Here, it is all about the protagonist, with no role for a *deus ex machina*.

In a novel, the third act finds a protagonist turning from reactive to proactive: when all else is lost, when she is far from help and friendship, her only option is to stand alone and find her strength. To throw herself body and soul into the battle.

When the reader reaches the final page, s/he expects to find the protagonist's challenges resolved, order restored to the world, and evil punished, or at least thwarted. More than that, however, the novel's solution must fit the characters who have worked so hard to get here: it must agree with the strengths and weakness the reader has come to see in them, with no sudden convenient changes in personality or new characters who contribute to the problem's solution.

The ideal ending not only finds the plot and subplots resolved, but finds the protagonist at peace, with herself and the world. The word *resolution* means both *solved* and *determined*: the hero stands firm again, doubt conquered, ready to resume her interrupted life.

- Intensity builds in the book's endgame: be ruthless with anything that undermines the protagonist's single-minded pursuit of his goal.

TOP TIP

The opening sells a book (to readers or editors) but the ending sells the following book. A book with a memorable closing scene lingers in the mind after the covers are shut or the off-button pressed.

Strong endings sound a clear note, not only of resolution, but of the future. They are strongest when they present a visual image of the chief character.

Be very wary of surprise endings, outside of short stories. A sudden twist that changes everything showcases the author's cleverness, but unless it's a comic novel to begin with, or deeply noir, the reader might feel you were not showing much respect to your characters, who have worked hard for 300 pages only to be told they weren't needed. And, if your surprise rests on the revelation of unexpected information, it violates that prime commandment of crime fiction: Thou shalt play fair with thy reader.

Closing and coda

Since the climax is, if you have done it right, a pulse-elevating experience for the reader, your book may want a scene or two afterwards, both to tidy up the explanations and to give the reader the sense of restoration. The questing hero must return to his home, and see how 'it' has changed – or rather, how his quest has changed *him*.

Consider the taste your ending leaves in the reader's mind. Does s/he close the covers with a shake of the head and a 'Whew!' at the thrill of it? Does s/he have a wistful smile, being sorry the story is over? Or a broad grin at the final comic kick? Whatever flavour you want your reader to be left with, this is your final chance.

EXAMPLE

Laurie says: In *O Jerusalem*, following an action-packed endgame involving a long underground pursuit, a mad overground chase, guns, bombs and the fate of the Middle East hanging in the balance, I wanted to end with a taste of the book's lighter side. So, a final salute is given to protagonist Mary Russell (who is disguised as a boy) by the novel's great authority figure, General Edmund Allenby, at a garden party attended by notables that include the Governor, heads of state, and T. E. Lawrence:

> But that was not the end of the adventure, for then (and here the expressions of astonishment and dismay turned to sheer, slack-jawed disbelief) 'Bull' Allenby – last of the Paladins, conqueror of Jerusalem, hero of the Middle East, and Commander in Chief of all the Holy Land – turned to the fourth noisome intruder, grasped that young Bedouin lad's black, bloodied, and bandaged hand gently in his own, raised it to his lips, and kissed it.

Strong final scenes often hold a trace of the beginning, reminding the reader where the journey began, and creating a sense of restoration in itself.

- *Coda* means 'tail', and that's what your closing words can be: a small bit of balance, and the last thing the reader sees as the characters depart.

When you're 'finished': the rewrite

So, you've finally typed THE END at the bottom of a long, long stretch of pages covered with 60,000 words, or 80,000, or 150,000. Congratulations! Take the rest of the day off, go out to dinner, pop open that bottle of champagne your brother-in-law gave you for your birthday.

And tomorrow? You go to work on the rewrite, naturally.

Some writers push to the end of a first draft; others are committed to edit-as-you-go, starting each day's writing stint with an edit of the entire piece, or at least the previous day's. Which you prefer depends on which permits you to get the job done: if pausing to reread and re-edit means you are getting no new material written, then that system isn't for you: lock away your existing Work in Progress and keep your eyes on the end.

Whether your 'finished' novel has 60,000 words or 150,000, the rewrite is the time when you go through every one of those words, to make sure it contributes to the whole.

- Orderly, or Organic? Did you scrupulously follow your outline? Or dive into the story with no intentions whatsoever – or follow the middle way of the Orderly Organic? No matter how you reached the first draft, the rewrite is the time you see if the story arc does what you intended.
- Does your novel maintain a position on the genre spectrum? A story that starts off as a simple detective mystery may slip into something darker and more psychologically complex than you had envisioned. The rewrite is the time to restore balance.
- If you are a writer of the Organic school, the rewrite is when you produce your outline, as an analytical tool instead of a tool for planning. It doesn't matter if your 'outline' is of the traditional outline format, or if it takes the form of a spreadsheet timeline, a branching tree-graph, or a wall covered with arrow-shaped sticky notes: breaking down just what

the plot and subplots do – and when – can shed strong light on any problems with the plot structure and the book's pace.

EXERCISE

Compare your book with its outline.

Do the major plot points of your outline actually coincide with the developments of the story, or are some of the high points submerged under peripheral material and sub-plots?

If there are scenes that distract readers away from the central thread of the story, would cutting them help to build momentum?

Do the key events build, then slacken off a little, then build again?

Do the chapters feel balanced – the number of scenes and number of pages?

Are all plot twists clear? Can the reader see not only where they are going and where they come from, but why they are there?

- Are all the motives clear? Does the reader understand why each character performs each act?
- Subplots both distract from the central storyline and lead the reader back into it. Tight plotting requires that any story elements that meander around and fail to strengthen the climax need to be cut off, or at least pruned back.
- If you think another set of eyes at this point would be of help, take a look at 'Working with others', above.

Reading aloud

TOP TIP

There is nothing like reading a piece of writing aloud to highlight its flaws. Professional copyeditors – the best ones – read their

> *assignment aloud as part of the job. Do not depend on yours to catch mistakes. Read your book out loud, to yourself or to a patient audience, working from a printed page, not a monitor. Do not murmur the words under your breath: pronounce each one. And take frequent breaks, to keep your mind and throat fresh.*

It can help to have a list of key concerns before starting the read-aloud, adding to it as things crop up. In the rewrite, perhaps you changed a subplot, or a character's nationality or sex. Watch for any vestigial elements of that earlier version. As you read, think about the following:

- **Words.** Test each word, every phrase: Is it necessary? Is it the best word for the job? It is a cliché? Is it strong and active? Does it feel like the work of a sure author? Listen for accidental rhymes, and for repetitions and overuse of words or phrases. Any time you have to repeat a sentence to get the sense of it, there may be some awkward phrasing to attend to. If you suspect you are using a word too often, make note of it, and later do a word search through the document with an eye to changing some of its appearances. Do the same with those thousand empty phrases and clutter words – *the fact that; clearly* – and the overuse of the verb to be – *there is; there are*; and especially *it was Mary who* ... (see 'Language' above). You might experiment with some of the software programs that catch word repetitions.
- **Sentence structure.** Am I hearing a lot of sentence fragments? Do I begin too many sentences with an infinitive phrase? ('Looking up, Mrs Hudson smiled at the little girl'). Both are good ways to vary the pace of the prose, but at a price: fragments distract, and infinitive beginnings create a brief catch in the forward action each time.
- **Spelling and punctuation.** Is it right? Perfectly, invisibly right?
- **Is there clutter?** Have I weighed my story down with unnecessary explanations and long-winded descriptions? Have I so loaded it with metaphors and imagery that the reader forgets what the characters were doing? Can I pare my prose down to the most vivid and essential points?
- **Are my point of view shifts clear?** Does the reader always know whose

eyes s/he is looking through? Are there any clumsy places, where a reader might have to check who is speaking?

- **Is my description awkward?** Have I given dialogue that belabours the view, or presented a character's looks by listing what she sees in the mirror? Is all that information necessary? Is there a smoother way I can give it?
- **Is my dialogue scalpel-sharp?** Does it carry the plot forward, reveal the characters, and plant doubts or clues – all at the same time?
- **Does my writing show, or tell?** Is the reader in the midst of the experience, or at a distance from it? Do I over-explain, over-describe?

EXERCISE: READING ALOUD

What is wrong with these sentences that the tongue has a better chance of catching than the eye?

1. In the rewrite, perhaps you changed a subplot, or a character's nationality, or sex.
2. In fact, he was the only boy who actually was right.
3. He was smaller then the dog.
4. This example is missing word.

Answers: 1. That last comma suggests that you, the writer changed sex, mid-book. 2. In fact; only; actually: why all three? 3. Then: than. 4. A dropped *a*.

How many drafts?

If you're a devoted outliner – some writers follow such tight outlines, their rewrite consists of little more than a read-through – or if you're one of the edit-as-you-go school who has rewritten early sections a hundred times by the time THE END comes about – your novel may have, strictly speaking, only one draft.

For most of us who write, then rewrite, a novel requires a minimum of three or four drafts. The first draft gets the story down on paper, in a more or less rough form, depending on your approach to outlining. Later drafts correct, improve and amend.

TOP TIP

When doing second, third and subsequent drafts, begin with the bigger issues (structure, storyline, progression, character development) and gradually moving towards the finer points – getting the pace right, sharpening up dialogue, making the language sing.

Print or e-doc? Traditionally, the editing process – involving both author and publisher – has worked via a master copy: a complete, printed single copy of the manuscript goes from the editor to the copyeditor to the author, each of whom writes notes and makes corrections in a different-colour pencil. The resulting mess of green, brown and graphite pencil is then given to an assistant who collates the notes from a couple of other copies that have circulated, and sends it to the typesetter. If anything happens to it – such as the manuscript of one writer, on its final return to the publishing house, that went up in flames in a Manhattan delivery van – the process starts all over, from the beginning.

More and more publishers are succumbing to the modern age and turning from master copies to electronic edits. An e-edit would appear to be far more efficient and lacking in drama ... until one considers the impossibility of getting two computers to agree on anything.

What next?

Congratulations, you've finished your book – until the editor and copy-editor send it back, scarred with pencil. Take the day off, go for a walk, maybe even read someone else's new book.

And tomorrow? Go back to work.

Because you're a writer, and that's what writers do: we write.

When you're *really* finished

The publishable manuscript

The purpose of this current book is crime *writing*, not crime *selling*. However, since most people interested in writing have an eventual sale in mind, it would be good to talk briefly about what a publisher expects of submissions.

First, you should be aware of the traditions of the industry. If you write a police procedural with paranormal elements, or the story of a Miss Marple type who comes up against a killer who dismembers small children, you may find it difficult to win a home for them with a commercial publishing house. Similarly, if your comfortable length is a piece of 30,000 words, you need to be aware that the industry is rarely interested in a piece that is neither short story nor novel.

Second, whether you are submitting to an agent or directly to a publishing house (where your manuscript will be placed on what is called the 'slush pile', generally a small room where the junior editors are locked in every so often and fed takeaway pizza until the shelves have been emptied), ensure that your manuscript is perfectly presented before you send it out. Above all, it must be: typed; double spaced; with margins wide enough for scribbled comments; scrubbed free of errors in spelling, grammar and syntax; and numbered continuously from the first page to the last. Make it attractive and easy to read. An online search of 'standard manuscript format' will give you further details.

E-publishing

The debate over online self-publishing – 'To E or not to E?' – is a pressing one in the writing world, given impetus in the spring of 2011 when two authors famously went different directions: best-seller Barry Eisler turned down a large offer in order to self-publish e-books, while Amanda

Hocking dropped her lucrative online self-publishing career in favour of the traditional route – same month, same publisher.

The question of whether or not to e-publish a book yourself is far too complicated to tackle here, since there is no one answer that applies to every writer. Yes, a writer receives a higher cut of the royalties, has more control over the finished work, and can determine how – and when – it is sold. On the downside, the writer is the publisher: everything from finding a good editor to creating professional-looking cover art to distributing any paperback editions becomes the writer's job – and that includes every aspect of marketing and promotion. Do you want to be a writer, or a writer/publisher?

The Eisler–Hocking debates (an online search will take you to them) make for thought-provoking reading, and can help you decide which is for you. But before you sign anything, with an e-publisher or a traditional house, make sure you have the contract examined by an agent or lawyer. You don't want to lock yourself into a bad situation, or to give away rights for ever.

The agent

Literary agents are a necessary part of traditional publishing, well worth the 15 per cent they charge for the expert knowledge they bring to your professional life. Make sure the agent you are considering is qualified, and experienced: your agent will be one of the most important people in your life. Ask around. Check up before entering into any agreement. And do not pay any fee up front: agents make their money from advances and royalties, not from readers' fees.

Contests

The gatekeepers who assess your manuscript, and decide whether or not it should be published, have a tough job. Editors and agents (and the readers who sometimes deputise for them) sift through huge numbers of manuscripts. (Michelle says: My agent in the UK receives 400 unsolicited manuscripts each month.) Anything you can do to show that your manuscript deserves careful scrutiny is worth a try. That's where contests come in.

If you can say in your covering letter that you have been selected as the Swindon Young Writer of the Year or that your short story won the William Shakespeare Memorial Prize, the gatekeeper is bound to be more attentive. Her job has just been made a little easier: someone else has judged your writing to be excellent.

So check out contests online, major ones and minor, and submit something, if you can.

In the UK, start by entering the Debut Daggers Award competition, organised by the (UK) Crime Writers' Association. You will be up against a great many other competitors, but it could be worthwhile: most winners and many of the shortlisted authors go on to achieve publication. Smaller, local competitions, or those associated with particular writing festivals or magazines, may offer smaller rewards, but they also give higher chances of success. Check out the informative website Prizemagic, and Writing Comps, run by Michael Shenton.

In the USA, several crime organisations sponsor contests for new writers, often with a prize of publication. St Martin's Press, with its imprint Minotaur Books, is especially supportive of new writers, sponsoring: the Best First Crime Novel Contest, through the Mystery Writers of America; Best First Traditional Mystery Novel, with the conference Malice Domestic; Best Private Eye Novel, with the Private Eye Writers of America; and the Hillerman Mystery contest, with the Tony Hillerman Writers Conference.

When to start the promotion wagon rolling?

Congratulations, you're published! What next?

Step one: keep writing. Remember this – a writer writes? Don't let the thrill of seeing your words in print keep you from your daily stint.

Step two depends on your publisher. If you're with a big house, you'll find a publicist has been assigned your book, one of dozens she handles during the year. Once upon a time, publishers rather preferred that the author not get involved with promoting the book, other than showing up and wowing the customers at a signing or radio interview. These days, most houses are grateful for any assistance you can give them – that is, if they don't leave it to you entirely.

Talk to your editor, find out if you have a publicist, and get in touch with her soon after the contract's ink is dry. Sales conferences take place months before a book is published, and if there's going to be a publicity budget for your book, everyone will know early. (Don't ask how much – more important is what kind.) Make clear that your interest is to coordinate and support what they are doing, and ask how.

And when you hear your granny's voice in your ear telling you it's time to write a thank-you letter, listen to it. Everyone likes to be appreciated, and everyone in publishing hears mostly complaints. You might even add a little box of chocolates, come pub day ...

Author's website

What do you invest in your writing business, by way of time and money? What are the basic requirements, when it comes to making yourself known out in the big cold world?

First and foremost, you need a website. An author website is absolutely essential: when people hear about you, they don't want to wade through your publisher's big, impersonal website to find you. It doesn't have to be fancy. You can build it yourself, or you can hire someone and spend your entire advance, as you like, but the minimum should be:

- **Biography.** Nothing elaborate; most people don't need to know about your childhood experiences or your divorce (unless that's what you're writing about) but they do want to know where you grew up and what your defining life experiences were, be they world travel, grad school, or twenty years as a carpenter. Keep it simple and friendly. Include a full-face photo suitable for downloading in case a newspaper or library needs one. If you can afford a professional portrait, it's a good investment. Take a close look at any snapshots and personal info: what do they say about you? Are they professional? And do they say too much?
- **List of publications.** Some writers prefer to do a new website for each book, but if you're planning a career at this, you want readers to identify the author, not just one book.
- **Contact information.** You might want to set up an email just for business, since it's sure to be exposed to spam. And think before you post a physical address online: it might be worth the peace of mind to hire a box at the post office or a mail collection agency.
- **Events page.** Because sooner or later, you'll be in front of an audience, and you want people to know where.

EXERCISE

Select three or four of your favourite crime or thriller writers, and check out their websites. Which one appeals to you most, and why? What works, and what doesn't?

Social media

Facebook, Twitter, Google+, Goodreads, and a myriad of other sites exist to get your name out there in exchange for sucking hours from your writing day. If you enjoy any of them, by all means continue, opening an author page for the purpose. If you hate it, you might open an author page anyway, and simply keep involvement to a bare minimum.

Guest blog tours can be a good way for new writers to get known. If you're thinking of offering a guest post, get involved with the blogs you're considering well in advance: nobody likes a stranger elbowing in.

Outreach

For the new writer, outreach should begin locally. Tell the bookshop you buy from (you *do* buy from them, don't you?) or library you haunt that you have a book coming out, and ask if they'd like to do an event – maybe a group event, with one or two other writers.

After you've talked with your publisher's publicist (duplicating her efforts makes you both look like rank amateurs) get in touch with your local paper or radio station, identifying the reporter most likely to write about local interest. If you can come up with an interesting hook – the story is set in the haunted house at the centre of town, you teach at the local high school – it means their job is half done.

Many authors love to give away what the publishing world calls tchotchkes – knick-knacks like key rings, refrigerator magnets, or pens with the name of the book on them. If you have a brother-in-law who can make them up for you cheap, fine, but don't expect they will ever sell a book. Postcards are the same, except that while the pens get used, the postcards get tossed into the recycling bin.

What about a book trailer? Again, unless you're related to Spielberg, they're a fun extra but not worth spending much money on. If you want to make a video that shows the book's setting, that might be of interest to readers.

Bookmarks, on the other hand, can be useful, simply because when someone asks what you do, it's nice to be able to put something in their hand so they remember your name – and, more important, the name of your book. Something with the cover, a line or two of description or review praise, your website URL, and a list of previous titles can be handy to give away to bookstores and libraries. You can also stick one in books at signings to remind the reader of what else you've written.

Join writing organisations, local and national. You need to know what is happening in the publishing world, and organisations of writers can not only help you form a community, they can improve your craft. Groups include: Mystery Writers of America, Crime Writers' Association, Sisters in Crime, International Thriller Writers and the International Association of Crime Writing.

The writer's public face

Public speaking terrifies some people – even people who do a lot of it. Being a writer can mean spending fifty weeks of the year sitting in a quiet room by yourself, followed by two weeks in and out of airports and hotels and evenings with dozens, even hundreds of people staring at you.

If that idea makes you break out in a sweat, you are not alone. Here's what you do:

TOP TIP

Prepare. A one-hour event doesn't mean one hour of reading, it means ten minutes of reading, half an hour of talking, and twenty minutes of Q&A. If you have a small crowd (or if you're in a part of the world where nobody will ask a question for fear of being thought assertive) you can do a longer reading – but, don't just extend it to half an hour of droning on. Choose two or three ten-minute sections and talk about each: the research you did for this part, the character exploration involved here, a battle you had with your editor there. You can even bring a little show-and-tell, if the item is easily visible to a crowd and not vulnerable to rough handling. Remember, people at signings are interested in you, and in the writing process.

Prepare your reading. Don't imagine you know how long it takes to read five pages: stand up and read those pages aloud, timing yourself.

When you have your pages – from the beginning, or later in the book if you can dig out a section that doesn't have spoilers and doesn't require lengthy explanation – read them aloud, several times. Pretend you're reading a bedtime story to a child. Go for presentation, go for drama or humour, tease out the meaning of the words.

A reading is performance art, without the hecklers. The audience is with you all the way. They want to be entertained, but they also want *you* to be entertained. It may be hard to believe, but your audience is in awe of you, the writer. Let them know that they're a good audience, by responding to them.

Put on a face. Never make a public admission of how nervous you are. It only makes the audience nervous.

Michelle says: Consider finding partners in crime. Earlier in our writing careers, six of us banded together to form a group called the Unusual Suspects. The benefits were substantial: together, we could afford to produce promotional material and send it out to libraries, festival organisers and the like, and this brought us many gigs; two or three or more of us together were more attractive to a venue organiser, and brought in larger crowds, than would have showed up for one of us on our own; we became very skilled at working together to put on an entertaining performance; when, as occasionally happened, few people turned out, none of us felt personally rejected, and together we could laugh off the disappointment on the homeward journey. Most of all, we had great fun; sharing the joys and angsts of a writer's public life was a powerful antidote to the isolation of writing.

Conferences and classes

Conferences can be expensive, exhausting, intimidating – and the best thing you've ever done for yourself as a writer. You'll meet writers and readers, make contact with agents and editors, hear suggestions that change the way you write, and come away recharged and excited.

Conferences are smart business, a great way of promoting and selling books. But be aware, some are primarily fan conferences, others zero in on the craft of writing. What you get varies.

For crime writers, conventions involve a lot of effort – panels, book signings, media interviews, greeting fans – but they're also an opportunity to meet friends in the writing community, to share a drink, tell jokes (only sometimes macabre ones) and talk shop (shorthand for dissing publishers). Even the macho men of the thriller world (you know, the ex-SAS types with their short-back-and-sides) have been known to let their hair down.

A typical convention provides a chance to have breakfast with Sara Paretsky, to do the Texas two-step with Val McDermid, to catch a glimpse of Ian Rankin's legs beneath his kilt. To hear Reginald Hill's apparently off-the-cuff witticisms at the opening of an awards banquet:

> *You can tell the writers. They are the ones who've tarted themselves up in the hopes that no one will guess that they're broke. And the publishers, who've dressed down, in a vain attempt to present themselves as something other than filthy rich. And then there's the agents. Well, we don't actually see a great deal of the agents at these events. Just the occasional fin knifing through the water ...*

Exhausting, exhilarating and irresistible.

US conferences include Bouchercon, which moves between big metropolitan areas in the US; Malice Domestic, celebrating the traditional mystery in Bethesda, MD; Left Coast Crime in the western half of the US; Magna cum Murder, in Muncie, Indiana; Sleuthfest in Florida; Love is Murder ('When chocolate and flowers aren't enough') in Rosemont, IL; and Thrillerfest, the International Thriller Writers convention in New York. In the UK one can join the richly attended Theakston Old Peculier Crime Festival in Harrogate; Crimefest in Bristol; or St Hilda's in the Oxford college of the same name. In Canada, one has Bloody Words and the Arthur Ellis Awards

Banquet, sponsored by the Crime Writers of Canada – Arthur Ellis is the pseudonym often adopted by Canada's official hangmen, and a favourite of Michelle, who says: To my very great delight, the CWC named *In the Midnight Hour* best novel of its year. And my award – a jointed wooden figure hanging from a gibbet, that dances when you pull a string – occupies pride of place on my mantelpiece still.

Crime conferences are listed online – in the UK, the Crime Writers' Association events page lists the major conferences.

TOP TIP

If you register early for any conference, you'll have a better chance to get a place on a panel. Telling the planners why the audience might like to listen to you – you're a forensic pathologist, the world's expert on Jack the Ripper, a New York Times *bestselling author – also improves your chance to be on a panel.*

When you take part in a conference, act like a professional. If you're on a panel, read something by each of your co-panellists (or at the very least, their online bio). And keep your answers short and sweet. Listen to what the others say. Talk about the ideas being discussed, not about your books. Do not begin every contribution on your panel with 'When I was writing [*name of novel*] I –.' Do not hog the microphone. If you are the moderator, keep your panellists in line. And finally, you can prop up your latest book and wear a t-shirt printed with your cover if you like, but both make your audience just a little wary.

Outside the panels, behave like a professional, too. Accept praise graciously. Accept also that many people won't have a clue who you are. Do not get drunk in the bar at night, unless that's a key part of your authorial identity. Do not thrust your promotional material in every hand you see.

Classes and workshops abound. Excellent instruction can be had in the Arvon classes, of course, in the UK, and in Creative Writing MA programmes – and increasingly, BAs and PhDs too – in most universities and colleges.

Across the US, you're spoiled for choice: Book Passage, just north of San Francisco, with a yearly mystery writing conference; Mystery Writers of America's 'MWA Universities'; the Tony Hillerman conference meets in Santa Fe; the Crime Fiction Academy run by the Center for Fiction at New York's Mercantile Library (where Edgar Allan Poe wrote); and the biennial California Crime Writers Conference in Pasadena.

Many conferences like Bouchercon and the Theakston's Old Peculier Crime Writing Festival have a 'writer's academy' attached, usually a one-day intensive, led by professionals. The Mystery Writers of America holds a symposium during the annual Edgars Week.

The Writer's Police Academy offers hands-on demonstrations of police techniques to fiction writers. Many police departments also sponsor 'police academies' and ridealongs for civilians interested in how things are done.

National Novel Writing Month – NaNoWriMo – calls for *Thirty days and nights of literary abandon.* Every November, an e-community of mad scribblers forms to urge each other into writing, the goal being a novel's first draft. Tips, pep talks, widgets and mass enthusiasm can push you forward through a highly caffeinated month.

Taking criticism

If you are published, you will be criticised. There will be people who dislike what you have written. They will say so, openly. Some of them will lurk in the darker recesses of the Amazon comments, others may emblazon your flaws across the pages of the *Times* (of London, New York, or Peoria – does it matter?), but the minute you put your work (and your heart) out there, someone will step on it.

Worse than being criticised, you will be ignored. One Booker Prize chair reportedly said that hell would freeze over before a crime novel made the Booker shortlist, while another explained that such books often weren't even submitted, since publishers felt it would be like entering a donkey for the Grand National. Val McDermid's *A Place of Execution* was praised, but dismissed because it was, in the end, a genre novel.

In either case, your response will be the same as it is when you lose a prize you thought you deserved or have a contract turned down by a publisher: gracious silence. You will politely listen while your friends, family and agent rage, and you will not respond. You will not rise up to counter the critic's points, you will not call the critic an idiot, you will not send him terse postcards or post about him on your Facebook page or challenge him to duelling Twitter feeds at dawn.

Step one is, do not read them. Delete your book's Amazon page from your computer, tell your editor that it's OK not to send you any really nasty reviews, hope that your well-meaning 'friends' don't forward too many examples of literary brutality, and delete from Facebook any 'Friends' who insist on doing so.

Step two is, take a deep breath and ask yourself if the criticism – be it active or by omission – is justified. Two books go up for a prize; the lesser one wins; can you summon your detachment and figure out why? It may simply have been the taste of the judges, in which case you shrug and go your way. It may have been that a couple of them heard stories about you (that lack of graciousness, perhaps?), in which case, the only thing you can do is work on your public face. Or it could be that yours was the lesser book. (Need we point out, this does not mean that you are the lesser person?)

Granted, the judges of literary prizes shy away from the contagion of genre. However, like a teenager who has fuchsia dreadlocks, multiple piercings and an exposed midriff yet becomes indignant when no bank will hire her, it may be time for the outraged author to consider goals.

What are you aiming for?

In a *Guardian* article, talking about the 2010 Australian literary Miles Franklin award, judge Morag Fraser is quoted:

> *Most crime novels that I have read (and I read one a week, often more) will never win the Miles Franklin or any other 'literary' prize because they do not work language hard enough, and they do not think originally and with sufficient depth and imagination ... They may gratify but they do not surprise the way great literature does.*
>
> *In the case of Peter Temple's* Truth*, the divide was so comprehensively crossed that we did not think much about the conventions of crime fiction except to note that Temple was able to observe them rather as a poet observes the 14-line convention of the sonnet or a musician the sonata form: as a useful disciplinary structure from which to expand, bend or depart.*

As writers, we need to ask ourselves hard questions: Does my novel wrestle with language, with ideas, with the human condition? Does my story surprise? Does it use its genre as a disciplinary structure, or is it limited by conventions?

We are story-tellers in a line of story-tellers that stretches back to the beginnings of language. We seek to entertain, to inform, and perhaps to disturb, just a little. We choose crime as a genre because that is where our kind of stories lie, in a place where death requires a response, where our protagonists embark on a quest that forces all of the good and some of the wicked to the surface, and where the reader may walk alongside.

We write crime, because it is human.

Acknowledgements

Michelle's acknowledgements
I'd like to acknowledge the support provided during the preparation of this book: by the Royal Literary Fund, and particularly by Steve Cook, the Director and extraordinary friend to writers; by colleagues at Magdalene College, Cambridge, where I have been a Bye-Fellow; and by Selina Walker whose advice and help was, as always, invaluable.

Permissions

The authors and publisher would like to thank the following for their kind permission to reproduce quotations:

Extract adapted from *Defending the Guilty* by Alex McBride reproduced by permission of Penguin Books 2010. Copyright © Alex McBride, 2010.

Alex McBride for his permission to reproduce the extract in the US and Canada.

Resources and reading

A writer's reference library

Because online reference goes only so far, a writer needs to build a library of familiar tools. What you need depends on what you are writing, but some of the basics are:

- **A good dictionary**, such as (UK) *The Chambers Dictionary* (12th edn, Chambers Harrap Publishers Ltd, Edinburgh, 2001) or in the US, *Merriam-Webster's Collegiate Dictionary* (10th edn, Springfield, MA, 2001).
- **A thesaurus:** Christine A. Lindberg (compiler), *The Oxford American Writer's Thesaurus* (2nd edn, Oxford University Press, New York, 2008); *Concise Oxford Thesaurus* (3rd edn, Oxford University Press, Oxford, 2007); *The Merriam-Webster Dictionary of Synonyms and Antonyms*, Merriam-Webster, New York, 2008 (for the subtle differences between similar words, e.g., prone, supine, prostrate, recumbent).
- **A basic grammar**, with clear description of the parts of speech, basic syntax and punctuation. *The Chicago Manual of Style*, University of Chicago Press, is the US publishing authority.
- For historical fiction, a **dictionary of slang** with dates of first usage such as *The Oxford Dictionary of Modern Slang* (John Ayto and John Simpson, Oxford University Press, New York, 1992) or *Dictionary of American Slang* (4th edn, eds Barbara Ann Kipfer and Robert L. Chapman, HarperCollins, New York, 2007).

Basic writing books

Strunk, William Jr and E. B. White, *The Elements of Style*, International edn/ 4th edn, Pearson Education, 2010.

Gardner, John, *The Art of Fiction: Notes on Craft for Young Writers*, Vintage Books, 2001; *On Becoming a Novelist*, Harper & Row, New York, 1983; *On Moral Fiction*, HarperCollins, NY, 1978.

Crime writing and reference

Benedict, Elizabeth, *The Joy of Writing Sex*, Souvenir Press Ltd, 2002.

Lawrence Block, *Telling Lies for Fun and Profit*, William Morrow, New York, 1981; *Writing the Novel*, Writer's Digest, Cincinnati, 1979.

Douglas, John and Mark Olshaker, *The Anatomy of Motive*, Simon and Schuster, New York, 1999; *Mind Hunter*, Scribner, New York, 1995.

Highsmith, Patricia, *Plotting and Writing Suspense Fiction*, St Martin's Press, New York, 2001.

James, P. D., *Talking About Detective Fiction*, Bodleian Library, Oxford, 2009.

Keating, H. R. F., *Writing Crime Fiction*, St Martin's Press, New York, 1986.

Kelly's Directories, published in the past as trade directories for many towns and cities in the UK, are often available in public libraries.

King, Stephen, *On Writing*, Pocket Books, New York, 2002.

Lamott, Anne, *Bird by Bird*, Anchor Books, New York, 1995.

Lukeman, Noah, *The First Five Pages*, Prentice Hall & IBD, 2000.

Lyle, Douglas P., MD, *Forensics and Fiction*, St Martin's Press, New York, 2007; *Forensics for Dummies*, Wiley, Hoboken, NJ, 2004; *Murder and Mayhem*, St Martin's Press, New York, 2003. Dr Lyle is also available through his website to answer writers' medical and forensic questions.

Mystery Writers of America, *Mystery Writer's Handbook* (ed. Lawrence Treat, Writer's Digest, Cincinnati, 1976) and *Writing Mysteries* (both the 1992 edition, ed. Sue Grafton, Writer's Digest, Cincinnati, and the 2002 book of the same title with new content, ed. Sue Grafton, Jan Burke and Barry Zeman, Writer's Digest, Cincinnati).

Writers' and Artists' Yearbook (for the current year), Bloomsbury, London (annual).

Writer's Digest Books (Cincinnati, OH) publishes the excellent HowDunit series, aimed at providing background to crime writers: *The Book of Poisons* by Serita Stevens and Anne Louise Bannon, 2007; *Forensics*, by Doug Lyle, 2008; *Police Procedure and Investigation*, by Lee Lofland, 2007. The publisher's many out-of-print (although occasionally out-of-date) titles can be found online or as e-books. Some of these are: *Armed and Dangerous*, a writer's guide to weapons by Michael Newton, 1990; *Body Trauma*, by David W. Page, 2006; *Cause of Death*, by Keith D. Wilson,

1992; *Just the Facts, Ma'am*, by Greg Fallis, 1998; *Howdunit*, ed. John Boertlein, 2001; *Malicious Intent*, by Sean Mactire, 1995; *Missing Persons*, by Fay Faron, 1997; *Modus Operandi*, by Mauro Corvasce and Joseph Paglino, 1995; *Murder One*, by Mauro Corvasce and Joseph Paglino, 1997.

Research tools

Maps are a joy. Ordnance Survey maps for all of Britain are available online, and the USGS offers Geologic Survey maps, including topographic and historical.

Antiquarian guidebooks such as Baedekers and Murray, written by people who sweated and froze their way through the country under consideration, can add a great deal of flavour to historical fiction.

The expert: as the Internet grows, the problem of winnowing through online material becomes ever greater. This means that you should keep watch for experts, whether on a Portuguese poet you're using in your historical novel or the specifics of the Glock your detective carries. For the most part, experts of all stripes are more than happy to share their knowledge with a writer, even a newbie.

Small regional museums can supply a wealth of telling detail, and the personal attention the writer can get from the staff is often extraordinary. Most small museums, whether they are regional or focus on some specific interest – toys, costume, cars – are run by people who love what they're doing, and want nothing better than to convert others to their own particular passion.

Before you confront a busy museum director, homicide cop or university professor with a list of questions, you need to make sure you've done some preliminary research beforehand. Don't waste their time with basics that you can find out with ten minutes online. And when you set up your interview, unless it's a public information officer paid by the city to do the job, offer to pay for their time. If they say it's not necessary, at least offer to take them to a good lunch. When you're finished, find out how they'd like their name to appear on the acknowledgement page. (And don't forget to send them a signed copy, when it's published!)

Video: for researching place, there's nothing like seeing it on the screen.

Cruise through YouTube, a wealth of historical oddities. An online search for 'movies set in X' can give you a strong sense of the ground. Google Earth is a great tool, particularly the street view function.

Newspaper and magazine archives, traditionally the realm of the dustier portions of research libraries, are more and more accessible online. For writers of historical fiction, the fee for using *The Times* of London or the *London Illustrated News* archives, among dozens of other archives both national and regional, can be worthwhile. Online archives can be found by searching such terms as 'list of online newspaper archives' and 'historical archives online'.

There are many online sites valuable for their insight into the business and the craft of writing. Because these change so rapidly, there is little point in giving a list – but then, learning about them is one of the main goals in joining the online crime fiction community.

Novels to study

We talked in Part One about the need for 'Reading like a writer', suggesting that you read widely in the genre and through the eras, keeping track of your reactions as you go.

Make friends with your local bookshop and library, looking for someone who knows crime, and whose taste you respect. If you're not lucky enough to have a specialist crime bookshop in your area, begin a relationship with one at a distance – Poisoned Pen in Scottsdale, USA, for example, ships all over the world, as does Heffer's Bookshop in Cambridge, UK, whose crime specialist is a real aficionado. A crime specialist can steer you not only to the best-sellers (anyone can do that) but also to the best.

We considered giving a list of must-read novels for would-be writers, and quickly ran into difficulties, not least in the space. Instead, we recommend that you do an online search for the Top 100 Crime (or Mystery) Novels, which gives you the 1990s lists compiled by the Crime Writers Association and the Mystery Writers of America. These lists date to the twentieth century, but include many classics providing vivid lessons in craftsmanship.

Bibliography

Books by Michelle Spring and Laurie R. King are noted on p. iii.

Ronald Knox's 'Decalogue of Crime Writing' first appeared in the introduction to *The Best Detective Stories of 1928–29*, and was reprinted in Haycraft, Howard, *Murder for Pleasure: The Life and Times of the Detective Story*, Biblio and Tannen, New York, 1976.

The Oath of the Detection Club, as writ by founding member Miss Dorothy L. Sayers, is referred to in her introduction to the club's serial novel, *The Floating Admiral* (ebook by HarperCollins, 2011).

Allingham, Margery, *Tiger in the Smoke*, Chatto and Windus, London, 1952.

Baden-Powell, Robert, *Pig-Sticking or Hog-Hunting*, rev. edn 1924, H. Jenkins, London.

Bloch, Robert, *Psycho*, Bloomsbury, London, 1997.

Brontë, Emily, *Wuthering Heights*, Wordsworth Editions, London, 1992.

Brown, Dan, *The Da Vinci Code*, Transworld, London, 2003.

Burke, James Lee, *Feast Day of Fools*, Simon and Schuster, New York, 2011; *The Neon Rain*, Henry Holt, New York, 1987.

Byatt, A. S., *The Children's Book*, Chatto & Windus, London, 2009.

Carr, Caleb, *The Alienist*, Random House, New York, 1994.

Chabon, Michael, *The Wonder Boys*, Harper Perennial, New York, 2008.

Chandler, Raymond, 'The Simple Art of Murder', in *Atlantic Monthly*, December 1944 (and widely collected).

— 'Red Wind', in Otto Penzler (ed.), *The Black Lizard Big Book of Pulps*, Vintage, New York, 2007; *The Big Sleep*, Vintage Crime/Black Lizard, 1988.

Christie, Agatha, *The Murder of Roger Ackroyd*, Harper, New York, 2007; *Murder on the Orient Express*, William Morrow Paperbacks, New York, 2011.

Connelly, Michael, *The Poet*, Orion, London, 2000.

Cooper, N. J., *Face of the Devil*, Simon and Schuster, London, 2011.

Crais, Robert, *L.A. Requiem*, Orion, London, 1999.

Dexter, Colin, *Dead in Jericho*, Pan, London, 2007; *Death is Now My Neighbour*, Pan, London, 2007.

Dickens, Charles, *Great Expectations*, Longman, 2004.

Dickinson, Peter, *Perfect Gallows*, Pantheon Books, 1998.
Doyle, Arthur Conan, the Sherlock Holmes stories (56 short stories, 4 novels).
Du Maurier, Daphne, *Rebecca*, Virago Modern Classics, 2003.
Dudley Edwards, Ruth, *Matricide at St Martha's*, Poisoned Pen Press, Scottsdale, 2002.
Eco, Umberto, *The Name of the Rose*, Harcourt, New York, 1983.
Forster, E. M., *A Passage to India*, Edward Arnold, London 1924.
— *The Hill of Devi*, Penguin, Harmondsworth, 1983.
French, Nikki, *Beneath the Skin*, Penguin, London, 2000.
Friedman, Micky and Otto Penzler (eds), *The Crown Crime Companion: The Top 100 Mystery Novels of All Time*, Three Rivers Press, New York, 1995.
Goddard, Robert, *Sea Change*, Corgi, London, 2001.
Grafton, Sue, *A is for Alibi*, Henry Holt, New York, 1982.
Guterson, David, *Snow Falling on Cedars*, Harcourt Brace, New York, 1994.
Hannah, Sophie, *Little Face*, Hodder Paperbacks, London, 2006.
Harris, Thomas, *Silence of the Lambs*, St Martin's Press, New York, 1988.
Highsmith, Patricia, *This Sweet Sickness*, Harper, New York, 1961.
Hillerman, Tony, 'Building without Blueprints', in (eds) Sue Grafton, Jan Burke, Barry Zeman, *Writing Mysteries*, Writer's Digest, Cincinnati, 2002.
Jackson, Shirley, *We Have Always Lived in the Castle*, Viking Press, New York, 1962.
Jahn, Ryan David, *Acts of Violence*, Macmillan New Writing, London, 2009.
James, P. D., *Death in Holy Orders*, Faber and Faber, London, 2001; *The Lighthouse*, Penguin, London, 2006; *Unnatural Causes*, Faber and Faber, London, 2010.
Keating, H. R. F., *The Perfect Murder*, Academy Chicago Publishers, 1964.
Kelly, Jim, *Death Wore White*, Penguin, London, New York and Toronto, 2010; *Death Watch*, Penguin, London, New York and Toronto, 2011.
Kelly, Nora, *Hot Pursuit*, Poisoned Pen Press, Scottsdale, 2002.
Larsson, Stieg, *Girl with the Dragon Tattoo*, Quercus, London, 2008.
Lee, Harper, *To Kill a Mockingbird*, J. B. Lippincott and Co., New York, 1960.
Leonard, Elmore, *10 Rules of Writing*, Morrow, New York, 2007.
McBain, Ed, 'She was Blond. She was in Trouble. And She Paid 3 Cents a Word', in *Writers [on Writing]: Collected Essays from the New York Times*, Henry Holt, New York, 2001.

McDermid, Val, *A Place of Execution*, HarperCollins, London, 1999; *The Mermaids Singing*, HarperCollins, London, 1995.
MacDonald, John D., *Darker than Amber*, Macmillan, Basingstoke, 1970; *The Executioners* (also titled, *Cape Fear*), Bloomsbury, London, 1997.
Miéville, China, *The City and The City*, Macmillan, London, 2009.
Moody, Susan (ed.), *Hatchard's Crime Companion: The Top 100 Crime Novels, Selected by the Crime Writers' Association*, Hatchard's, London, 1990.
Paretsky, Sara, *Hard Time*, Penguin, London, 2000.
Pelecanos, George, *The Night Gardener*, Little, Brown, New York, 2007.
Poe, Edgar Allan, 'The Purloined Letter', 1845, widely collected.
Rinehart, Mary Roberts, *The Wall*, Kensington, 1988.
Robinson, Peter, *Aftermath*, Macmillan, London, 2002.
Rubenfeld, Jeb, *The Interpretation of Murder*, Headline, London, 2007.
Sansom, C. J., *Dissolution*, Pan, London, 2007.
Saville, Guy, *Afrika Reich*, Hodder and Stoughton, London, 2011.
Sayers, Dorothy, *Gaudy Night*, Gollancz, London, 1935; *Busman's Honeymoon*, Gollancz, London, 1937; *Five Red Herrings*, New English Library, 1959.
Shah, Tahir, *Sorcerer's Apprentice*, Arcade Publishing, New York, 2002.
Sjöwall, Maj and Per Wahlöö, the Martin Beck series, from *Roseanna* to *The Terrorists*.
Simm, Chris, *Outside the White Lines*, Arrow Books, London, 2004.
Taylor, Andrew, *The American Boy*, Harper Perennial, London, 2004.
Temple, Peter, *Truth*, Quercus, London, 2010.
Tey, Josephine, *To Love and be Wise*, Macmillan, New York, 1951.
Travers, Robert, *Anatomy of a Murder*, Penguin, London, 1960.
Uhnak, Dorothy, *Victims*, Simon and Schuster, New York, 1986.
White, T. H., *Darkness at Pemberley*, Ostara Publishing, Colchester, 2011.
Wilson, Laura, *The Lover*, Orion, 2005; *Hello Bunny Alice*, Orion, 2003.

Index

Printed in Great Britain
by Amazon.co.uk, Ltd.,
Marston Gate.